INTELLECTUAL ROOTS

OF THE

WELFARE STATE:

A Reader for Students of

Social Policy and

Development Theory

INTELLECTUAL ROOTS OF THE WELFARE STATE:

A Reader for Students of Social Policy and Development Theory

Edited by Bill Kirwin

Canadian Scholars' Press   Toronto   1991

Intellectual Roots of the Welfare State

First published in 1991 by
Canadian Scholars' Press Inc.
339 Bloor Street West, Suite 220
Toronto, M5S 1W7
Canada

Copyright © Bill Kirwin 1991. No copy, reproduction or transmission of this material may be made without written permission.

Canadian Cataloguing in Publication Data

Main entry under title:

Intellectual roots of the welfare state

ISBN 0-921627-87-4

1. Welfare state - Philosophy. 2. Public welfare - Philosophy.
3. Social service - Philosophy. I. Kirwin, Bill, 1937-.

HN5.I57 1991   361.6'5'01   C91-095039-3

ACKNOWLEDGEMENTS

I would like to thank those people who helped me in this effort. First to Dr. Joe Hudson for his encouragement and to Professor Ron Levin for his support and consultation. A big vote of thanks to Barbara Messenger and Karen Braid for their many hours of typing. A special thanks is in line for Karen Braid who managed to get the document camera ready. A final thanks to Professor Peter Boothroyd for his article and his dedication to scholarship.

Edmonton Bill Kirwin
June 1991

To

Pamela Kirwin Adams

and

Pamela Weinlick

because they both have an appreciation of history

TABLE OF CONTENTS

Introduction   i

Plato – Government by Philosophers   1

Marcus Aurelius – Mediations   3

Sir Thomas More's – Utopia   5

Thomas Hobbes – State and Sovereignty   15

Jean-Jaques Rousseau's – The Social Contract and
    Discourse on the Origin of Inequality   29

Daniel Defoe – A Journal of the Plague Year   33

Niccolo Machiavelli – Promises and Princes   48

General Poorhouse – Paris Regulations   51

Gerrard Winstanley – The Law or Freedom in a Platform;
    or True Magistracy Restored   53

Thomas Robert Malthus – Population   56

Francois Marie Aronet de Voltaire – Philosophical Dictionary   64

Georg Wilhelm Friedrich Hegel – Reason in History   67

Edmund Burke – On Public Discontents   76

Mary Wollstonecraft – A Vindication of the Rights Woman   78

David Ricardo – Wages   87

Adam Smith – The Nature and Causes of the Wealth of Nations   92

J(Jean) B(Baptiste) Say – A Treatise on Political Economy or The Production, Distribution & Consuption of Wealth 99

Max Weber – The Protestant Ethnic and the Spirit of Capitalism 103

John Stuart Mill – On Liberty 109

Jeremy Bentham – Pleasure and Pain 114

Robert Owen – Man's Character is Formed for Him 117

Proudhon – What is Property? 120

The New Poor Law of 1834 123

Benjamin Disraeli – Sybil: Or The Two Nations 131

Claude Henri De Rouvroy Comte De Saint-Simon – The Organizer 138

Prince Peter Kropotkin – Anarchism 141

Arthur Schopenhauer – Studies in Pessimism 144

Karl Marx & Friedrich Engels – Manifesto of the Communist Party 148

Otto Von Bismarck – A Speech on State Socialism 157

Charles B.P. Bonsanquet – London: Some Account of its Growth, Charitable Agencies and Wants 160

Ferdinand Lassalle – The Law of Wages 166

Eduard Bernstein – The Case For Reform 168

Rosa Luxemburg – Reform or Revolution 173

Herbert Spencer – The Study of Society 178

TABLE OF CONTENTS

Introduction	i
Plato – Government by Philosophers	1
Marcus Aurelius – Mediations	3
Sir Thomas More's – Utopia	5
Thomas Hobbes – State and Sovereignty	15
Jean-Jaques Rousseau's – The Social Contract and Discourse on the Origin of Inequality	29
Daniel Defoe – A Journal of the Plague Year	33
Niccolo Machiavelli – Promises and Princes	48
General Poorhouse – Paris Regulations	51
Gerrard Winstanley – The Law or Freedom in a Platform; or True Magistracy Restored	53
Thomas Robert Malthus – Population	56
Francois Marie Aronet de Voltaire – Philosophical Dictionary	64
Georg Wilhelm Friedrich Hegel – Reason in History	67
Edmund Burke – On Public Discontents	76
Mary Wollstonecraft – A Vindication of the Rights Woman	78
David Ricardo – Wages	87
Adam Smith – The Nature and Causes of the Wealth of Nations	92

J(Jean) B(Baptiste) Say – A Treatise on Political Economy or The Production, Distribution & Consuption of Wealth 99

Max Weber – The Protestant Ethnic and the Spirit of Capitalism 103

John Stuart Mill – On Liberty 109

Jeremy Bentham – Pleasure and Pain 114

Robert Owen – Man's Character is Formed for Him 117

Proudhon – What is Property? 120

The New Poor Law of 1834 123

Benjamin Disraeli – Sybil: Or The Two Nations 131

Claude Henri De Rouvroy Comte De Saint-Simon – The Organizer 138

Prince Peter Kropotkin – Anarchism 141

Arthur Schopenhauer – Studies in Pessimism 144

Karl Marx & Friedrich Engels – Manifesto of the Communist Party 148

Otto Von Bismarck – A Speech on State Socialism 157

Charles B.P. Bonsanquet – London: Some Account of its Growth, Charitable Agencies and Wants 160

Ferdinand Lassalle – The Law of Wages 166

Eduard Bernstein – The Case For Reform 168

Rosa Luxemburg – Reform or Revolution 173

Herbert Spencer – The Study of Society 178

Friedrich Wilhelm Nietzsche – The Will to Power as Society and Individual … 182

Henry George – Social Problems … 189

Georges Sorel – Reflections on Violence … 200

Oscar Wilde – The Soul of Man … 205

Vladmir Ilyich Lenin – "Left Wing" Communism, An Infantile Disorder … 207

Jane Addams – Peace & Bread in Time of War … 210

Thorstein Veblen – The Theory of the Leisure Class … 222

Benito Mussolini – The Doctrine of Fascism … 230

The Fabian Society … 237

Jakob Burckhardt – Reflections on History … 242

Randolph Bourne – Twilight of Idols … 246

Peter Boothroyd – From Keynes to Buddhist Ecology: Rationalizing and Criticizing the Welfare State … 249

Bibliography … 295

INTRODUCTION

These readings, will serve as a introductory anthology that will create a beginning understanding for the student of social work and the development of social policy. The popular historical idea of social welfare is, too often, presented as a collection of do-good liberal social legislation that gradually has produced an ameliorative society. The ideological concept of social welfare, on the other hand, is often seen by many thinkers as a bothersome annoyance on the road to Paradise. The readings presented in this volume represent some of the basic writings of the great thinkers of the world and their attempts to understand and do something about the social inequities that they saw around them. Most of the readings pre-date, the originator of the modern welfare state, Otto von Bismarck. Since most of the writers pre-dating this time were not specifically addressing the idea of social welfare as we know it today, they serve as a pre-welfare state group of thinkers. In contrast, the article by Peter Boothroyd serves as an expanded annotated bibliographical introduction to the great thinkers of this century. It is important for the student of social welfare to have a general understanding of the origin of philosophical thought concerning their profession. It is with this goal in mind that these collection of readings have been selected.

The idea of social welfare is often mistakenly thought of as being a phenomenon of this century; however many of the ideas have their origin from a variety of thinkers who lived and wrote prior to the 20th century. This collection of readings is a brief introduction to some of the more notable philosophical thinkers and their ideas about social welfare. Goethe, the great German writer once said that "thinking is a thousand things in one's head," he certainly was correct if he was thinking about social welfare. No other field of study has so many self-proclaimed experts; from the Beggars Law of Henry VIII in 1536 to the present day, there is practically no one who would shy away from expressing a definite opinion about what should or should not be done about "welfare." These opinions are often paraded as new wisdom or dependable shibboleths when, in reality, they are often bits and pieces of ideas distorted and repacked without knowledge or the where-abouts of the origin of these ideas.

The scientific method has increased our knowledge of the pure sciences. However, despite the rather, at times, extravagant claims of social scientists the area of human understanding is still largely dependent on general observation and intuition not to mention introspection. As any practising social worker knows these three methods of learning are both necessary and fraught with danger. From the time of Plato there have been no revolutionary philosophical method; new ideas, certainly, but no new method, that is why the philosophy of Aristotle still means something to us to this very day; whereas his ideas of the sciences serve only to illustrate what was once thought. Yet with our infatuation with the scientific method we, to our peril, open ourselves to the notion that by merely accumulating data (at ever faster computer rates) that we may soon no longer need general observation, intuition and introspection. To better understand the human condition social workers need to strive to broaden their introspective and intuitive skills. Thus the importance of studying some of the great thinkers. The need to deal with the great questions and the small are the common chore of both the philosopher and the social worker. To try to begin to understand the world, the state, the family, the person is both for the philosopher and the social worker an impossible but necessary chore. The reader of this collection of thinkers will observe the writers were not merely engaging in social philosophy but most combined philosophy with history and economics. Hegel was the first to combine philosophy with history. Plato, Hobbes and Rousseau commented on the historical process and their ideas are important for those wishing to gain a fuller understanding of the history of ideas. However, it was the union of philosophy and history by Hegel that has influenced almost every political movement since. With the introduction of economic analysis Smith and Say completed the triangular form which used by most thinkers since that time. Nietzsche, who was impacted by Schopenhauer, enhanced the process by adding psychology to the process.

Louis XIV once said "It is in my person alone that the legislative power resides...I am the state." The power of the sovereign was also clear to Hobbes who argued that if citizens did not subject themselves to the authority of the crown they would be little more than "flies of the summer." Underlying this aristocratic view of the state was a basic fear that left to their own devices any person other than the monarch would fail to consider the general welfare of the community. The fear of anarchy and the need for social institutions that were larger than life, or at least appeared to be, required a society to unfold according to a grand design. The sovereign was maintained, it was generally believed, by the dignified subservience of the serf and the discipline and self regulation of the guilds coupled with the moral authority of the church.

By the late 1780's France was beset by bankruptcy due, in part, to rising inflation, a cumbersome and increasingly corrupt feudal system and a string of poor harvests. With the outbreak of the French Revolution middle-class liberalism began its's successful campaign against the privilege of aristocratic rule. In England people like Robert Owen insisted that the environment in which one found themselves, determined their status rather than the one that they had inherited. Edmund Burke had previously insisted that the landed aristocracy were the natural leaders and that a revolutionary mob could destroy a hundred years of progress in one day; yet the tumult of the French Revolution served as a dynamic ideological catalyst. Many of the ideas and fears about population control we have derived from the gloomy predictions of Thomas Malthus. Adam Smith thoughts about the intervention of the state into the every day affairs of commerce are, in part, still held in reverence as are David Ricardo's pessimistic Law of Iron Wages.

The liberal but gloomy views of Ricardo and Malthus contrast sharply with the liberal optimism of Adam Smith and J.B. Say yet they all embraced the liberal notion of progress independent of aristocratic regulation and a sense of progress attained in a free society. The conservative Burke on the other hand, thought that "the march of the human mind was slow" and that "abstract liberty, like other mere abstractions was not to be found": whereas Disraeli thought that social institutions alone created a nation. Disraeli's idea was not lost on Bismarck who insisted that only through social imperialism could a nation become great.

The triumph of liberalism in the nineteenth century, of course, sparked an ideological reaction of socialism, communism, and anarchism as well as a host of utopian movements. Marx and Engels call for the abolishment of private property was neither new or original, Proudhon, for instance, had announced eight years earlier that property was theft and indeed even their call for proletarian rule was an echo of Gerrard Winstanley's mid-seventeenth century plea. Yet the proliferation of socialist ideas in the nineteenth century is a testimony to both the collapse of classical conservatism and the overall practical poverty of liberalism. However, before Marx had even completed his exhaustive studies of capitalism he was taken to task by revisionists like Bernstein and Lassalle that the idea of class war was unnecessary and unwanted.

Most of the thinkers in this volume were long on criticism of the existing order and short of practical ideas as to how to correct them. Yet, it was their critical thoughts, no matter how fragmentary, or how diluted, or how camouflaged that form much of the way we view social welfare today. Malthus arguments for instance, of two centuries ago for population control have their base on a fear of global famine; a fear that is still very much within the human psyche. His proposal of sexual abstinence seems slightly ridiculous when viewed from the present day and the advances of the pharmaceutical industry. However, his notion that any assistance to the poor of the world would merely be an act of cruelty disguised as charity finds its way into contemporary thinkers of today such as Guilder and Friedman. Or Malthus theory of gluts, was virtually ignored when he was alive but embraced by Keynes in this century.

Malthus serves as an example of the legacy that some of the thinkers in this book have left to us. It has become fashionable, in some circles, to reject the study of great thinkers of the past because it might in some way contaminate the surety of present day thought. This is, of course, unfortunate not only for the obvious anti-intellectualism but also for the historical poverty that such thinking engenders. For intellectual history, no matter how great or small, is the link that binds, for good or bad, the generations. We have much to learn from our mistakes of the past. It is also important to remember today's heresy is often tomorrow's orthodoxy. Most of the thinkers in this volume led lonely, misunderstood lives. It has only been through historical retrospect that we have managed to see how they have given us insight into the era in which they lived and the evolution of their thinking to our beliefs of today.

PLATO
(Approx. 427-347 B.C.)

To Plato order and rational thought was all important and disorder was evil. Therefore the best state was the one that was ruled by a philosopher. The notion of a benevolent philosopher-king comes from Plato.

GOVERNMENT BY PHILOSOPHERS

We were inquiring into the nature of absolute justice and into the character of the perfectly just, and into injustice and the perfectly unjust, that we might have an ideal. We were to look at these in order that we might judge of our own happiness and unhappiness according to the standard which they exhibited and the degree in which we resembled them, but not with any view of showing that they could exist in fact.

True, he said.

Would a painter be any the worse because, after having delineated with consummate art an ideal of a perfectly beautiful man, he was unable to show that any such man could ever have existed?

He would be none the worse.

Well, and were we not creating an ideal of a perfect state?

To be sure.

And is our theory a worse theory because we are unable to prove the possibility of a city being ordered in the manner described?

Surely not, he replied.

That is the truth, I said. But if, at your request, I am to try and show how and under what conditions the possibility is highest, I must ask you, having this in view, to repeat your former admissions.

What admissions?

I want to know whether ideals are ever fully realized in language? Does not the word express more than the fact, and must not the actual, whatever a man may think, always, in the nature of things, fall short of the truth? What do you say?

I agree.

Then you must not insist on my proving the actual state will in every respect coincide with the ideal: if we are only able to discover how a city may be governed nearly as we proposed, you will admit that we have discovered the possibility which you deans; and will be contented. I am sure that I should be contented - will not you?

Yes, I will.

Let me next endeavor to show what is that fault in states which is the cause of their present maladministration, and what is the least change which will enable a state to pass into the truer form; and let the change, if possible, be of one thing only, or, if not, of two; at any rate, let the changes be as few and slight as possible.

Certainly, he replied.

I think, I said, that there might be a reform of the state if only one change were made, which is not a slight or easy though still a possible one.

What is it? he said.

Now then, I said, I go to meet that which I liken to the greatest of the waves; yet shall the word be spoken, even though the wave break and drown me in laughter and dishonor; and do you mark my words.

Proceed.

I said: *Until philosophers are kings, or the kings and princes of this world have the spirit and power of philosophy, and political greatness and wisdom meet in one, and those commoner natures who pursue either to the exclusion of the other are compelled to stand aside, cities will never have rest from their evils, - no, nor the human race, as I believe, - and then only will this our state have a possibility of life and behold the light of day.* Such was the thought, my dear Glaucon, which I would fain have uttered if it had not seemed too extravagant; for to be convinced that in no other state can there be happiness private or public is indeed a hard thing.

MARCUS AURELIUS
(121-180)

The Roman Emperor (169-180) Marcus Aurelius was a devout stoic. He believed that one's action should be in accord with his nature and his surroundings and that our primary obligation on earth was to get along with each other. To live life according to these basic principles would enable us to rise above our fears of death.

MEDITATIONS

Men seek retreats for themselves, houses in the country, sea-shores and mountains; and thou too art wont to desire such things very much. But this is altogether a mark of the most common sort of men, for it is in they power whenever thou shalt choose to retire into thyself. For nowhere, either with more quiet or more freedom from trouble, does a man retire than into his own soul, particularly when he has within him such thoughts that by looking into them he is immediately in perfect tranquility; and I affirm that tranquility is nothing else than the good ordering of the mind. Constantly then give to thyself this retreat, and renew thyself; and let thy principles be brief and fundamental, which, as soon as thou shalt recur to them, will be sufficient to cleanse the soul completely, and to send thee back free from all discontent with the things to which thou returnest.

Time is like a river made up of the events which happen, and a violent stream; for as soon as a thing has been seen, it is carried away, and another comes in its place, and this will be carried away too.

Observe constantly that all things take place by change, and accustom thyself to consider that the nature of the Universe loves nothing so much as to change the things which are to make new things like them. For everything that exists is in a manner the seed of that which will be.

Think continually how many physicians are dead after often contracting their eyebrows over the sick; and how many astrologers after predicting with great pretensions the deaths of others; how many philosophers after endless discourses on death or immortality; how many heroes after killing thousands; and how many tyrants who have used their power over men's lives with terrible insolence as if they were immortal. Pass then through this little space of time conformably to nature, and end they journey in content, just as an olive falls when it is ripe, blessing nature who produced it, and thanking the tree it grew on.

SIR THOMAS MORE
(1478-1535)

His book Utopia laid the groundwork for social criticism. Utopia, from the Greek meaning no where, proposes a fictional model of a perfect society. Utopia subtlely juxtaposed his fictional paradise with that of contemporary England of the 15th Century. His own personal life reflects the dilemma of those who try to live the utopian life. Although he enjoyed a brilliant career, as both a politician and a writer and appeared to be a conformist, he opposed Henry VIII and his desire to secede from the church. His opposition to the King resulted in his beheading and eventual elevation to saint hood.

UTOPIA

On Their Lives Together

But now I must explain the interrelationships of the citizens, what mutual intercourse they have and what method there is for dividing everything up. Now, the city is composed of households and generally blood ties make up households. For when the women have matured, they are married and go to live in their husbands' homes. But male children and grandchildren remain in the household and obey the oldest of the parents, unless his mind is feeble from old age. Then the next in age takes his place.

Each city has six thousand such households, not counting the surrounding districts. To prevent the population from decreasing or expanding above the limit, no household is allowed to have fewer than ten or more than sixteen adults. No limit can be put upon the number of children. This number is easily maintained by transferring to smaller households those that are above the limit in larger ones. But if ever the number is exceeded for the whole city, they use the surplus to fill the gaps in their other cities. But if by any chance the numbers swell beyond the limit for the whole island, they choose citizens from any city and with their own laws set up a colony on the nearby mainland, wherever the inhabitants have too much land to cultivate. They take in any of the inhabitants of the country who wish to live with them. Thus joined with men who are willing, they easily merge into the same way of life and the same habits. That is advantageous for both peoples; for by their practices they bring it about that the land which appeared insufficient and niggardly to the others is now more than enough for both. But those who refuse to live by the laws they drive out of the boundaries they mark out for themselves. If they resist, they go to war against them. For they think it the justest reason for war when any nation refuses to others the use and possession of that land which it does not use itself, but owns in idle emptiness, when the others by the law of nature ought to be nourished from it. It is said to have happened only twice ever, from a plague, that some of their cities are so reduced in numbers that they cannot be replenished from other parts of the island if each city is to keep its level. In that case citizens return from a colony to make up the numbers. For they prefer their colonies to die out rather than let any of the cities in the island decrease.

But to come back to the common lives of the citizens, as I said, the oldest member is head of each household. Wives serve their husbands, children their parents, and, in short, the younger serve the elder. Each city is divided into four equal parts. In the middle of each pair is a marketplace for everything. There the produce of each household is brought and put in certain buildings. Each different kind of product is put separately into barns. From these each family head seeks what he and his family need, and he carries off whatever he seeks, without any money or exchange of any kind. For why should anything be refused him? There is more than enough of everything and there is no fear that anyone will ask for more than he needs. For why would he be likely to seek too much, when he knows for certain that his needs will always be met? A man is made greedy and grasping either by the fear of need (a fear common to all creatures) or else (in man alone) by pride, which thinks it glorious to surpass others in superfluous show. This kind of vice has no place at all in the ways of the Utopians.

Next to the markets I have mentioned are provision markets, where they bring vegetables, fruits and bread, as well as fish and the animals and birds that can be eaten. These markets are outside the city where the filth and muck can be washed away in the river. From there they bring the animals that have been killed and cleaned by the hands of their slaves. For they do not allow their own citizens to grow accustomed to the slaughter of animals, as they think that constant practice in this gradually destroys the kindness and gentle feeling of our soul. Nor do they allow anything filthy and impure to be brought into the city, whose corruption could pollute the air and carry in some disease.

Moreover, each street has certain large halls set at an equal distance apart, each one known by a separate name. The syphogrants live in these. Thirty households, fifteen from either side, are assigned to each hall and take their meals there. The caterers of each hall go into the market at a fixed hour and after telling the number of their charges, get the food.

But chief consideration is given to the sick, who are looked after in public hospitals. For they have four hospitals in the range of the city, a little outside the walls. These are so large that they could match as many small towns, and no number of patients, however great, would be cramped for lack of space. They also allow the isolation of patients who are suffering from a contagious disease. These hospitals are so well arranged, and so fully supplied with all things conducive to health, such tender and constant treatment is given, and the best doctors are so constantly in attendance, that while no one is sent there against his will, yet there is practically no one in the whole city who would not prefer to lie there when ill rather than at his own home. When the caterer for the sick has received the food in accordance with the doctor's prescription, then all the best remaining portions are divided equally among the halls, depending on the number in each. The only distinction is that some consideration is given to the President, the Bishop and the tranibores, and also to ambassadors and all foreigners - if there are any, as very rarely happens. These too, if there are any, are provided with certain houses properly equipped.

To these halls at the fixed hours of lunch and dinner comes the whole syphograntia, summoned by the sound of a bronze trumpet, except for those who are sick in the hospitals or at home. Yet no one is prevented, after the halls have had enough, from taking food home from the market. For they know that no one does it for no reason. Although there is no rule forbidding eating at home, yet no one does this willingly, since it is not considered honorable, and in any case it is foolish to take the pains to prepare an inferior meal, when a rich and plentiful one is to be had at a nearby hall. In this hall, the slaves do all the tasks that are dirty or burdensome. But the job of cooking and preparing the food and making ready the whole meal is left to the women alone, each household taking its turn. Depending on their number, the people sit at three or more tables. The men are placed near the wall, the women nearer the door, so that if any sudden illness comes upon them (as occasionally happens in pregnancy) they may get up without disturbing the company and find their way to the nurses.

These nurses sit apart with the suckling children in a room set aside especially for that purpose. There is always a fire and clean water and also cradles, so that they can put the children down to rest and, when they wish, take off their swaddling clothes in front of the fire and refresh them with play. Each mother is nurse to her own child, except where death or illness prevents this. When that happens, the wives of the syphogrants quickly find a nurse, and this is not difficult. For the women who can fulfil this function offer themselves to no task more willingly; since everyone praises this act of mercy and the child so brought up regards his nurse as his mother. In the nurses' room sit all the children under five years of age. All the other children of either sex who are below the age of marriage either serve at table or, if they are too young, stand nearby in absolute silence. Both classes of children eat what is offered to them by those at table, and they have no other set time for eating. The syphogrant and his wife sit in the middle of the first table, as this is the most distinguished place and from it can be seen the whole assembly, since this table runs across the highest part of the dining room. These are joined by two of the eldest present, as they sit four at a table. If there is a church located in that syphograntia, the priest and his wife sit wit the syphogrant to preside. On each side sit the younger people and after them the older members, and so on throughout the whole hall. People of the same age sit together, but yet are mixed in with other age groups. They say that the reason for this practice is to allow the dignity and reverence of the old to check the young from unnecessary license in words and actions, since nothing can be done or said at table without being noticed by those nearby in one direction or another. The dishes are not served from the first place on, but first of all the older people, whose places are marked out in some special way, are given the choicest food; then the others are served impartially. If there are not enough tidbits to distribute to the whole company, the old people share theirs at their discretion with those sitting near them. In this way respect for the elderly is preserved and at the same time all have the same advantages.

They begin every lunch and dinner with some reading suitable for forming the character. This is kept short to avoid boredom. Using this as a basis, the old men indulge in moral conversation, which nevertheless is not gloomy or lacking in wit. But they do not occupy the whole meal with lengthy dissertations. Rather, they gladly listen to the younger members also and even deliberately provoke them to speak so that they may discover the nature and mind of each, as these betray themselves in the freedom of the table. Their lunches are rather brief, their dinners more lavish. For lunch is succeeded by work, but dinner by sleep and rest for the night. This, they think, is more conducive to a healthy digestion. No dinner passes without music, nor is the second course without its delights. They burn sweet-scented spices and scatter unguents and do everything to make the diners merrier. For they are readily inclined in this direction and think no kind of pleasure forbidden, as long as no inconvenience for it.

In this way, then, they live together in the city. In the country, as they are more widely scattered, they eat in their own homes. For no household lacks for as they are the source of supply for the city.

On the Occupations of the Utopians

All the men and women have one occupation in common - agriculture, in which everyone is skilled. They are all trained in this from childhood, partly by learning rules in school, and partly from being taken to the countryside near the city as if in play. As well as watching, they use the opportunity for exercise to gain some practical experience.

Besides agriculture (which, as I have said, is shared by all), each man is taught one occupation as his own specialty. This is usually weaving of wool or flax, or the craft of a mason, a smith, an ironworker or a carpenter. Nor is there any other trade there that occupies any number of men worth mentioning. For throughout the island there is only one style of clothing, except that one sex is distinguished from another and unmarried from married people by their dress. This style is retained all through life. It is attractive, allows easy movement and is designed to be equally suitable for cold and hot weather. Each household makes its own clothes. But of those other crafts each person learns one or another, not merely men, but women too. But because of their comparative weakness, the women do lighter tasks. They usually work wool or flax. To the men are assigned the other, more laborious crafts. A person is generally trained to the craft of his father, as most men are naturally inclined that way. But if anyone's bent lies in a different direction, he is adopted into a household concerned with the craft he wants to practice. His father and the magistrates as well see to it that the new father he goes to is a worthy and honorable head of a family. If anyone learns one craft thoroughly and wishes to know another as well, he is likewise allowed. When he has a command of both, he practices whichever he wishes, unless the state happens to need one more than the other.

It is the chief and almost the only task of the syphogrants to see that no one is idle, but that everyone diligently sets about his craft, but not like a beast, worn out by constant toil from early morning until late at night. For even a slave is not as hard pressed as that. Nevertheless, this is the life of workmen practically everywhere except in Utopia. The Utopians divide night and day into twenty-four hours of equal length and assign only six to work: three before midday, after which they go to lunch; after lunch they have two hours in the afternoon for rest; after that they work for another three hours before dinner. Counting their first hour from midday, they go to bed around eight o'clock. Sleep claims eight hours. They are allowed to do as they please with the hours in between their work and sleep and meals. The purpose is not to allow them to waste this free time in wild living or idleness, but to enable them to apply their minds to whatever useful pursuit they wish in their free time. Most men devote their intervening hours to literature. For it is customary to hold public lectures every day before dawn. Only those are compelled to go who have been chosen by name to study literature. But a great number of men and women alike, from all classes, attend the lectures, their choice, depending on their natural inclination. If anyone would prefer to spend this time in the practice of his trade (as happens to many who are not inspired by the thought of learning) he is not prevented. In fact, he is even praised as being beneficial to the state.

After dinner they devote one hour to games, in the gardens during the summer, and in the winter in the common halls where they eat. There they practice music, or refresh themselves with conversation. They do not even know dice and such foolish and pernicious games. But they play two games not unlike chess: one is a battle of numbers in which one number makes booty of another; the second is a game where, in battle array, vices fight with virtues. In this game a clever demonstration is given of the mutual discord of vices and their unity against virtues. It is also shown what vices oppose what virtues, with how much strength they openly assault, the wiles they use for oblique attack, the defenses virtues use to break the power of vices, the means they employ to foil their attempts and the ways in which either side gains victory.

But at this point, to avoid giving you a wrong impression, we must examine one aspect more closely. For as they spend only six hours in work, it might be that you think a shortage of supplies must follow. This is quite the reverse of the truth. In fact, this period of time is enough and more than enough to provide everything needed to support life or make it more comfortable. You will easily understand this if you remember how large a part of the population is idle in other countries. In the first place, there are all the women, a half of the total number; or if women are occupied in business anywhere, the men usually snore in their place. On top of this, there is a large and idle number of priests and religious, as they are called. Add to this all the rich men, especially the owners of estates, who are commonly called gentlemen, and the nobles. Add to these their servants, all that sewage of swashbuckling villains. Then count in the strong and healthy beggars, who use some sickness as a cloak for their laziness. You will certainly find that all these are far more numerous than the men whose labor provides all that human needs require. Of these latter, consider how few are engaged in necessary trades. For where we measure everything by money, many crafts are bound to be practiced which are quite useless and superfluous, merely the servants of luxury and vice. For if this large number now engaged in work were divided up to practice as few crafts as the convenient use of nature requires, then in the great abundance that would necessarily ensue, the prices would be too small to allow the craftsmen to earn a living. But take all those who now waste their time in idle occupations, and also all that mob enjoying the leisure of laziness and sloth, each one of whom consumes as much as two workmen who provide the goods; if they were all put to useful occupations, you can easily see how little time would amply suffice for supplying everything demanded by considerations of necessity or comfort, and of pleasure too if it is real and natural.

This is made clear by the state of affairs in Utopia. For there in the whole city and the surrounding neighborhood, scarcely five hundred persons of all the men and women strong and young enough to work are exempted. Among these are the syphogrants, who are legally released from work; but they do not use this privilege, so that by their example they may more easily attract people to their occupations. The same immunity is enjoyed by those to whom the people, persuaded by the recommendation of the priests and secret election of the syphogrants, give a perpetual release to allow them to devote themselves to learning. If any one of these falls short of the hopes entertained of him, he is thrust back among the workers. Contrariwise, it often happens that a mechanic spends his leisure time in such hard work on literature and makes such progress that he is taken from his trade and promoted to the class of scholars.

From this order are chosen ambassadors, priests, tranibores, and even the President himself, who is called in their old language Barzanes and in the newer one Ademus. Since the remainder of the population is neither idle nor engaged in useless trades, it is easy to estimate how few hours produce so much good work. In addition to what I have said, there is also this advantage: they have to spend less time in the necessary crafts than other people. For in the first place, building repairing houses requires the constant work of so many men everywhere simply because a spendthrift heir allows the house his father built gradually to crumble. So his successor must at great cost begin all over again what could have been safeguarded for so little It also often happens that a man fastidiously turns his nose up at a house that cost another a great deal. So it is neglected and soon falls down. Then he builds another elsewhere at no less a price. But in Utopia, where everything is in good order and the state well established, it happens only very infrequently that a new site is chosen for building. They quickly repair present faults and also take precautionary measures against those that are likely to arise. So the buildings last for a very long time with only a slight expenditure of labor, and workmen in that field occasionally have practically nothing to do - except that they are given timber to cut at home and stones to square and shape in the meanwhile, so that if any work does come it can rise more quickly.

Now see how few workmen they need for their clothing. When they are at work they are carelessly clothed in leather or skins, which will last seven years. When they go out of doors, they put a cloak on top to cover up their simple clothes. Throughout the whole island these cloaks are of the same natural color. So they need much less woollen cloth than is required in other countries and it also costs them much less. But linen is easier to produce and so is used more commonly. But in linen cloth only whiteness is observed, in woollen only cleanliness. No value is put upon a finer thread. Thus, while elsewhere four or five woollen cloaks of different colors are not enough for one man, and as many silk tunics, and for a more fastidious man not even ten are enough, in Utopia each man is content with one and it generally lasts him two years. For there is no reason why he should want more; if he obtained them, he would not be any better protected against the cold, nor would he seem one jot more attractive in his clothing.

So with everyone practicing useful crafts and fewer men needed for each, as there is a great abundance of supplies, occasionally they lead out a huge crowd to repair the public roads if any are worn away. Very often not even such work is required and so they make a public announcement of fewer working hours. For the magistrates do not exercise the citizens against their will in unnecessary work, since the institution of the republic has this one chief aim - that, as far as public necessity allows, all citizens should be given as much time as possible away from bodily service for the freedom and cultivation of the mind. For there, they think, lies happiness in life.

THOMAS HOBBES
(1588-1679)

Hobbes was the first of the great English political theorists. His views that people in their natural state were nasty and brutish offended the religious point of view. To escape this natural state of anarchy, Hobbes believed that everyone had to submit themselves absolutely to the sovereign. This selection comes from his most famous work <u>The Leviathan</u> which was published in 1651.

STATE AND SOVEREIGNTY

The final cause, end, or design of men, who naturally love liberty, and dominion over others, in the introduction of that restraint upon themselves, in which we see them live in commonwealths, is the foresight of their own preservation, and of a more contended life thereby; that is to say, of getting themselves out from that miserable condition of war, which is necessarily consequent...to the natural passions of men, when there is no visible power to keep them in awe, and tie them by fear of punishment to the performance of their covenants, and observation of those laws of nature set down in the fourteenth and fifteenth chapters.

For the laws of nature, as "justice," "equity," "modesty," "mercy," and, in sum, "doing to others as we would be done to," of themselves, without the terror of some power to cause them to be observed, are contrary to our natural passions, that carry us to partiality, pride, revenge, and the like. And covenants, without the sword, are but words and of no strength to secure a man at all. Therefore notwithstanding the laws of nature which every one hath then kept, when he has the will to keep them, when he can do it safely, if there be no power erected, or not great enough for our security, every man will and may lawfully rely on his own strength and art, for caution against all other men. And in all places where men have lived by small families, to rob and spoil one another has been a trade, and so far from being reputed against the law of nature, that the greater spoils they gained, the greater was their honor; and men observed no other laws, therein, but the laws of honor; that is, to abstain from cruelty, leaving to men their lives, and instruments of husbandry. And as small families did then, so now do cities and kingdoms, which are but greater families, for their own security, enlarge their dominions, upon all pretences of danger, and fear of invasion, or assistance that may be given to invaders, and endeavor as much as they can to subdue or weaken their neighbors, by open force and secret arts, for want of other caution, justly; and are remembered for it in after ages with honor.

Nor is it the joining together of a small number of men that gives them this security; because in small numbers, small additions on the one side or the other make the advantage of strength so great as is sufficient to carry the victory; and therefore gives encouragement to an invasion. The multitude sufficient to confide in for our security is not determined by any certain number, but by comparison with the enemy we fear, and is then sufficient, when the odds of the enemy is not of so visible and conspicuous moment to determine the event of war, as to move him to attempt.

And be there never so great a multitude; yet if their actions be directed according to their particular judgements and particular appetites, they can expect thereby no defence, nor protection, neither against a common enemy, nor against the injuries of one another. For being distracted in opinions concerning the best use and application of their strength, they do not help but hinder one another; and reduce their strength by mutual opposition to nothing: whereby they are easily, not only subdued by a very few that agree together; but also when there is no common enemy, they make war upon each other, for their particular interests. For if we could suppose a great multitude of men to consent in the observation of justice, and other laws of nature, without a common power to keep them all in awe, we might as well suppose all mankind to do the same; and then there neither would be nor need to be any civil government or commonwealth at all; because there would be peace without subjection.

Nor is it enough for the security, which men desire should last all the time of their life, that they be governed and directed by one judgment for a limited time: as in one battle, or one war. For though they obtain a victory by their unanimous endeavor against a foreign enemy; yet afterwards, when either they have no common enemy, or he that by one part is held for an enemy is by another part held for a friend, they must needs by the difference of their interests dissolve, and fall again into a war amongst themselves.

It is true that certain living creatures, as bees and ants, live sociably one with another, which are therefore by Aristotle numbered amongst political creatures; and yet have no other direction than their particular judgments and appetites; nor speech, whereby one of them can signify to another what he thinks expedient for the common benefit: and therefore some man may perhaps desire to know why mankind cannot do the same. To which I answer,

First, that men are continually in competition for honor and dignity, which these creatures are not; and consequently amongst men there ariseth on that ground, envy and hatred, and finally war; but amongst these not so.

Secondly, that amongst these creatures, the common good differeth not from the private; and being by nature inclined to their private, they procure thereby the common benefit. But man, whose joy consisteth in comparing himself with other men, can relish nothing but what is eminent.

Thirdly, that these creatures, having not, as man, the use of reason, do not see, nor think they see any fault in the administration of their common business; whereas amongst men there are very many that think themselves wiser and abler to govern the public better than the rest; and these strive to reform and innovate, one this way, another that way, and thereby bring it into distraction and civil war.

Fourthly, that these creatures, though they have some use of voice, in making known to one another their desires and other affections; yet they want that art of words by which some men can represent to others that which is good in the likeness of evil, and evil in the likeness of good, and augment or diminish the apparent greatness of good and evil; discontenting men, and troubling their peace at their pleasure.

Fifthly, irrational creatures cannot distinguish between injury and damage; and therefore as long as they be at ease, they are not offended with their fellows: whereas man is then most troublesome when he is most at ease; for then it is that he loves to show his wisdom, and control the actions of them that govern the commonwealth.

Lastly, the agreement of these creatures is natural; that of men is by covenant only, which is artificial: and therefore it is no wonder if there by somewhat else required, besides covenant, to make their agreement constant and lasting; which is a common power, to keep them in awe, and to direct their actions to the common benefit.

The only way to erect such a common power as may be able to defend them from the invasion of foreigners and the injuries of one another, and thereby to secure them in such sort as that by their own industry, and by the fruits of the earth, they may nourish themselves and live contentedly, is to confer all their power and strength upon one man, or upon one assembly of men, that may reduce all their wills, by plurality of voices, unto one will: which is as much as to say, to appoint one man, or assembly of men, to bear their person; and every one to own and acknowledge himself to be author of whatsoever he that so beareth their person shall act, or cause to be acted, in those things which concern the common peace and safety; and therein to submit their wills, every one to his will, and their judgments to his judgment. This is more than consent, or concord; it is a real unity of them all in one and the same person, made by covenant of every man with every man, in such a manner as if every man should say to every man, "I authorize and give up my right of governing myself, to this man or to this assembly of men, on this condition, that thou give up they right to him and authorize all his actions in like manner." This done, the multitude so united in one person is called a "commonwealth," in Latin *civitas*. This is the generation of that great leviathan, or rather, to speak more reverently, of that mortal god, to which we owe under the immortal God, our peace and defence. For by this authority, given him by every particular man in the commonwealth, he hath the use of so much power and strength conferred on him, that by terror thereof, he is enabled to perform the wills of them all, to peace at home, and mutual aid against their enemies abroad. And in him consisteth the essence of the commonwealth; which, to define it, is "one person, of whose acts a great multitude, by mutual covenants one with another, have made themselves every one the author, to the end he may use the strength and means of them all, as he shall think expedient, for their peace and common defence."

And he that carrieth this person is called sovereign, and said to have sovereign power; and every one besides, his subject.

The attaining to this sovereign power is by two ways. One, by natural force; as when a man maketh his children to submit themselves, and their children, to his government, as being able to destroy them if they refuse; or by war subdueth his enemies to his will, giving them their lives on that condition. The other is when men agree amongst themselves to submit to some man, or assembly of men, voluntarily, on confidence to be protected by him against all others. This latter may be called a political commonwealth, or commonwealth by institution; and the former, a commonwealth by acquisition.

* * *

A commonwealth is said to be instituted when a multitude of men do agree and covenant, every one with every one, that to whatsoever man or assembly of men shall be given by the major part the right to present the person of them all, that is to say, to be their representative; every one, as well he that voted for it as he that voted against it, shall authorize all the actions and judgments of that man or assembly of men in the same manner as if they were his own, to the end to live peaceably amongst themselves and be protected against other men.

From this institution of a commonwealth are derived all the rights and faculties of him, or them, on whom sovereign power is conferred by the consent of the people assembled.

First, because they covenant, it is to be understood, they are not obliged by former covenant to anything repugnant hereunto. And consequently that they have already instituted a commonwealth, being thereby bound by covenant to anything repugnant hereunto. And consequently that they have already instituted a commonwealth, being thereby bound by covenant to own the actions and judgments of one, cannot lawfully make a new covenant amongst themselves, to be obedient to any other in any thing whatsoever, without his permission. And therefore, they that are subjects to a monarch, cannot without his leave cast off monarchy, and return to the confusion of a disunited multitude; nor transfer their person from him that beareth it, to another man, or other assembly of men: for they are bound, every man to every man, to own and be reputed author of all that he that already is their sovereign shall do, and judge fit to be done: so that any one man dissenting, all the rest should break their covenant made to that man, which is injustice: and they have also every man given the sovereignty to him that beareth their person; and therefore if they depose him, they take from him that which is his own, and so again it is injustice. Besides, if he that attempteth to depose his sovereign be killed, or punished by him for such attempt, he is author of his own punishment, as being by the institution author of all his sovereign shall do: and because it is injustice for a man to do anything for which he may be punished by his own authority, he is also upon that title unjust. And whereas some men have pretended for their disobedience to their sovereign, a new covenant, made not with men, but with God, this also is unjust: for there is no covenant with God but by meditation of somebody that representeth God's person; which none doth but God's lieutenant, who hath the sovereignty under God. But this pretence of covenant with God is so evident a lie, even in the pretenders' own consciences, that it is not only an act of an unjust, but also of a vile and unmanly disposition.

Secondly, because the right of bearing the person of them all is given to him they make sovereign, by covenant only of one to another, and not of him to any of them, there can happen no breach of covenant on the part of the sovereign: and consequently none of his subjects, by any pretence of forfeiture, can be freed from his subjection. That he which is made sovereign maketh no covenant with his subjects beforehand, is manifest; because either he must make it with the whole multitude, as one party to the covenant, or he must make a several covenant with every man. With the whole, as one party, it is impossible; because as yet they are not one person; and if he make so many several covenants as there be men, those covenants after he hath the sovereignty are void; because what act soever can be pretended by any one of them for breach thereof, is the act both of himself and of all the rest, because done in the person and by the right of every one of them in particular. Besides, if any one or more of them pretend a breach of the covenant made by the sovereign at his institution; and other, or one other of his subjects, or himself alone, pretend there was no such breach, there is in this case no judge to decide the controversy; it returns therefore to the sword again, and every man recovereth the right of protecting himself by his own strength, contrary to the design they had in the institution. It is therefore in vain to grant sovereignty by way of precedent covenant. The opinion that any monarch receiveth his power by covenant, that is to say, on condition, proceedeth from want of understanding this easy truth, that covenants being but words and breath, have no force to oblige, contain, constrain, or protect any man, but what they have from the public sword; that is, from the united hands of that man or assembly of men that hath the sovereignty, and whose actions are avouched by them all, and performed by the strength of them all, in him united. But when an assembly of men is made sovereign, then no man imagineth any such covenant to have passed in the institution; for no man is so dull as to say, for example, the people of Rome made a covenant with the Romans to hold the sovereignty on such or such conditions; which not performed, the Romans might lawfully depose the Roman people. That men see not the reason to be alike in a monarchy and in a popular government, proceedeth from the ambition of some that are kinder to the government of an assembly, whereof they may hope to participate, than of monarchy, which they despair to enjoy.

Thirdly, because the major part hath by consenting voices declared a sovereign, he that dissented must now consent with the rest, that is, be contented to avow all the actions he shall do, or else justly be destroyed by the rest. For if he voluntarily entered into the congregation of them that were assembled, he sufficiently declared thereby his will, and therefore tacitly covenanted to stand to what the major part should ordain: and therefore if he refuse to stand thereto, or make protestation against any of the decrees, he does contrary to his covenant, and whether his consent be asked or not, he must either submit to the decrees, or be left in the condition of war he was in before; wherein he might without injustice be destroyed by any man whatsoever.

Fourthly, because every subject is by this institution author of all the actions and judgments of the sovereign instituted, it follows that whatsoever he doth it can be no injury to any of his subjects, nor ought he to be by any of them accused of injustice. For he that doth anything by authority from another doth therein no injury to him by whose authority he acteth: but by this institution of a commonwealth every particular man is author of all the sovereign doth; and consequently, he that complaineth of injury from his sovereign complaineth of that whereof he himself is author and therefore ought not to accuse any man but himself; no, nor himself of injury, because to do injury to one's self is impossible. It is true that they that have sovereign power may commit iniquity, but not injustice or injury in the proper signification.

Fifthly, and consequently to that which was said last, no man that hath sovereign power can justly be put to death, or otherwise in any manner by his subjects punished. For seeing every subject is author of the actions of his sovereign, he punisheth another for the actions committed by himself.

And because the end of this institution is the peace and defence of them all, and, whosoever has right to the end has right to the means, it belongeth of right to whatsoever man or assembly that hath the sovereignty to be judge both of the means of peace and defence, and also of the hindrances and disturbances of the same, and to do whatsoever he shall think necessary to be done, both beforehand, for the preserving of peace and security, by prevention of discord at home and hostility from abroad; and, when peace and security are lost, for the recovery of the same.

Sixthly, it is annexed to the sovereignty to be judge of what opinions and doctrines are averse and what conducting to peace; and consequently, on what occasions, how far, and what men are to be trusted withal, in speaking to multitudes of people, and who shall examine the doctrines of all books before they be published. For the actions of men proceed from their opinions, and in the well governing of opinions consisteth the well governing of men's actions, in order to their peace and concord. And though in matter of doctrine nothing ought to be regarded but the truth; yet this is not repugnant to regulating the same by peace. For doctrine repugnant to peace can be no more true than peace and concord can be against the law of nature. It is true that in a commonwealth, where, by the negligence or unskilfulness of governors and teachers, false doctrines are by time generally received, the contrary truths may be generally offensive. Yet the most sudden and rough bursting in of a new truth that can be, does never break the peace, but only sometimes awake the war. For those men that are so remissly governed, that they dare take up arms to defend or introduce an opinion, are still in war; and their condition not peace, but only a cessation of arms for fear of one another; and they live, as it were, in the precincts of battle continually. It belongeth therefore to him that hath the sovereign power to be judge, or constitute all judges, of opinions and doctrines, as a thing necessary to peace, thereby to prevent discord and civil war.

Seventhly, is annexed to the sovereignty, the whole power of prescribing the rules whereby every man may know what goods he may enjoy and what actions he may do, without being molested by any of his fellow subjects; and this is it men call "propriety." For before constitution of sovereign power, as hath already been shown, all men had right to all things, which necessarily causeth war: and therefore this propriety, being necessary to peace, and depending on the sovereign power, is the act of that power, in order to the public peace. These rules of propriety, or *meum* and *tuum*, and of good, evil, lawful, and unlawful in the actions of subjects, are the civil laws, that is to say, the laws of each commonwealth in particular; though the name of civil law be now restrained to the ancient civil laws of the city of Rome, which being the head of a great part of the world, her laws at that time were in these parts the civil law.

Eighthly, is annexed to the sovereignty, the right of judicature, that is to say, of hearing and deciding all controversies which may arise concerning law, either civil or natural, or concerning fact. For without the decision of controversies, there is no protection of one subject against the injuries of another; the laws concerning *meum* and *tuum* are in vain, and to every man remaineth, from the natural and necessary appetite of his own conservation, the right of protecting himself by his private strength, which is the condition of war, and contrary to the end for which every commonwealth is instituted.

Ninethly, is annexed to the sovereignty, the right of making war and peace with other nations and commonwealths, that is to say, of judging when it is for the public good, and how great forces are to be assembled, armed, and paid for that end, and to levy money upon the subjects to defray the expenses thereof. For the power by which the people are to be defended consisteth in their armies, and the strength of an army, in the union of their strength under one command, which command the sovereign instituted, therefore hath; because the command of the "militia," without other institution, maketh him that hath it sovereign. And therefore whosoever is made general of an army, he that hath the sovereign power is always generalissimo.

Tenthly, is annexed to the sovereignty, the choosing of all counsellors, ministers, magistrates, and officers, both in peace and war. For seeing the sovereign is charged with the end, which is the common peace and defence, he is understood to have power to use such means as he shall think most fit for his discharge.

Eleventhly, to the sovereign is committed the power of rewarding with riches or honor, and of punishing with corporal or pecuniary punishment, or with ignominy, every subject according to the law he hath formerly made; or if there be no law made, according as he shall judge most to conduce to the encouraging of men to serve the commonwealth, or deferring of them from doing disservice to the same.

Lastly, considering what value men are naturally apt to set upon themselves, what respect they look for from others, and how little they value other men, from whence continually arise amongst them, emulation, quarrels, factions, and at least war, to the destroying of one another and diminution of their strength against a common enemy, it is necessary that there be laws of honor, and a public rate of the worth of such men as have deserved or are able to deserve well of the commonwealth; and that there be force in the hands of some or other, to put these laws in execution. But it hath already been shows that not only the whole "militia," or forces of the commonwealth, but also the judicature of all controversies, is annexed to the sovereignty. To the sovereign therefore it annexed to the sovereignty. To the sovereign therefore it belongeth also to give titles of honor; and to appoint what order of place and dignity each man shall hold; and what signs of respect, in public or private meetings, they shall give to one another.

These are the rights which make the essence of sovereignty, and which are the marks whereby a man may discern in what man, or assembly of men, the sovereign power is placed and resideth. For these are incommunicable, and inseparable. The power to coin money, to dispose of the estate and persons of infant heirs, to have preemption in markets, and all other statute prerogatives, may be transferred by the sovereign, and yet the power to protect his subjects be retained. But if he transfer the "militia," he retains the judicature in vain, for want of execution of the laws: or if he grant away the power of raising money, the "militia" is in vain; or if he give away of the government of doctrines, men will be frighted into rebellion with the fear of spirits. And so if we consider any one of the said rights, we shall presently see that the holding of all the rest will produce no effect in the conservation of peace and justice, the end for which all commonwealths are instituted. And this division is it whereof it is said, "a kingdom divided into itself cannot stand:" for unless this division precede, division into opposite armies can never happen. If there had not first been an opinion received of the greatest part of England that these powers were divided between the King, and the Lords, and the House of Commons, the people had never been divided and fallen into this civil war, first between those that disagreed in politics, and after between the dissenters about the liberty of religion; which have so instructed men in this point of sovereign right, that there be few now in England that do not see that these rights are inseparable, and will be so generally acknowledged at the next return of peace, and so continue, till their miseries are forgotten; and no longer, except the vulgar be better taught than they have hitherto been.

And because they are essential and inseparable rights, it

follows necessarily that in whatsoever words any of them seem to be granted away, yet if the sovereign power itself be not in direct terms renounced, and the name of sovereign no more given by the grantees to him that grants them, the grant is void: for when he has granted all he can, if we grant back the sovereignty, all is restored, as inseparably annexed thereunto.

This great authority being indivisible and inseparably annexed to the sovereignty, there is little ground for the opinion of them that say of sovereign kings, though they be *universis minores*, of less power than them all together. For if by "all together" they mean not the collective body as one person, then "all together" and "every one" signify the same; and the speech is absurd. But if by "all together," they understand them as one person, which person the sovereign bears, then the power of all together is the same with the sovereign's power; and so again the speech is absurd: which absurdity they see well enough, when the sovereignty is in an assembly of the people; but in a monarch they see it not; and yet the power of sovereignty is the same in whomsoever it be placed.

And as the power, so also the honor of the sovereign, ought to be greater than that of any or all the subjects. For in the sovereignty is the fountain of honor. The dignities of lord, earl, duke, and prince are his creatures. As in the presence of the master the servants are equal, and without any honor at all; so are the subjects in the presence of the sovereign. And though they shine some more, some less, when they are out of his sight; yet in his presence, they shine no more than the stars in the presence of the sun.

But a man may here object that the condition of subjects is very miserable; as being obnoxious to the lusts, and other irregular passions of him or them that have so unlimited a power in their hands. And commonly they that live under a monarch, think it the fault of monarchy; and they that live under the government of democracy, or other sovereign assembly, attribute all the inconvenience to that form of commonwealth; whereas the power in all forms, if the be perfect enough to protect them, is the same: not considering that the state of man can never be without some incommodity or other; and that the greatest, that in any form of government can possibly happen to the people in general, is scarce sensible, in respect of the miseries and horrible calamities that accompany a civil war, or that dissolute condition of masterless men, without subjection to laws and a coercive power to tie their hands from rapine and revenge: nor considering that the greatest pressure of sovereign governors proceedeth not from any delight or profit they can expect in the damage of weakening of their subjects, in whose vigor consisteth their own strength and glory; but in the restiveness of themselves, that unwillingly contributing to their own defence, make it necessary for their governors to draw from them what they can in time of peace, that they may have means on any emergent occasion, or sudden need, to resist, or take advantage on their enemies. For all men are by nature provided of notable multiplying glasses, that is their passions and self-love, through which every little payment appeareth a great grievance; but are destitute of those prospective glasses, namely moral and civil science, to see afar off the miseries that hang over them, and cannot without such payments be avoided.

JEAN-JAQUES ROUSSEAU
(1712-78)

A troubled paranoid person that quarreled bitterly with just about everyone. His ideas about the social contract between the ruler and the ruled were to provide a system of government and education that would offset the natural tendency of institutions to become corrupt. He also believed that humanity was by nature a pure animal that is neither good nor bad.

THE SOCIAL CONTRACT AND DISCOURSE ON THE ORIGIN OF INEQUALITY

Subject of the First Book

Man was born free, and everywhere he is in chains. Many a one believes himself the master of others, and yet he is a greater slave than they. How has this change come about? I do not know. What can render it legitimate? I believe that I can settle this question.

If I considered only force and the results that proceed from it, I should say that so long as a people is compelled to obey and does obey, it does well; but that, so soon as it can shake off the yoke and does shake it off, it does better; for, if men recover their freedom by virtue of the same right by which it was taken away, either they are justified in resuming it, or there was no justification for depriving them of it. But the social order is a sacred right which serves as a foundation for all others. This right, however, does not come from nature. It is therefore based on conventions. The question is to know what these conventions are. Before coming to that, I must establish what I have just laid down.

The Right of the Strongest

The strongest man is never strong enough to be always master, unless he transforms his power into right, and obedience into duty. Hence the right of the strongest - a right apparently assumed in irony, and really established in principle. But will this phrase never be explained to us? Force is a physical power; I do not see what morality can result from its effects. To yield to force is an act of necessity, not of will; it is at most an act of prudence. In what sense can it be a duty?

Let us assume for a moment this pretended right. I say that nothing results from it but inexplicable nonsense; for if force constitutes right, the effect changes with the cause, and any force which overcomes the first succeeds to its rights. As soon as men can disobey with impunity, they may do so legitimately; and since the strongest is always in the right, the only thing is to act in such a way that one may be the strongest. But what sort of a right is it that perishes when force ceases? If it is necessary to obey by compulsion, there is no need to obey from duty; and if men are no longer forced to obey, obligation is at an end. We see, then, that this work *right* adds nothing to force; it here means nothing at all.

Obey the powers that be. If that means, Yield to force, the precept is good but superfluous; I reply that it will never be violated. All power comes from God, I admit; but every disease comes from Him too; does it follow that we are prohibited from calling in a physician? If a brigand should surprise me in the recesses of a wood, am I bound not only to give up my purse when forced, but am I also morally bound to do so when I might conceal it? For, in effect, the pistol which he holds is a superior force.

Let us agree, then, that might does not make right, and that we are bound to obey none but lawful authorities. Thus my original question ever recurs.

The Social Pact

I assume that men have reached a point at which the obstacles that endanger their preservation in the state of nature overcome by their resistance the forces which each individual can exert with a view to maintaining himself in that state. Then this primitive condition can no longer subsist, and the human race would perish unless it changed its mode of existence.

Now, as men cannot create any new forces, but only combine and direct those that exist, they have no other means of self-preservation than to form by aggregation a sum of forces which may overcome the resistance, to put them in action by a single motive power, and to make them work in concert.

This sum of forces can be produced only by the combination of many; but the strength and freedom of each man being the chief instruments of his preservation, how can he pledge them without injuring himself, and without neglecting the cares which he owes to himself? This difficulty, applied to my subject, may be expressed in these terms:-

"To find a form of association which may defend and protect with the whole force of the community the person and property of every associate, and by means of which each, coalescing with all, may nevertheless obey only himself, and remain as free as before." Such is the fundamental problem of which the social contract furnishes the solution.

The clauses of this contract are so determined by the nature of the act that the slightest modification would render them vain and ineffectual; so that, although they had never perhaps been formally enunciated, they are everywhere the same, everywhere tacitly admitted and recognized, until, the social pact being violated, each man regains his original rights and recovers his natural liberty, while losing the conventional liberty for which he renounced it.

These clauses, rightly understood, are reducible to one only, viz., the total alienation to the whole community of each associate with all his rights; for, in the first place, since each gives himself up entirely, the conditions are equal for all; and, the conditions being equal for all, no one has any interest in making them burdensome to others.

Further, the alienation being made without reserve, the

union is as perfect as it can be, and an individual associate can no longer claim anything; for, if any rights were left to individuals, since there would be no common superior who could judge between them and the public, each, being on some point in his own judge, would soon claim to be so on all; the state of nature would still subsist, and the association would necessarily become tyrannical or useless.

In short, each giving himself to all, gives himself to nobody; and as there is not one associate over whom we do not acquire the same rights which we concede to him over ourselves, we gain the equivalent of all that we lose, and more power to preserve what we have.

If, then, we set aside what is not of the essence of the social contract, we shall find that it is reducible to the following terms: "Each of us puts in common his person and his whole power under the supreme direction of the general will; and in return we receive every member as an indivisible part of the whole."

Forthwith, instead of the individual personalities of all the contracting parties, this act of association produces a moral and collective body, which is composed of as many members as the assembly has voices, and which receives from this same act its unity, its common self (*moi*), its life, and its will. This public person, which is thus formed by the union of all the individual members, formerly took the name of *city*, and now takes that of *republic or body politic*, which is called by its members *State* when it is passive, *sovereign* when it is active, *power* when it is compared to similar bodies. With regard to the associates, they take collectively the name of *people*, and are called individually *citizens*, as participating in the sovereign power, and *subjects*, as subjected to the laws of the State. But these terms are often confused and are mistaken one for another; it is sufficient to know how to distinguish them when they are used with complete precision.

DANIEL DEFOE
(1660-1731)

The author of <u>Robinson Crusoe</u> wrote a fictional reconstruction of the 1722 plague. His journal portrays the trials of living and dying in a society dominated by a plague mentality. His writings strike a receptive chord among people of today concerning their attitudes regarding the AIDS epidemic.

A JOURNAL OF THE PLAGUE YEAR

ORDERS CONCEIVED AND PUBLISHED BY THE LORD MAYOR AND ALDERMEN OF THE CITY OF LONDON CONCERNING THE INFECTION OF THE PLAGUE, 1665.

'Whereas in the reign of our late Sovereign King James, of happy memory, an Act was made for the charitable relief and ordering of persons infected with the plague, whereby authority was given to justices of the peace, mayors, bailiffs, and other headofficers to appoint within their several limits examiners searchers, watchmen, keepers, and buriers for the persons and places infected, and to minister unto them oaths for the performance of their offices. And the same statute did also authorise the giving of other directions, as unto them for the present necessity should seem good in their directions. It is now, upon special consideration, thought very expedient for preventing and avoiding of infection of sickness (if it shall so please Almighty God) that these officers following be appointed, and these orders hereafter duly observed.

Examiners to be appointed in every Parish
'First, it is thought requisite, and so ordered, that in every parish there be one, two, or more persons of good sort and credit chosen and appointed by the alderman, his deputy, and common council of every ward, by the name of

examiners, to continue in that office the space of two months at least. And if any fit person so appointed shall refuse to undertake the same, the said parties so refusing to be committed to prison until they shall conform themselves accordingly.

The Examiner's Office

'That these examiners be sworn by the aldermen to inquire and learn from time to time what houses in every parish be visited, and what persons be sick, and of what diseases, as near as they can inform themselves; and upon doubt in that case, to command restraint of access until it appear what the disease shall prove. And if they find any person sick of the infection, to give order to the constable that the house be shut up; and if the constable shall be found remiss or negligent, to give present notice thereof to the alderman of the ward.

Watchmen

'That to every infected house there be appointed two watchmen, one for every day, and the other for the night; and that these watchmen have a special care that no person go in or out of such infected houses whereof they have the charge, upon pain of severe punishment. And the said watchmen to do such further offices as the sick house shall need and require; and if the watchman be sent upon any business, to lock up the house and take the key with him; and the watchman by day to attend until ten of the clock at night, and the watchman by night until six in the morning.

Searchers

'There there be special care to appoint women searchers in every parish, such as are of honest reputation, and of the best sort as can be got in this kind; and these to be sworn to make due search and true report to the utmost of their knowledge whether the persons whose bodies they are appointed to search do die of the infection, or of what other diseases, as near as they can. And that the physicians who shall be appointed for cure and prevention of the infection do call before them the said searchers who are, or shall be, appointed for the several parishes under their respective cares, to the end they may consider whether they are fitly qualified for that employment, and charge them from time to time as they shall see cause, if they appear defective in their duties.

'That no searcher during this time of visitation be permitted to use any public work or employment, or keep any shop or stall, or be employed as a laundress, or in any other common employment whatsoever.

Chirurgeons

'For better assistance of the searchers, forasmuch as there hath been heretofore great abuse in misreporting the disease, to the further spreading of the infection, it is therefore ordered that there be chosen and appointed able and discreet chirurgeons, besides those that do already belong to the pest-house, amongst whom the city and Liberties to be quartered as the places lie most apt and convenient; and every of these to have one quarter for his limit; and the said chirurgeons in every of their limits to join with the searchers for the view of the body, to the end there may be a true report made of the disease.

'And further, that the said chirurgeons shall visit and search such-like persons as shall either send for them or be named and directed unto them by the examiners of every parish, and inform themselves of the disease of the said parties.

'And forasmuch as the said chirurgeons are to be sequestered from all other cures, and kept only to this disease of the infection, it is ordered that every of the said chirurgeons shall have twelve-pence a body searched by them, to be paid out of the goods of the party searched, if he be able, or otherwise by the parish.

Nurse-keepers

'If any nurse-keeper shall remove herself out of any

infected house before twenty-eight days after the decease of any person dying of the infection, the house to which the said nurse-keeper doth so remove herself shall be shut up until the said twenty-eight days be expired.'

ORDERS CONCERNING INFECTED HOUSES AND PERSONS SICK OF THE PLAGUE

Notice to be given of the Sickness

'The master of every house, as soon as any one in his house complaineth, either of blotch or purple, or swelling in any part of his body, or falleth otherwise dangerously sick, without apparent cause of some other disease, shall give knowledge thereof to the examiner of health within two hours after the said sign shall appear.

Sequestration of the Sick

'As soon as any man shall be found by this examiner, chirurgeon, or searcher to be sick o the plague, he shall the same night be sequestered in the same house; and in case he be so sequestered, then, though he afterwards die not, the house wherein he sickened should be shut up for a month, after the use of the due preservatives taken by the rest.

Airing the Stuff

'For sequestration of the goods and stuff of the infection, their bedding and apparel and hangings of chambers must be well aired with fire and such perfumes as are requisite within the infected house before they be taken again to use. This to be done by the appointment of an examiner.

Shutting up of the House

'If any person shall have visited any man known to be infected of the plague, or entered willingly into any known infected house, being not allowed, the house wherein he inhabiteth shall be shut up for certain days by the examiner's direction.

None to be removed out of infected Houses, but, &c.
'Item, that none be removed out of the house where he falleth sick of the infection into any other house in the city (except it be to the pest-house or a tent, or unto some such house which the owner of the said visited house holdeth in his own hands and occupieth by his own servants); and so as security be given to the parish whither such remove is made, that the attendance and charge about the said visited persons shall be observed and charged in all the particularities before expressed, without any cost of that parish to which any such remove shall happen to be made, and this remove to be done by night. And it shall be lawful to any person that hath two houses to remove either his sound or his infected people to his spare house at his choice, so as, if he send away first his sound, he not after send thither his sick, nor again unto the sick the sound; and that the same which he sendeth be for one week at the least shut up and secluded from company, for fear of some infection at the first not appearing.

Burial of the Dead
'That the burial of the dead by this visitation be at most convenient hours, always either before sun-rising or after sun-setting, with the privity of the churchwardens or constable, and not otherwise; and that no neighbours nor friends be suffered to accompany the corpse to church, or to enter the house visited, upon pain of having his house shut up or be imprisoned.

'And that no-corpse dying of infection shall be buried, or remain in any church in time of common prayer, sermon, or lecture. And that no children be suffered at time of burial of any corpse in any church, churchyard, or burying-place to come near the corpse, coffin, or grave. And that all the graves shall be at least six feet deep.[*]

'And further, all public assemblies at other burials are to be forborne during the continuance of this visitation.

---

[*]The beginning of the six-foot-deep grave policy.

No infected Stuff to be uttered

'That no clothes, stuff, bedding, or garments be suffered to be carried or conveyed out of any infected houses, and that the criers and carriers abroad of bedding or old apparel to be sold or pawned be utterly prohibited and restrained, and no brokers of bedding or old apparel be permitted to make any outward show, or hang forth on their stalls, shop-boards, or windows, towards any street, lane, common way, or passage, any old bedding or apparel to be sold, upon pain of imprisonment. And if any broker or other person shall buy any bedding, apparel, or other stuff out of any infected house within two months after the infection hath been there, his house shall be shut up as infected, and so shall continue shut up twenty days at the least.

No Person to be conveyed out of any infected House

'If any person visited do fortune, by negligent looking unto, or by any other means, to come or be conveyed from a place infected to any other place, the parish from whence such party hath come or been conveyed, upon notice thereof given, shall at their charge cause the said party so visited and escaped to be carried and brought back again by night, and the parties in this case offending to be punished at the direction of the alderman of the ward, and the house of the receiver of such visited person to be shut up for twenty days.

Every visited House to be marked

'That every house visited be marked with a red cross of a foot long in the middle of the door, evident to be seen, and with these usual printed words, that is to say, "Lord, have mercy upon us," to be set close over the same cross, there to continue until lawful opening of the same house.

Every visited House to be watched

'That the constables see every house shut up, and to be attended with watchmen, which may keep them in, and minister necessaries unto them at their own charges, if they be able, or at the common charge, if they are unable; the shutting up to be for the space of four weeks after all be whole.

'That precise order to be taken that the searchers, chirurgeons, keepers, and buriers are not to pass the streets without holding a red rod or wand of three feet in length in their hands, open and evident to be seen, and are not to go into any other house than into their own, or into that whereunto they are directed or sentfor; but to forbear and abstain from company, especially when they have been lately used in any such business or attendance.

Inmates

'That where several inmates are in one and the same house, and any person in that house happens to be infected, no other person or family of such house shall be suffered to remove him or themselves without a certificate from the examiners of health of that parish; or in default thereof, the house whither he or they so remove shall be shut up as in case of visitation.

Hackney-Coaches

'That care be taken of hackney-coachmen, that they may not (as some of them have been observed to do after carrying of infected persons to the pest-house and other places) be admitted to common use till their coaches be well aired, and have stood unemployed by the space of five or six days after such service.'

ORDERS FOR CLEANSING AND KEEPING OF THE STREETS SWEET

The Streets to be kept Clean

'First, it is thought necessary, and so ordered, that every householder do cause the street to be daily prepared before his door, and so to keep it clean swept all the week long.

That Rakers take it from out the Houses
'That the sweeping and filth of houses be daily carried away by the rakers, and that the raker shall give notice of his coming by the blowing of a horn, as hitherto hath been done.

Laystalls to be made far off from the City
'That the laystalls be removed as far as may be out of the city and common passages, and that no nightman or other be suffered to empty a vault into any garden near about the city.

Care to be had of unwholesome Fish or Flesh, and of musty Corn
'That special care be taken that no stinking fish, or unwholesome flesh, or musty corn, or other corrupt fruits of what sort soever, be suffered to be sold about the city, or any part of the same.

'That the brewers and tippling-houses be looked unto for musty and unwholesome casks.

'That no hogs, dogs, or cats, or tame pigeons, or conies, be suffered to be kept within any part of the city, or any swine to be or stray in the streets or lanes, but that such swine be impounded by the beadle or any other officer, and the owner punished according to Act of Common Council, and that the dogs be killed by the dog-killers appointed for that purpose.'

ORDERS CONCERNING LOOSE PERSONS AND IDLE ASSEMBLIES

Beggars
'Forasmuch as nothing is more complained of than the multitude of rogues and wandering beggars that swarm in every place about the city, being a great cause of the spreading of the infection, and will not be avoided, notwithstanding any orders that have been given to the

contrary: It is therefore now ordered, that such constables, and others whom this matter may any way concern, take special care that no wandering beggars be suffered in the streets of this city in any fashion or manner whatsoever, upon the penalty provided by the law, to be duly and severely executed upon them.

Plays

'That all plays, bear-baitings, games, singing of ballads, buckler-play, or such-like causes of assemblies of people be utterly prohibited, and the parties offending severely punished by every alderman in his ward.

Feasting prohibited

'That all public feasting, and particularly by the companies of this city, and dinners at taverns, ale-houses, and other places of common entertainment, be forborne till further order and allowance; and that the money thereby spared be preserved and employed for the benefit and relief of the poor visited with the infection.

Tippling-houses

'That disorderly tippling in taverns, ale-houses, coffee-houses, and cellars be severely looked unto, as the common sin of this time and greatest occasion of dispersing the plague. And that no company or person be suffered to remain or come into any tavern, ale-house, or coffee-house to drink after nine of the clock in the evening, according to the ancient law and custom of this city, upon the penalties ordained in that behalf.

'And for the better execution of these orders, and such other rules and directions as, upon further consideration, shall be found needful: It is ordered and enjoined that the aldermen, deputies, and common councilmen shall meet together weekly, once, twice, thrice or oftener (as cause shall require), at some one general place accustomed in their respective wards (being clear from infection of the plague), to consult how the said orders may be duly put in execution; not intending that any dwelling in or near places infected shall come to the said meeting while their coming may be doubtful. And the said aldermen, and deputies, and common councilmen in their several wards may put in execution any other good orders that by them at their said meetings shall be conceived and devised for preservation of his Majesty's subjects from the infection.

   'SIR JOHN LAWRENCE, Lord Mayor.
   SIR GEORGE WATERMAN,
   SIR CHARLES DOE, Sheriffs.'

  I need not say that these orders extended only to such places as were within the Lord Mayor's jurisdiction, so it is requisite to observe that the Justices of Peace within those parishes and places as were called the Hamlets and out-parts took the same method. As I remember, the orders for shutting up of houses did not take place so soon on our side, because, as I said before, the plague did not reach to these eastern parts of the town at least, nor begin to be very violent, till the beginning of August. For example, the whole bill from the 11th to the 18th of July was 1761, yet there died but 71 of the plague in all those parishes we call the Tower Hamlets, and they were as follows: -

		The next week was thus:	*And to the 1st of Aug. thus:*
Aldgate	14	34	65
Stepney	33	58	76
Whitechappel	21	48	79
St Katherine, Tower	2	4	4
Trinity, Minories	1	1	4
	71	145	228

It was indeed coming on amain, for the burials that same week were in the next adjoining parishes thus: -

		The next week prodigiously increased, as:	*To the 1st of Aug. thus*
St Leonard's, Shoreditch	64	84	110
St Botolph's, Bishopsgate	65	105	116
St Giles's, Cripplegate	213	421	554
	342	610	780

This shutting up of houses was at first counted a very cruel and unchristian method, and the poor people so confined made bitter lamentations. Complaints of the severity of it were also daily brought to my Lord Mayor, of houses causelessly (and some maliciously) shut up. I cannot say; but upon inquiry many that complained so loudly were found in a condition to be continued; and others again, inspection being made upon the sick person, and the sickness not appearing infectious, or if uncertain, yet on his being content to be carried to the pest-house, were released.

It is true that the locking up the doors of people's houses, and setting a watchman there night and day to prevent their stirring out or any coming to them, when perhaps the sound people in the family might have escaped if they had been removed from the sick, looked very hard and cruel; and many people perished in these miserable confinements which, 'tis reasonable to believe, would not have been distempered if they had had liberty, though the plague was in the house; at which the people were very clamorous and uneasy at first, and several violences were committed and injuries offered to the men who were set to watch the houses so shut up; also several people broke out by force in many places, as I shall observe by-and-by. But it was a public good that justified the private mischief, and there was no obtaining the least mitigation by any application to magistrates or government at that time, at least not that I heard of. This put the people upon all manner of stratagem in order, if possible, to get out; and it would fill a little volume to set down the arts used by the people of such houses to shut the eyes of the watchmen who were employed, to deceive them, and to escape or break out from them, in which frequent scuffles and some mischief happened; of which by itself.

As I went along Houdsditch one morning about eight o'clock there was ag great noise. It is true, indeed, there was not much crowd, because people were not very free to gather together, or to stay long together when they were there; nor did I stay long there. But the outcry was loud enough to prompt my curiosity, and I called to one that looked out of a window, and asked what was the matter.

A watchman, it seems, had been employed to keep his post at the door of a house which was infected, or said to be infected, and was shut up. He had been there all night for two nights together, as he told his story, and the day-watchman had been there one day and was now come to relieve him. All this while no noise had been heard in the house, no light had been seen; they called for nothing, sent him of no errands, which used to be the chief business of the watchmen; neither had they given him any disturbance, as he said, from the Monday afternoon, when he heard great crying and screaming in the house, which, as he supposed, was occasioned by some of the family dying just at that time. It seems, the night before, the dead-cart, as it was called, had been stopped there, and a servant-maid had been brought down to the door dead, and the buriers or bearers, as they were called, put her into the cart, wrapt only in a green rug, and carried her away.

The watchman had knocked at the door, it seems, when he heard that noise and crying, as above, and nobody answered a great while; but at last one looked out and said with an angry, quick tone; and yet a kind of crying voice, or a voice of one that was crying, 'What d'ye want, that ye make such a knocking?' He answered, 'I am the watchman! How do you do? What is the matter?' Thye person answered, 'What is that to you? Stop the dead-cart.' This, it seems, was about one o'clock. Soon after, as the fellow said, he stopped the dead-cart, and then knocked again, but nobody answered. He continued knocking, and the bellman called out several times, 'Bring out your dead'; but nobody answered, till the man that drove the cart, being called to other houses, would stay no longer, and drove away.

The watchman knew not what to make of all this, so he let them alone till the morning-man or day-watchman, as they called him, came to relieve him. Giving him an account of the particulars, they knocked at the door a great while, but nobody answered; and they observed that the window or casement at which the person had looked out who had answered before continued open, being up two pair of stairs.

Upon this the two men, to satisfy their curiosity, got a long ladder, and one of them went up to the window and looked into the room, where he saw a woman lying dead upon the floor in a dismal manner, having no clothes on her but her shift. But though he called aloud, and putting in his long staff, knocked hard on the floor, yet nobody stirred or answered; neither could he hear any noise in the house.

He came down again upon this, and acquainted his fellow, who went up also; and finding it just so, they resolved to acquaint either the Lord Mayor or some other magistrate of it, but did not offer to go in at the window. The magistrate, it seems, upon the information of the two men, ordered the house to be broke open, a constable and other persons being appointed to be present, that nothing might be plundered; and accordingly it was do done, when nobody was found in the house but that young woman, who having been infected and past recovery, the rest had left her to die by herself, and were every one gone, having found some way to delude the watchman, and to get open the door, or get out at some back-door, or over the tops of the houses, so that he knew nothing of it; and as to those cries and shrieks which he heard, it was supposed they were the passionate cries of the family at the bitter parting, which, to be sure, it was to them all, this being the sister to the mistress of the family. The man of the house, his wife, several children, and servants, being all gone and fled, whether sick or sound, that I could never learn; nor, indeed, did I make much inquiry after it.

Many such escapes were made out of infected houses, as particularly when the watchman was sent of some errand; for it was his business to go of any errand that the family sent him of; that is to say, for necessaries, such as food and physic; to fetch physicians, if they would come, or surgeons, or nurses, or to order the dead-cart, and the like; but with this condition, too, that when he went he was to lock up the outer door of the house and take the key away with him. To evade this, and cheat the watchmen, people got two or three keys made to their locks, or they found ways to unscrew the locks such as were screwed on, and so take off the lock, being in the inside of the house, and while they sent away the watchman to the market, to the bakehouse, or for one trifle or another, open the door and go out as often as they pleased. But this being found out, the officers afterwards had orders to padlock up the doors on the outside, and place bolts on them as they thought fit.

At another house, as I was informed, in the street next within Aldgate, a whole family was shut up and locked in because the maid-servant was taken sick. The master of the house had complained by his friends to the next alderman and to the Lord Mayor, and had consented to have the maid carried to the pest-house, but was refused; so the door was marked with a red cross, a padlock on the outside, as above, and a watchman set to keep the door, according to public order.

After the master of the house found there was no remedy, but that he, his wife, and his children were to be locked up with this poor distempered servant, he called to the watchman, and told him he must go then and fetch a nurse for them to attend this poor girl, for that it would be certain death to them all to oblige them to nurse her; and told him plainly that if he would not do this, the maid must perish either of the distemper or be starved for want of food, for he was resolved none of his family should go near her; and she lay in the garret four storey high, where she could not cry out, or call to anybody for help.

The watchman consented to that, and went and fetched a nurse, as he was appointed, and brought her to them the same evening. During this interval the master of the house took his opportunity to break a large hole through his shop into a bulk or stall, where formerly a cobbler had sat, before or under his shopwindow; but the tenant, as may be supposed at such a dismal time as that, was dead or removed, and so he had the key in his own keeping. Having made his way into this stall, which he could not have done if the man had been at the door, the noise he was obliged to make being such as would have alarmed the watchman; I say, having made his way into this stall, he sat still till the watchman returned with the nurse, and all the next day also. But the night following, having contrived to send the watchman of another trifling errand, which, as I take it, was to an apothecary's for a plaister for the maid, which he was to stay for the making up, or some other such errand that might secure his staying some time; in that time he conveyed himself and all his family out of the house, and left the nurse and the watchman to bury the poor wench - that is, throw her into the cart - and take care of the house.

I could give a great many such stories as these, diverting enough, which in the long course of that dismal year I met with - that is, heard of - and which are very certain to be true, or very near the truth; that is to say, true in the general: for no man could at such a time learn all the particulars. There was likewise violence used with the watchmen, as was reported, in abundance of places; and I believe that from the beginning of the visitation to the end, there was not less than eighteen or twenty of them killed, or so wounded as to be taken up for dead, which was supposed to be done by the people in the infected houses which were shut up, and where they attempted to come out and were opposed.

NICCOLO MACHIAVELLI
(1469-1527)

While in political exile Machiavelli wrote The Prince *which was the world's first amoral non-partisan study of the political process.*

PROMISES AND PRINCES

How honorable it is for a prince to keep his word, and act rather with integrity than collusion, I suppose everybody understands: nevertheless, experience has shown in our times that those princes who have not pinned themselves up to that punctuality and preciseness have done great things, and by their cunning and subtility have not only circumvented those with whom they had to deal, but have overcome and been too hard for those who have been so superstitiously exact. For further explanation you must understand there are two ways of contending - by law and by force: the first is proper to men; the second to beasts; but because many times the first is insufficient, recourse must be had to the second. It belongs, therefore, to a prince to understand both - when to make use of the rational and when of the brutal way; and this is recommended to princes, though abstrusely, by ancient writers, who tell them how Achilles and several other princes were committed for education to Chiron the Centaur, who was half man and half beast - thus showing how necessary it is for a prince to be acquainted with both natures, for one without the other will be of little duration. Seeing, therefore, it is of such importance to a prince to take upon him the nature and disposition of a beast, of all the whole flock he ought to imitate the lion and the fox; for the lion is in danger of toils and snares, and the fox of the wolf; so that he must be a fox to find out the snares, and a lion to fight away the wolves, but they who keep wholly to the lion have no true notion of themselves. A prince, therefore, who is wise and prudent, cannot or ought not to keep his word, when the keeping of it is to his prejudice, and the causes for which he promised removed. Were men all good this doctrine would not be taught, but because they are wicked and not likely to be punctual with you, you are not obliged to any such strictness with them; nor was there ever any prince that lacked lawful pretence to justify his breach of promise. I might give many modern examples, and show how many confederations, and peaces, and promises have been broken by the infidelity of princes, and how he that best personated the fox had the better success. Nevertheless, it is of great consequence to disguise your inclination, and to play the hypocrite well; and men are so simple in their temper and so submissive in their present necessities that he that is neat and cleanly in his collusions shall never want people to practice them upon. I cannot forbear one example which is still fresh in our memory. Alexander VI never did, nor thought of, anything but cheating, and never wanted matter to work upon; and though no man promised a thing with greater asseveration, nor confirmed it with more oaths and imprecations, and observed them less, yet understanding the world well he never miscarried.

A prince, therefore, is not obliged to have all the forementioned good qualities in reality, but is necessary he have them in appearance; nay, I will be bold to affirm that, having them actually, and employing them upon all occasions, they are extremely prejudicial, whereas, having them only in appearance, they turn to better account; it is honorable to seem mild, and merciful, and courteous, and religious, and sincere and indeed to be so, provided your mind be so rectified and prepared that you can act quite contrary upon occasion. And this must be premised, that a prince, especially if come but lately to the throne, cannot observe all those things exactly which cause men to be esteemed virtuous, being oftentimes necessitated, for the preservation of his state, to do things inhuman, uncharitable, and irreligious; and, therefore, it is convenient for his mind to be at his command, and flexible to all the puffs and variations of fortune; not forbearing to be good while it is in his choice, but knowing how to be evil when there is a necessity. A prince, then, is to have particular care that nothing falls from his mouth but what is full of the five qualities aforementioned, and that to see and hear him he appears all goodness, integrity, humanity, and religion, which last he ought to pretend to more than ordinarily, because more men do judge by the eye than by the touch; for everybody sees but few understand; everybody sees how you appear, but few know what in reality you are, and those few dare not oppose the opinion of the multitude, who have the majesty of their prince to defend them; and in the actions of all men, especially princes, where no man has power to judge, everyone looks to the end. Let a prince, therefore, do what he can to preserve his life, and continue his supremacy, the means which he uses shall be thought honorable, and be commended by everybody; because the people are always taken with the appearance and event of things, and the greatest part of the world consists of the people; those few who are wise taking place when the multitude has nothing else to rely upon. There is a prince at this time in being (but his name I shall conceal) who has nothing in his mouth but fidelity and peace: and yet had he exercised either the one or the other, they had robbed him before this both of his power and reputation.

GENERAL POORHOUSE

The poorhouse was the chief instrument of English poor law policy. It was to be a place of the last resort. Those that were sent to the workhouse were often those who could not look after themselves. The sick, the aged, the abandoned. Never the less all inmates, as they were then called, were treated by the guiding principle of "least eligibility" which stated that no residence of the poorhouse would receive more than the least paid worker.

REGULATIONS FOR THE ADMINISTRATION OF THE GENERAL POORHOUSE OF PARIS DURING THE REIGN OF LOUIS XIV

23 MARCH 1680

As there were no general poorhouses for shutting up the poor and for punishing able-bodied but idle beggars, at the time when that in our great city of Paris was established in 1656, and as those which have since been created in other towns on our orders were not instituted until some years later, the Paris house has received a large number of paupers from other towns and provinces who presented themselves at its gates; but as there are at the moment general poorhouses in almost every considerable town in the kingdom; and as the ordinances of the Kings our predecessors have stated that each town should succour its own poor, and as we have been informed that the penalties contained in our edict of April 1656 against able-bodied but idle beggars have not been sufficiently rigorous to abolish this disorder altogether, and as there is no more effective remedy than to shut them up in the institutions designed for the purpose, in order to punish them by the loss of their liberty, but the kind of food which they are given, and by the essential work which they are compelled to do:

We have therefore thought it reasonable to regulate on the one hand the kinds of people who must be received and looked after charitably inside this Poorhouse, and on the other to create new penalties which will make a rather stronger impact on these vagabonds....

To this end we order that there shall be freely received into this Poorhouse of our great city of Paris all poor children and the aged of either sex, those suffering from epilepsy, fits and other ills of this nature, provided that they were born or have lived for a number of years in the said city of Paris, its suburbs or environs, and are unable to subsist without the aid of the said Poorhouse....

We further order that all able-bodied persons of either sex, and over sixteen years old, who have the necessary strength to gain their own livelihood, and who are found begging in the city, suburbs and environs of Paris, and at Saint-Germain-en-Laye or at Versailles when we reside there, or on the roads leading thereto, shall be confined in separate buildings for each sex, for a fortnight or any other length of time which the directors shall determine, where they shall be given only what is absolutely necessary for their existence, and shall be employed on the harshest work which their bodies will support; if such people are found begging a second time, they shall be confined in the same place for three months; if a third time, for a year, and if a fourth time, we order that they shall be confined for the rest of their lives, never going out, no matter what the pretext, even in case of illness....

To ensure that this present regulation, those which have already been issued and those which will be published in the future, are obeyed to the letter..., we shall appoint every year six directors who will visit these poorhouses at least once in each month, and make a report on their findings....

GERRARD WINSTANLEY
(Approx. 1609-1660)

Winstanley was the leader of a religious economic group in England. In 1649 and 1650 the Diggers attempted to establish an egalitarian community that was based on a co-operative effort for a common good. Believing that humans were not normally aggressive, but only acted in an aggressive manner, when they were forced to be competitive. Ironically the poorer neighbors surrounding the Digger community harrassed the group into oblivion; however Winstanley's ideas found their way into the thoughts of Owen and Godwin.

THE LAW OF FREEDOM IN A PLATFORM;
OR
TRUE MAGISTRACY RESTORED

The great searching of heart in these days, is to finde out where true Freedom lies, that the Commonwealth of *England* might be established in Peace.

Some say, it lies in the free use of trading, and to have all patents, licenses, and restraints removed: But this is a *Freedom* under the Will of a Conqueror.

Others say, It is true Freedom to have Ministers to preach, and for people to hear whom they will, without being restrained or compelled from or to any form of worship: But this is an unsetled Freedom.

Others say, It is true Freedom to have Community with all Women, and to have liberty to satisfie their lusts and greedy appetitues: But this is the *Freedom*, that the elder Brother shall be Landlord of the Earth, and the younger Brother a Servant: And this is but a half Freedom, and begets murmurings, wars, and quarrels.

All these, and such like, are Freedoms: but they lead to Bondage, and are not the true *Foundation-Freedom* which settles a Commonwealth in Peace.

True Commonwealths Freedom lies in the free Enjoyment of the Earth.

True *Freedom* lies where a man receives his nourishment and preservation, and that is in the use of the Earth: For as Man is compounded of the four Materials of the Creation, *Fire, Water, Earth, and Ayr*; so is he preserved by the compounded bodies of these four, which are the fruits of the Earth; and he cannot live without them: for take away the free use of these, and the body languishes, the spirit is brought into bondage, and at length departs, and ceaseth his motional action in the body.

All that a man labors for, saith *Solomon*, is this, That he may enjoy the free use of the Earth, with the fruits thereof. *Eccles. 2.24.*

Do not the Ministers preach for maintenance in the Earth? the Lawyers plead causes to get the possessions of the Earth? Does not the Soldier fight for the Earth? And doth not the Landlord require Rent, that he may live in the fulness of the Earth by the labor of his Tenants?

And so, from the Thief upon the high way to the King who sits upon the throne, do not every one strive, either by force of Arms, or secret cheats, to get the possessions of the Earth one from another, because they see their Freedom lies in plenty, and their bondage lies in poverty?

Surely then, oppressing Lords of Manors, exacting Landlords, and Tythe-takers, may as well say, their brethren shall not breathe in the ayr, nor enjoy warmth in their bodies, nor have the moyst waters to fall upon them in showres, unless they will pay them Rent for it: As to say, Their brethren shall not work upon Earth, nor eat the fruits thereof, unless they will hire that liberty of them: for he that takes upon him to restrain his brother from the liberty of the one, may upon the same ground restrain him from the liberty of all four; *viz.* Fire, Water, Earth, and Ayr.

A man had better to have had no body, then to have no food for it; therefore this restraining of the Earth from brethren by brethren, is oppression and bondage; but the free enjoyment thereof is true Freedom.

I speak now in relation between the Oppressor and the oppressed; the inward bondages I meddle not with in their place, though I am assured that if it be rightly searched into, the inward bondages of the minde, as covetousness, pride, hypocrisie, envy, sorrow, fears, desperation, and madness, are all occasioned by the outward bondage, that one sort of people lay upon another.

And thus far natural experience makes it good, That true Freedom lies in the free enjoyment of the Earth.

THOMAS ROBERT MALTHUS
(1766-1834)

The pioneer of population studies, Malthus in his Essay on the Principle of Population written in 1798 addresses that poverty is inevitable because population increases geometrically whereas food production increases arithmetically. He believed that the only way people could control population increases was through "moral restraint," that is sexual abstinence.

POPULATION

It has been said that a tendency in mankind to increase at such a rate as would double the population in twenty-five years, and, if it had full scope, would fill the habitable globe with people in a comparatively short period, cannot be the law of nature, as the very different rate of increase which is actually found to take place must imply such an excessive degree of mortality and destruction of life as to be quite irreconcilable with actual facts and appearances. But the peculiar advantage of a law of increase in a geometrical progression is that though its power be absolutely immense if it be left unchecked, yet when this becomes impossible, it may be restrained by a comparatively moderate force. It can never, of course, happen that any considerable part of that prodigious increase which might be produced by an uninterrupted geometrical progression should exist and then be destroyed. The laws of nature which make food necessary to the life of man, as well as of plants and animals, prevent the continued existence of an excess which cannot be supported, and thus either discourage the production of such an excess, or destroy it in the bud in such a way as to make it scarcely perceptible to a careless observer. It has been seen that in some countries of Europe where the actual progress of the population is slower than in many others, as in Switzerland and Norway, for instance, the mortality is considerably less. Here, then, the necessity of a greater check to the natural progress of population produces no increase of mortality. And it appears, farther, that even the degree of mortality which is each year would be sufficient to destroy that excess of births which would naturally be produced if all married young and all could be supported, might take place, and often does take place in particular situations, and yet is very little noticed. About the middle of last century, the mortality of Stockholm and London was about 1 in 19 or 20. This is a degree of mortality which would probably keep the births on a level with the deaths even though all married at twenty. And yet numbers resorted both the Stockholm and London from choice, the grater part probably not aware that by so doing, they would shorten their own lives and those of their children, and the rest thinking that the difference was not worth attending to, or was at least balanced by the advantages of society and employment which the town presented. There is nothing, therefore, in the actual state of the mortality observed to take place in different countries and situations which, in the slightest degree, contradicts the supposition of a natural tendency to increase quite as great as that which has been stated.

It has been further remarked that as, in point of fact, it very rarely happens that mankind continue to increase in a geometrical progression of any kind, and only in a single instance in such a one as to double the population in twenty-five years, it is useless and absurd to lay any stress upon tendencies which never, for any length of time together, produce their natural effects. But it might really as well be said that we are not to estimate the natural rate of increase in wheat or sheep, as it is quite certain that their natural tendency to increase has never practically continued to develop itself for so long a time together as that of mankind. Both as a physical, and even economical question, it is curious and desirable to know the natural law of increase which prevails among the most important plants and animals. In the same view, it must be still more interesting to know the natural law of increase with respect to man. It may be said, indeed with truth, that the actual appearances all around us - the varying rate of increase in different countries, its very slow progress, or stationary state in some, and its very rapid progress in others - must be a mass of anomalies, and quite contrary to the analogies of all the rest of animated nature, if the natural tendency of mankind to increase be not, at the least, as great as that which is developed under the most favourable circumstances, while in all others it is kept down by the varying difficulties which the state of the soil and other obstacles oppose to it. But the question as it applies to man assumes at once a tenfold importance in reference to the moral and political effects which must result from those checks to increase, the existence and operation of which, in some form or other, no human exertions can by possibility prevent. A field is here opened for the most interesting inquiries which can engage the friends of human happiness.

But as a preliminary to these inquiries, it is obvious that we must know the degree of force to be overcome, and the varying character of the checks which, in the different countries of the world, are practically found to overcome it; and, for this purpose, the first step must be an endeavour to ascertain the natural law of population, or the rate at which mankind would increase under the fewest known obstacles. Nor can this tendency to increase every safely be lost sight of in the subsequent inquiries, which have for their object the improvement of the moral condition of man in society.

The existence of a tendency in mankind to increase, if unchecked, beyond the possibility of an adequate supply of food in a limited territory, must at once determine the question s to the natural right of the poor to full support in a state of society where the law of property is recognized. The question, therefore, resolves itself chiefly into a question relating to the necessity of those laws which establish and protect private property. It has been usual to consider the right of the strongest as the law of nature among mankind as well as among brutes; yet in so doing, we at once give up the peculiar and distinctive superiority of man as a reasonable being and class him with the beasts of the field. In the same language, it may be said that the cultivation of the earth is not natural to man. It certainly is not to man, considered merely as an animal without reason. But to a reasonable being, able to look forward to consequences, the laws of nature dictate the cultivation of the earth, both as the means of affording better support to the individual and of increasing the supplies required for increasing numbers, the dictates of those laws of nature being thus evidently calculated to promote the general good and increase the mass of human happiness. It is precisely in the same way, and in order to attain the same object, that the laws of nature dictate to man the establishment of property and the absolute necessity of some power in the society capable of protecting it. So strongly have the laws of nature spoken this language to mankind and so fully has the force of it been felt, that nothing seems to be thought so absolutely intolerable to reasonable beings as the prevalence in the same society of the right of the strongest; and the history of all ages shows that if men see no other way of putting and end to it than by establishing arbitrary power in an individual, there is scarcely any degree of tyranny, oppression, and cruelty which hey will not submit to from some single person and his satellites rather than be at the mercy of the first stronger man who may wish to possess himself of the fruit of their labour. The consequence of this universal and deeply seated feeling inevitably produced by the laws of nature, as applied to reasonable beings, is that the almost certain consequence of anarchy is despotism.

Allowing, then, distinctly, that the right of property is the creature of positive law, yet this law is so early and so imperiously forced on the attention of mankind that if it cannot be called a natural law, it must be considered as the most natural as well as the most necessary of all positive laws; and the foundation of this pre-eminence is its obvious tendency to promote the general good, and the obvious tendency of the absence of it to degrade mankind to the rank of brutes.

As property is the result of positive law, and the ground

on which the law which establishes it rests is the promotion of the public good and the increase of human happiness, it follows that it may be modified by the same authority by which it was enacted, with a view to the more complete attainment of the objects which it has in view. It may be said, indeed, that every tax for the use of the government, and every country or parish rate, is a modification of this kind. But there is no modification of the law of property, having still for its object the increase of human happiness, which must not be defeated by the concession of a right of full support to all that might be born. It may be safely said, therefore, that the concession of such a right, and a right of property, are absolutely incompatible and cannot exist together.

To what extent assistance may be given, even by law, to the poorer classes of society when in distress without defeating the great object of the law of property, is essentially a different question. It depends mainly upon the feelings and habits of the labouring classes of society, and can only be determined by experience. If it be generally considered as so discreditable to receive parochial relief, that great exertions are made to avoid it, and few or none marry with a certain prospect of being obliged to have recourse to it, and there is no doubt that those who were really in distress might be adequately assisted with little danger of a constantly increasing proportion of paupers; and, in that case, a great good would be attained without any proportionate evil to counterbalance it. But if, from the numbers of the dependent poor, the discredit of receiving relief is so diminished as to be practically disregarded, so that many marry with the almost certain prospect of becoming paupers, and the proportion of their numbers to the whole population is, in consequence, continually increasing, it is certain that the partial good attained must be much more than counterbalanced by the general deterioration in the condition of the great mass of the society and the prospect of its daily growing worse: so that, though from the inadequate relief which is in many cases granted, the manner in which it is conceded, and other counteracting causes, the operation of poor-laws such as they exist in England might be very different from the effects of a full concession of the right,[1] and a complete fulfilment of the duties resulting from it, yet such a state of things ought to give the most serious alarm to every friend to the happiness of society, and every effort consistent with justice and humanity ought to be made to remedy it. But whatever steps may be taken on this subject, it will be allowed that with any prospect of legislating for the poor with success, it is necessary to be fully aware of the natural tendency of the labouring classes of society to increase beyond the demand for their labour or the means of their adequate support, and the effect of this tendency to throw the greatest difficulties in the way of permanently improving their condition.

It would lead far beyond the limits which must be prescribed to this summary to notice the various objections which have been made by different writers to the principles which have been here explained. Those which contain in them the slightest degree of plausibility have been answered in the late editions of the *Essay on Population*, particularly in the appendix to the fifth and sixth, to which we refer the reader.[2] We will only, therefore, further notice the objection

---

[1] The grand objection to the language used respecting the *right of the poor to suppose* is that, as a matter of fact, we do not perform what we promise, and the poor may justly accuse us of deceiving them.

[2] In the answer to Mr. Arthur Young, the question of giving land to cottagers is discussed; and it is a curious fact, that after proposing a plan of this kind, Mr. A. Young is obliged to own, "that it might be prudent to consider the misery to which the progressive population might be subject as an evil which it is absolutely and physically impossible to prevent." The whole of the difficulty, in fact, lies here. The grand distinction between colonies in England and Ireland a colonies in Canada is that in the one case there will be no demand for the progressive population from the colonists, and the redundancy of labour after a short time will be aggravated; in the other, the demand will be great and certain for a long time, and the redundancy in the emigrating countries essentially relieved.

which has been made by some persons on religious grounds; for, as it is certainly of great importance that the answer which has been given to it should be kept in mind, we cannot refuse a place to a condensed statement of it at the end of this summary.

It has been thought that a tendency in mankind to increase beyond the greatest possible increase of food which could be produced in a limited space impeaches the goodness of the Deity, and is inconsistent with the letter and spirit of the Scriptures. If this objection were well founded, it would certainly be the most serious one which has been brought forwards; but the answer to it appears to be quite satisfactory, and it may be compressed into a very small compass.

First, it appears that the evils arising from the principle of population are exactly of the same kind as the evils arising from the excessive or irregular gratification of the human passions in general, and may equally be avoided by moral restraint. Consequently, there can be no more reason to conclude, from the existence of these evils, that the principle of increase is too strong than to conclude, from the existence of the vices arising from the human passions, that these passions are all too strong and require diminution or extinction instead of regulation and direction.

Secondly, it is almost universally acknowledged that both the letter and spirit of Revelation represent this world as a state of moral discipline and probation. But a state of moral discipline and probation cannot be a state of unmixed happiness, as it necessarily implies difficulties to be overcome and temptations to be resisted. Now, in the whole range of the laws of nature, not one can be pointed out which so especially accords with this scriptural view of the state of man on earth, as it gives rise to a greater variety of situations and exertions than any other, and marks, in a more general and stronger manner, and nationally as well as individually, the different effects of virtue and vice - of the proper government of the passions, and the culpable indulgence of them. It follows, then, that the principle of population, instead of being inconsistent with Revelation, must be considered as affording strong additional proofs of its truth.

Lastly, it will be acknowledged that in a state of probation, those laws seem best to accord with the views of a benevolent Creator, which, while they furnish the difficulties and temptations which form the essence of such a state, are of such a nature as to reward those who overcome them with happiness in this life as well as in the next. But the law of population answers particularly to this description. Each individual has, to a great degree, the power of avoiding the evil consequences to himself and society resulting from it, by the practice of a virtue dictated to him by the light of nature and sanctioned by revealed religion. And, as there can be no question that this virtue tends greatly to improve the condition and increase the comforts both of the individual who practice it, and through them, of the whole society, the ways of God to man with regard to this great law are completely vindicated.

FRANCOIS MARIE ARONET DE VOLTAIRE
(1694-1778)

Voltaire was one of the first authors to take cultural and economic developments seriously. He was a masterful satirist and rationalist best symbolized by his sweeping statements such as "If God did not exist, He would have to be invented."

PHILOSOPHICAL DICTIONARY

General Reflection on Man

It needs twenty years to lead man from the plant state in which he is within his mother's womb, and the pure animal state which is the lot of his early childhood, to the state at which the maturity of his reason begins to appear. It has taken some thirty centuries to learn a little about his structure. It would need an eternity to learn something about his soul. It takes but an instant to kill him.

Tolerance

What is tolerance? It is the consequence of humanity. All of us are formed of frailty and error. Let us mutually pardon each other's folly. that is the first law of nature.

It is quite clear that the individual who persecutes a man, his brother, because he is not of the same opinion, is nothing more than a monster. That admits of no difficulty. But the Government! The Magistrates! The Princes! How do they treat those who have different worships from theirs? If they are powerful strangers, it is certain that a prince will make an alliance with them. Francois I, very Christian, will unite with Muslims against Charles V, very Catholic.

Francois I will give money to the Lutherans of Germany to support them in their revolt against the emperor, but, in accordance with custom, he will commence by having Lutherans burnt at home. He pays them in Saxony for political reasons, but in Paris he burns them for political reasons. But what will happen? Persecutions make proselytes? Soon France will be filled with new Protestants. At first they will let themselves be hanged, later will come their turn to hang. There will be civil wars, then will come the Night of St. Bartholomew, then this corner of the world will be worse than all that the ancients and moderns have ever told of hell.

Madmen, who have never been able to give worship to the God who made you! Miscreants, whom the examples of the Noachides, the learned Chinese, the Parseems, and all the sages, have never been able to lead! Monsters, who have need of superstitions as crows' gizzards have need of carrion! You have been told it already, and there remains nothing else to tell you - if you have two religions in your countries, they will cut each other's throat; if you have thirty religions, they will dwell in peace. Look at the great Turk. He governs Guebres, Banians, Greek Christians, Nestorians, Romans. The first who dare to stir up trouble would be impaled. Hence everyone is tranquil.

Of all religions, the Christian is no doubt the one which should inspire tolerance most, although to this point in history the Christians have been the most tolerant of men. The Christian Church was divided in its cradle, and was divided even in the persecutions which under the first emperors it sometimes endured. Often the martyr was regarded as an apostate by his brethren, and the Carpocratian Christian expired beneath the sword of the Roman executioners, excommunicated by the Edionite Christian, which in turn was anathema to the Sabellian.

This terrible discord, which has lasted for so many centuries, is a very striking lesson that we should pardon each other's errors. Discord is the great ill of mankind. Tolerance is the only remedy.

Every sect, as one knows, is a ground of error; there are no sects of geometers, algebraist, arithmeticians, because all the propositions of geometry, algebra, and arithmetic are true. In every other science one may be deceived. What Thomist or Scotist theologian would dare say seriously that he is certain of his case?

If it were permitted to reason consistently in religious matters, it is clear that we all ought to become Jews, because Jesus Christ our Savior was born a Jew, lived a Jew, died a Jew, and because he said expressly that he was accomplishing and fulfilling the Jewish religion. But it is clearer still that we ought to be tolerant of one another, because we are all weak, inconsistent, liable to fickleness and error. Shall a reed laid low in the mud by the wind say to a fellow reed fallen in the opposite direction: "Crawl as I crawl, wretch, or I shall petition that you be torn up by the roots and burned!"

GEORG WILHELM FRIEDRICH HEGEL
(1770-1831)

Hegel has contributed greatly to the world of knowledge. Of his many achievements none surpass his ideas about dialectical thinking. The dialectical process consists of one idea (thesis) inevitably creating an opposite idea (anti-thesis) and the interaction of the two forms a new concept (synthesis). Thus the universe of ideas is in a state of perpetual motion. Many scholars, Karl Marx and John Dewey included, are indebted to Hegel's basic intellectual formula.

REASON IN HISTORY

The Dialectic of National Principles

World history in general is the development of spirit in *Time*, just a nature is the development of the Idea is *Space*.

When we cast a glance at world history in general, we see a tremendous picture of transformations and actions, an infinite of varied formations of peoples, states, individuals, in restless succession. Everything that can enter and interest the mind of man, every sentiment of goodness, beauty, greatness is called into play. Everywhere aims are adopted and pursued which we recognize, whose accomplishment we desire; we hope and fear for them. In all these events and accidents we see human activity and suffering in the foreground, everywhere something which is part and parcel of ourselves, and therefore everywhere our interest takes sides for or against. At times we are attracted by beauty, freedom, and richness, at others by energy, by which when vice knows how to make itself important. At other times we see the large mass of a universal interest move heavily along, only to be abandoned to and pulverized by an infinite complexity of trifling circumstances. Then again we see trivial results from gigantic expenditures of forces or tremendous results from seemingly insignificant causes. Everywhere the motliest throng which draws us into its circle; when the one disappears, the other swiftly takes its place.

This restless succession of individuals and peoples, who exist for a time and then disappear, presents to us a universal thought, a category: that of *change* in general. To comprehend this change from its negative side, all we have to do is to look at the ruins of past splendor. What traveller has not been moved by the ruins of Carthage, Palmyra, Persepolis, Rome to think of the transitoriness of empires and men, to mourn the passing of once vigorous and flourishing life? This sadness does not dwell on personal loss and the transitoriness of one's own purposes; it is disinterested sadness about the passing of splendid and highly developed human life. But then we pass on to another thought just as intimately connected with the idea of change, the positive fact, namely, that ruin is at the same time emergence of a new life, that out of life arises death, but out of death, life. This is a great thought which the Orientals fully understood and which is the highest thought of their metaphysics. In the conception of the migration of souls it refers to individuals. In the better known image of the *Phoenix*, however, it refers to all natural life, continuously preparing its own pyre and consuming itself so that from its ashes the new, rejuvenated, fresh life continually arises. This picture, however, is Asiatic; oriental, not occidental. The Spirit, devouring its worldly envelope, not only passes into another envelope, not only arises rejuvenated from the ashes of its embodiment, but it emerges from them exalted, transfigured, a purer Spirit. It is true that it acts against itself, devours its own existence. But in so doing it elaborates upon this existence; its embodiment becomes material for its work to elevate itself to a new embodiment.

We must, then, consider the spirit in this respect. Its transformations are not merely rejuvenating transitions, returns to the same form. They are elaborations upon itself, by which it multiplies the material for its endeavors. Thus it experiments in a multitude of dimensions and directions, developing itself, exercising itself, enjoying itself in inexhaustible abundance. For each of its creations, satisfying for the moment, presents new material, a new challenge for further elaborations. The abstract thought of mere change gives place to the thought of Spirit manifesting, developing, and differentiating its powers in all the directions of its plenitude. What powers it possesses in itself we understand by the multiplicity of its products and formations. In this lust of activity it only deals with itself. Though involved with the conditions of nature, both inner and outer, it not only meets in them opposition and hindrance, but often failure and defeat through the complications into which it becomes involved through them or through itself. But even when it perishes it does so in the course of its function and destiny, and even then it offers the spectacle of having proved itself as spiritual activity.

The very essence of spirit is *action*. It makes itself what it essentially is; it is its own product, its own work. Thus it becomes object of itself, thus it is presented to itself as an external existence. Likewise the spirit of a people: it is a definite spirit which builds itself up to an objective world. This world, then, stands and continues in its religion, its cult, its customs, its constitution and political laws, the whole scope of its institutions, its events and deeds. This is its work: this *one* people! Peoples are what their deeds are. Every Englishman will say, we are the ones who navigate the ocean and dominate world commerce, who own East India and its wealth, who have a parliament, juries, and so on. The function of the individual is to appropriate to himself this substantial being, make it part of his character and capacity, and thus to become something in the world. For he finds the existence of the people as a ready-made, stable world, into which he must fit himself. The spirit of the people, then, enjoys and satisfies itself in its work, in its world.

The people is moral, virtuous, strong when it brings forth

what it wills. It defends its product against outside powers through the work of its objectification. The tension between (its potentiality and its actuality) what it is in itself, subjectively, in its inner purpose and essence, and what it really is (objectively), is thus abolished. It is with itself (actualized), it has itself objectively before itself. But then this activity of spirit is no longer necessary; it has what it wanted. The people can still do a great deal in war and peace, internally and externally. But the living, substantial soul itself is, so to speak, no longer active. The deepest, highest interest thus has gone out of life; for interest is only where there is opposition. The people lives like an individual passing from manhood to old age, enjoying himself, for he is exactly what he wanted to be and was able to achieve. Even though his imagination may have gone further, it has abandoned more far-reaching purposes; if reality did not fit them, he fits the purposes to reality. It is this life of *habit* - the watch is wound up and goes by itself - which brings about natural death. Habit is tensionless activity. Only formal duration is left to it, in which plenitude and depth of purpose need no longer to be heard. Existence has become, so to speak, external, sensuous; it is not absorbed any more in its purpose. Thus individuals die, thus peoples die a natural death. Although the latter continue in existence, it is an uninterested, lifeless existence; its institutions are without necessity, just because the necessity has been satisfied - all political life is triviality and boredom. If a truly general interest is desired, then the spirit of the people would have to come to the point of wanting something new - but whence this something new? It would be a higher, more universal idea of itself, transcending its present principle; but this, precisely, would manifest the presence of a wider principle, a new spirit.

Such a new principle does indeed come into the spirit of a people which has arrived at its completion and actualization. It not merely dies a natural death, for it is no merely single individual, but has spiritual, universal life. Its natural death appears rather as the killing of itself by itself.

The reason for this difference from the single, natural individual is that the national spirit exists as a genus, and consequently carries its own negation within itself, the very universality of its existence. A people can die a violent death only when it has become naturally dead in itself, such as the German Imperial Cities (*Reichsstadte*) or the German Imperial Constitution.

The universal spirit does not merely die a natural death; it does not simply vanish in the senile life of mere habit. Insofar as it is a national spirit and a part of world history itself, it also comes to know its work and to think itself. It is world-historical only insofar as in its fundamental elements, its essential purpose, there is a *universal* principle; only insofar is the work which such a spirit produces a moral, political organization. If it is mere desires which impel peoples to actions, then such actions pass without leaving traces, or rather, its traces are mere corruption and ruin.

Thus at first Cronos ruled, Time itself - the golden age without moral works. What it produced, its children, were devoured by it. Only Zeus, who gave birth to Athene out of his head and whose circle included Apollo and the Muses, conquered Time and set a limit to its lapse. He is the political God who has produced a moral work, the State.

In work itself is implied the elemental character of universality, of Thought. Without Thought it has no objective; thought is its fundamental definition. The highest point of a people's development is the rational consciousness of its life and conditions, the scientific understanding of its laws, its system of justice, its morality. For in this unity (of subjective and objective) lies the most intimate unity in which Spirit can be with itself. The purpose of its work is to have itself as object. But Spirit can have itself as object only by thinking itself.

At this point, then, Spirit knows its principles, the universal element of its actions. But this work of Thought, being universal, is at the same time different in form from the particular, real work, and from the concrete life which brings the work about. When this point is attained, we have both a real and an ideal existence. If (for example) we want to gain a general representation and a concept of the Greeks and their life, we find it in Sophocles and Aristophanes, in Thucydides and Plato. In these individuals the Greek spirit grasped itself in thought and representation. This is its deeper satisfaction (its consummation); but it is at the same time ideal and different from its active reality.

In such a time, a people, therefore, necessarily finds a satisfaction in the idea of virtue. Talk about virtue partly accompanies, partly replaces real virtue. On the other hand, pure universal Thought, being universal, is apt to bring the particular and unreflected - faith, confidence, custom - to reflection about itself and its immediate (simple and unreflected) existence. It thus shows up the limitation of unreflected life, partly by giving it reasons on hand by which to secede from its duties, partly by asking about reasons and the connection with universal thought. Then, in not finding the latter, it tries to shatter duty itself as without foundation.

Therewith appears the isolation of the individuals from each other and the whole, their aggressive selfishness and vanity, their seeking of advantage and satisfaction at the expense of the whole. For the inward principle of such isolation (not only produces the content but) the *form* of subjectivity - selfishness and corruption in the unbound passions and egotistic interests of men.

Thus Zeus and his race were themselves devoured, Zeus who set an end to the devouring action of Time and stayed this transiency by firmly establishing something lasting in itself. He was devoured by the generative agent, namely, the principle of Thought, of knowledge, of reasoning, of insight from and demand for reasons.

Time is the negative element in the sensuous world. Thought is the same negativity, but its deepest, its infinite form. It therefore resolves all existence in general, but first in its finite, its definite form. For existence in general is determined as objective. It therefore appears as given and immediate, as authority. It is finite and limited either as content or (as form; the latter) as the bound for the thinking subject and its infinite reflection in itself.

[*The resolution of existence through thought is at the same time necessarily the arising of a new principle. Thought as universal is resolving, but this resolution actually contains the preceding principle within it, though no longer in its original form but transfigured through universality.*] Thus life emerges out of death; but it is only individual life. If we consider the genus as the substantial in this transformation, then the death of the individual is a falling back of the genus into individuality. The preservation of the genus is then nothing but the monotonous repetition of the same kind of existence. Cognition, the thinking comprehension of being, is the source and birthplace of a new spiritual form, a higher form, whose principle is partly preserving, partly transfiguring its material. For Thought is the universal, the genus which is immortal and preserves its identity. The particular form of Spirit not only passes away naturally in time, but is abolished through the self-acting, self-mirroring activity of self-consciousness. Since this abolition is activity of Thought, it is both preservation and transfiguration. While thus Spirit, on the one hand, abolishes the actuality, the subsistence of what it is, on the other hand, it gains thereby the essence, the Thought, the universal of that which it *only was* (of its transient condition). Its principle is no longer this immediate content and purpose of what it previously was, but the essence of it.

The result of this process, then, is that the Spirit in objectifying itself and thinking its own being, on the one hand, destroys this (particular) determination of its own being and, on the other hand, grasps its universality. It thus gives a new determination to its principle. The substantial determination of this national spirit is therewith changed; its principle passes into a new and higher one.

It is most important for the full understanding and comprehension of history to grasp and possess the thought of this transition. An individual as unity traverses various stages and remains the same individual. So also a people, up to the stage which is the universal stage of its spirit. In this consists the inner, the conceptual necessity of its change. Here we have the essence, the very soul of the philosophical understanding of history.

Spirit is essentially the result of its own activity. Its activity is transcending the immediately given, negating it, and returning into itself. We can compare it with the seed of a plant, which is both beginning and result of the plant's whole life. The powerlessness of life manifests itself precisely in this falling apart of beginning and end. Likewise in the lives of individuals and peoples. The life of a people brings a fruit to maturity, for its activity aims at actualizing its principle. But the fruit does not fall back into the womb of the people which has produced and matured it. On the contrary, it turns into a bitter drink for this people. The people cannot abandon it, for it has an unquenchable thirst for it. But imbibing the drink is the drinker's destruction, yet, at the same time the rise of a new principle.

We have already seen what the final purpose of this process is. The principles of the national spirits progressing through a necessary succession of stages are only moments of the one universal Spirit which through them elevates and completes itself into a self-comprehending *totality*.

Thus, in dealing with the idea of Spirit only and in considering the whole of world history as nothing but its manifestation, we are dealing only with the *present* - however long the past may be which we survey. [*There is no time where it (the Spirit) has not been nor will not be; it neither was nor is it yet to be. It is forever now.*] The Idea is ever present, the Spirit immortal. [*What is true is eternal in and for itself, neither yesterday nor tomorrow but now in the sense of absolute presence. In the Idea, what may seem lost is eternally preserved.*] This implies that the present stage of Spirit contains all previous stages within itself. These, to be sure, have unfolded themselves successively and separately, but Spirit still is what it has in itself always been. The differentiation of its stages is but the development of what it is in itself. The life of the ever-present Spirit is a cycle of stages, which, on the one hand, co-exist side by side, but, on the other hand, seem to be past. The moments which Spirit seems to have left behind, it still possesses in the depth of its present.

EDMUND BURKE
(1729-97)

The father of conservatism, Burke resisted political reform. He wrote against the French revolution believing that more damage could be done to society in one day of revolution than one-hundred years of rule.

ON PUBLIC DISCONTENTS

It is an undertaking of some degree of delicacy to examine its the cause of public disorders. If a man happens not to succeed in such an inquiry, he will be thought weak and visionary; if he touches the true grievance, there is a danger that he may come near to persons of weight and consequence, who will rather be exasperated at the discovery of their errors, than thankful for the occasion of correcting them. If he should be obliged to blame favorites of the people, he will be considered as the tool of power; if he censures those in power, he will be looked on as an instrument of faction. But in all exertions of duty something is to be hazarded. In cases of tumult and disorder, our law has invested every man, in some sort, with the authority of a magistrate. When the affairs of the nation are distracted, private people are by the spirit of that law, justified in stepping a little out of their ordinary sphere. They enjoy a privilege, of somewhat more dignity and effect, than that of idle lamentation over the calamities of their country. They may look into them narrowly; they may reason upon them liberally; and if they should be so fortunate as to discover the true source of the mischief, and to suggest any probable method of removing it, though they may displease the rulers for the day, they are certainly of service to the cause of Government. Government is deeply interested in everything which, even through the medium of some temporary uneasiness, may tend finally to compose the minds of the subjects, and to conciliate their affections. I have nothing to do here with the abstract value of the voice of the people. But as long as reputation, the most precious possession of every individual, and as long as opinion, the great support of the State, depend entirely upon that voice, it can never be considered as a thing of little consequence either to individuals or to Government. Nations are not primarily ruled by laws; less by violence. Whatever original energy may be supposed either in force or regulation; the operation of both is, in truth, merely instrumental. Nations are governed by the same methods, and on the same principles, by which an individual without authority is often able to govern those who are his equals or his superiors; by a knowledge of their temper, and by a judicious management of it; I mean - when public affairs are steadily and quietly conducted: not when the Government is nothing but a continued scuffle between the magistrate and the multitude; in which sometimes the one and sometimes the other is uppermost; in which they alternately yield and prevail, in a series of contemptible victories and scandalous submissions. The temper of the people amongst whom he presides ought therefore to be the first study of a Statesman. And the knowledge of this temper it is by no means impossible for him to attain, if he has not an interest in being ignorant of what it is his duty to learn.

To complain of the age we live in, to murmur at the present possessors of power, to lament the past, to conceive extravagant hopes of the future, are the common dispositions of the greatest part of mankind; indeed the necessary effects of the ignorance and levity of the vulgar. Such complaints and humors have existed in all times; yet as all times have not been alike, true political sagacity manifests itself, in distinguishing that complaint which only characterizes the general infirmity of human nature, from those which are symptoms of the particular distemperature of our own air and season.

MARY WOLLSTONECRAFT
(1759-97)

<u>Her Vindication of the Rights of Woman</u> was the first great feminist work. It was written in 1790 in response to Edmund Burke's thoughts about human rights in his <u>Reflections on the Revolution in France</u>. She was married to the anarchist William Godwin and died an early death due to childbirth complications associated with the birth of her daughter Mary Wollstonecraft-Godwin Shelley the author of Frankenstein.

A VINDICATION OF THE RIGHTS WOMAN

My own sex, I hope, will excuse me, if I treat them like rational creatures, instead of flattering their *fascinating* graces, and viewing them as if they were in a state of perpetual childhood, unable to stand alone. I earnestly wish to point out in what true dignity and human happiness consists--I wish to persuade women to endeavour to acquire strength, both of mind and body, and to convince them that the soft phrases, susceptibility of heart, delicacy of sentiment, and refinement of taste, are almost synonymous with epithets of weakness, and that those beings who are only the objects of pity and that kind of love, which as been termed its sister, will soon become objects of contempt.

Dismissing, then, those pretty feminine phrases, which the men condescendingly use to soften our slavish dependence, and despising that weak elegancy of mind, exquisite sensibility, and sweet docility of manners, supposed to be the sexual characteristics of the weaker vessel, I wish to shew that elegance is inferior to virtue, that the first object of laudable ambition is to obtain a character as a human being, regardless of the distinction of sex; and that secondary views should be brought to this simple touchstone.

I may be accused of arrogance; still I must declare what I firmly believe, that all the writers who have written on the subject of female education and manners, from Rousseau to Dr. Gregory, have contributed to render women more artificial, weak characters, than they would otherwise have been; and consequently, more useless members of society. I might have expressed this conviction in a lower key; but I am afraid it would have been the whine of affectation, and not the faithful expression of my feelings, of the clear result which experience and reflection have led me to draw. When I come to that division of the subject, I shall advert to the passages that I more particularly disapprove of, in the works of the authors I have just alluded to; but it is first necessary to observe, that my objection extends to the whole purport of those books, which tend, in my opinion, to degrade one half of the human species, and render women pleasing at the expense of every solid virtue.

Though, to reason on Rousseau's ground, if man did attain a degree of perfection of mind when his body arrived at maturity, it might be proper, in order to make a man and his wife *one*, that she should rely entirely on his understanding; and the graceful ivy, clasping the oak that supported it, would form a whole in which strength and beauty would be equally conspicuous. But, alas! husbands, as well as their helpmates, are often only overgrown children; nay, thanks to early debauchery, scarcely men in their outward form--and if the blind lead the blind, one need not come from heaven to tell us the consequence.

Many are the causes that, in the present corrupt state of society, contribute to enslave women by cramping their understandings and sharpening their senses. One, perhaps, that silently does more mischief than all the rest, is their disregard of order.

To do everything in an orderly manner, is a most important precept, which women, who, generally speaking, receive only a disorderly kind of education, seldom attend to with that degree of exactness that men, who from their infancy are broken into method, observe. This negligent kind of guess-work, for what other epithet can be used to point out the random exertions of a sort of instinctive common sense, never brought to the test of reason? prevents their generalizing matters of fact--so that they do today, what they did yesterday, merely because they did it yesterday.

This contempt of the understanding in early life has more baneful consequences than is commonly supposed; for the little knowledge which women of strong minds attain, is, from various circumstances, of a desultory kind than the knowledge of men, and it is acquired more by sheer observations on real life, than from comparing what has been individually observed with the results of experience generalized by speculation. Led by their dependent situation and domestic employments more into society, what they learn is rather by snatches; and as learning is with them, in general, only a secondary thing, they do not pursue any one branch with that persevering ardour necessary to give vigour to the faculties, and clearness to the judgment. In the present state of society, a little learning is required to support the character of a gentleman; and boys are obliged to submit to a few years of discipline. But in the education of women, the cultivation of the understanding is always subordinate to the acquirement of some corporeal accomplishment; even while enervated by confinement and false notions of modesty, the body is prevented from attaining that grace and beauty which relaxed half-formed limbs never exhibit. Besides, in youth their faculties are not brought forward by emulation; and having no serious scientific study, if they have natural sagacity if is turned too soon on life and manners. They dwell on effects, and modifications, without tracing them back to causes; and complicated rules to adjust behaviour are a weak substitute for simple principles.

As a proof that education gives this appearance of weakness to females, we may instance the example of military men, who are, like them, sent into the world before their minds have been stored with knowledge or fortified by principles. The consequences are similar; soldiers acquire a little superficial knowledge, snatched from the muddy current of conversation, and, from continually mixing with society, they gain, what is termed a knowledge of the world; and this acquaintance with manners and customs has frequently been confounded with a knowledge of the human heart. But can the crude fruit of casual observation, never brought to the test of judgment, formed by comparing speculation and experience, deserve such a distinction? Soldiers, as well as women, practice the minor virtues with punctilious politeness. Where is then the sexual difference, when the education has been the same? All the difference that i can discern, arises from the superior advantage of liberty, which enables the former to see more of life.

It is wandering from my present subject, perhaps, to make a political remark; but, as it was produced naturally by the train of my reflections, I shall not pass it silently over.

Standing armies can never consist of resolute robust men; they may be well disciplined machines, but they will seldom contain men under the influence of strong passions, or with very rigorous faculties. And as for any depth of understanding, I will venture to affirm, that it is as rarely to be found in the army as amongst women; and the cause, I maintain, is the same. It may be further observed, that officers are also particularly attentive to their persons, fond of dancing, crowd rooms, adventures, and ridicule. Like the *fair* sex, the business of their lives is gallantry. they were taught to please, and they only live to please. Yet they do not lose their rank in the distinction of sexes, for they are still reckoned superior to women, though in what their superiority consists, beyond what I have just mentioned, it is difficult to discover.

The great misfortune is this, that they both acquire manners before morals, and a knowledge of life before they have, from reflection, any acquaintance with the grand ideal outline of human nature. The consequence is natural; satisfied with common nature, they become a prey to prejudices, and taking all their opinions on credit, they blindly submit to authority. So that, if they have any sense, it is a kind of instinctive glance, that catches proportions, and decides with respect to manners; but fails when arguments are to be pursued below the surface, or opinions analyzed.

May not the same remarks be applied to women? Nay, the argument may be carried still further, for they are both thrown out of a useful station by the unnatural distinctions established in civilized life. Riches and hereditary honours have made cyphers of women to give consequence to the numerical figure; and idleness has produced a mixture of gallantry and despotism into society, which leads the very men who are slaves of their mistresses to tyrannize over their sisters, wives, and daughters. This is only keeping them in rank and file, it is true. Strengthen the female mind by enlarging it, and there will be an end to blind obedience; but, as blind obedience is ever fought for by power, tyrants and sensualists are in the right when they endeavour to keep women in the dark, because the former only want slaves, and the latter a plaything. The sensualist, indeed, has been the most dangerous of tyrants, and women have been duped by their lovers, as princes by their ministers, whilst dreaming that they reigned over them.

I now principally allude to Rousseau, for his character of Sophia is, undoubtedly, a captivating one, though it appears to me grossly unnatural; however it is not the superstructure, but the foundation of her character, the principles on which her education was built, that I mean to attack; nay, warmly as I admire the genius of that able writer, whose opinions I shall often have occasion to cite, indignation always takes place of admiration, and the rigid frown of insulted virtue effaces the smile of complacency, which his eloquent periods are wont to raise, when I read his voluptuous reveries. Is this the man, who, in his ardour for virtue, would banish all the soft arts of peace, and almost carry us back to Spartan discipline? Is this the man who delights to paint the useful struggles of passion, the triumphs of good dispositions, and the heroic flights which carry the glowing soul out of itself?--How are these mighty sentiments lowered when he describes the pretty foot and enticing airs of his little favourite! But, for the present, I waive the subject, and, instead of severely reprehending the transient effusions of overweening sensibility, I shall only observe, that whoever has cast a benevolent eye on society, must often have been gratified by the sight of humble mutual love, not dignified by sentiment, or strengthened by a union in intellectual pursuits. The domestic trifles of the day have afforded matters for cheerful converse, and innocent caresses have softened toils which did not require great exercise of mind or stretch of though: yet, has not the sight of this moderate felicity excited more tenderness than respect? An emotion similar to what we feel when children are playing, or animals sporting, whilst the contemplation of the noble struggles of suffering merit has raised admiration, and carried our thoughts to that world where sensation will give place to reason.

Women are, therefore, to be considered either as moral beings, or so weak that they must be entirely subjected to the superior faculties of men.

Let us examine this question. Rousseau declares that a woman should never, for a moment, feel herself independent, that she should be governed by fear to exercise her *natural* cunning, and made a coquettish slave in order to render her a more alluring object of desire, a *sweeter* companion to man, whenever he chooses to relax himself. He carries the arguments, which he pretends to draw from the indications of nature, still further, and insinuates that truth and fortitude, the corner stones of all human virtue should be cultivated with certain restrictions, because, with respect to the female character, obedience is the grand lesson which ought to be impressed with unrelenting rigour.

What nonsense! When will a great man arise with sufficient strength of mind to puff away the fumes which pride and sensuality have thus spread over the subject! If women are by nature inferior to men, their virtues must be the same in quality, if not in degree, or virtue is a relative idea; consequently, their conduct should be founded on the same principles, and have the same aim.

Connected with man as daughters, wives, and mothers, their moral character may be estimated by their manner of fulfilling those simple duties; but the end, the grand end of their exertions should be to unfold their own faculties and acquire the dignity of conscious virtue. They may try to render their road pleasant; but ought never to forget, in common with man, that life yields not the felicity which can satisfy an immortal soul. I do not mean to insinuate that either sex should be so lost in abstract reflections or distant views, as to forget the affections and duties that lie before them, and are, in truth, the means appointed to produce the fruit of life: on the contrary, I would warmly recommend them, even while I assert, that they afford most satisfaction when they are considered in their true, sober light.

Probably the prevailing opinion, that woman was created for man, may have taken its rise from Moses's poetical story; yet, as very few, it is presumed, who have bestowed any serious thought on the subject, ever supposed that Eve was, literally speaking, one of Adam's ribs, the deduction must be allowed to fall to the ground; or, only be so far admitted as it proves that man, from the remotest antiquity, found it convenient to exert his strength to subjugate his companion, and his invention to show that she ought to have her neck bent under the yoke, because the whole creation was only created for his convenience or pleasure.

Let it not be concluded that I wish to invert the order of things; I have already granted, that, from the constitution of their bodies, men seem to be designed by Providence to attain a greater degree of virtue. I speak collectively of the whole sex; but I see not the shadow of a reason to conclude that their virtues should differ in respect to their nature. In fact, how can they, if virtue has only one eternal standard? I must therefore, if I reason consequentially, as strenuously maintain that they have the same simple direction, as that there is a God.

It follows then that cunning should not be opposed to wisdom, little cares to great exertions, or insipid softness, varnished over with the name of gentleness, to that fortitude which grand views alone can inspire.

I shall be told that woman would then lose many of her peculiar graces, and the opinion of a well-known poet might be quoted to refute my unqualified assertion. For Pope has said, in the name of the whole male sex,

"Yet ne'er so sure our passion to create,
As when she touch'd the brink of all we hate."

In what light this sally places men and women, I shall leave to the judicious to determine; meanwhile I shall content myself with observing, that I cannot discover why, unless they are mortel, females should always be degraded by being made subservient to love or lust.

To speak disrespectfully of love is, I know, high treason against sentiment and fine feelings; but I wish to speak the simple language of truth, and rather to address the head than the heart. To endeavour to reason love out of the world, would be to out Quixote Cervantes, and equally offend against common sense; but an endeavour to restrain this tumultuous passion, and to prove that it should not be allowed to dethrone superior powers, or to usurp the sceptre which the understanding should ever coolly wield, appears less wild.

Youth is the season for love in both sexes; but in those days of thoughtless enjoyment provision should be made for the more important years of life, when reflection takes place of sensation. But Rousseau, and most of the male writers who have followed his steps, have warmly inculcated that the whole tendency of female education ought to be directed to one point:--to render them pleasing.

Let me reason with the supporters of this opinion who have any knowledge of human nature, do they imagine that marriage can eradicate the habitude of life? The woman who has only been taught to please will soon find that her charms are oblique sunbeams, and that they cannot have much effect on her husband's heart when they are seen every day, when the summer is passed and gone. Will she then have sufficient native energy to look into herself for comfort, and cultivate her dormant faculties? or, is it not more rational to expect that she will try to please other men; and, in the emotions raised by the expectation of new conquests, endeavour to forget the mortification her love or pride has received? When the husband ceases to be a lover--and the time will inevitably come, her desire of pleasing will then grow languid, or become a spring of bitterness; and love, perhaps, the lost evanescent of all passions, gives place to jealousy or vanity.

I now speak of women who are restrained by principle or prejudice; such women, though they would shrink from an intrigue with real abhorrence, yet, nevertheless, wish to be convinced by the homage of gallantry that they are cruelly neglected by their husbands; or, days and weeks are spent in dreaming of the happiness enjoyed by congenial souls till their health is undermined and their spirits broken by discontent. How then can the great art of pleasing be such a necessary study? It is only useful to a mistress; the chaste wife, and serious mother, should only consider her power to please as the polish of her virtues, and the affection of her husband as one of the comforts that render her talk less difficult and her life happier. But, whether she be loved or neglected, her first wish should be to make herself respectable, and not to rely for all her happiness on a being subject to like infirmities with herself.

DAVID RICARDO
(1772-1823)

He stated wages cannot, for long, rise above the lowest level of subsistence. Although he deplored the parasitic activity of the landlord, he was to amass his own private fortune through property. His works greatly influenced Marx and Engels.

"WAGES" from
Principles of Political Economy

When wages rise, it is generally because the increase of wealth and capital have occasioned a new demand for labour, which will infallibly be attended with an increased production of commodities. To circulate these additional commodities, even at the same prices as before, more money is required, more of this foreign commodity from which money is made, and which can only be obtained by importation. Whenever a commodity is required in greater abundance than before, its relative value rises comparatively with those commodities with which its purchase is made. If more hats were wanted, their price would rise, and more gold would be given for them. If more gold were required, gold would rise, and hats would fall in price, as a greater quantity of hats and of all other things would then be necessary to purchase the same quantity of gold. But in the case supposed, to say that commodities will rise, because wages rise, is to affirm a positive contradiction; for we first say that gold will rise in relative value in consequence of demand, and secondly, that it will fall in relative value because prices will rise, two effects which are totally incompatible with each other. To say that commodities are raised in price, is the same thing as to say that money is lowered in relative value; for it is by commodities that the relative value of gold is estimated. If then all commodities rose in price, gold could not come from abroad to purchase those dear commodities, but it would go from home to be employed with advantage in purchasing the comparatively cheaper foreign commodities. It appears, then, that the rise of wages will not raise the prices of commodities, whether the metal from which money is made be produced at home or in a foreign country. All commodities cannot rise at the same time without an addition to the quantity of money. This addition could not be obtained at home, as we have already shewn; nor could it be imported from abroad. To purchase any additional quantity of gold from abroad, commodities at home must be cheap, not dear. The importation of gold, and a rise in the price of all home-made commodities with which gold is purchased or paid for, are effects absolutely incompatible. The extensive use of paper money does not alter this question, for paper money conforms, or ought to conform, to the value of gold, and therefore its value is influenced by such causes only as influence the value of that metal.

These then are the laws by which wages are regulated, and by which the happiness of far the greatest part of every community is governed. Like all other contracts, wages should be left to the fair and free competition of the market, and should never be controlled by the interference of the legislature.

The clear and direct tendency of the poor laws, is in direct opposition to these obvious principles: it is not, as the legislature benevolently intended, to amend the condition of the poor, but to deteriorate the condition of both poor and rich; instead of making the poor rich, they are calculated to make the rich poor; and whilst the present laws are in force, it is quite in the natural order of things that the fund for the maintenance of the poor should progressively increase, till it has absorbed all the net revenue of the country, or at least so much of it as the state shall leave to us, after satisfying its own never failing demands for the public expenditure.

This pernicious tendency of these laws is no longer a mystery, since it has been fully developed by the able hand of Mr. Malthus; and every friend to the poor must ardently wish for their abolition. Unfortunately, however, they have been so long established, and the habits of the poor have been so formed upon their operation, that to eradicate them with safety from our political system, requires the most cautious and skilful management. It is agreed by all who are most friendly to a repeal of these laws, that if it be desirable to prevent the most overwhelming distress to those for whose benefit they were erroneously enacted, their abolition should be effected by the most gradual steps.

It is a truth which admits not a doubt, that the comforts and well-being of the poor cannot be permanently secured without some regard on their part, or some effort on the part of the legislature, to regulate the increase of their numbers, and to render less frequent among them early and improvident marriages. The operation of the system of poor laws has been directly contrary to this. They have rendered restraint superfluous, and have invited imprudence, by offering it a portion of the wages of prudence and industry.[1]

The nature of the evil points out the remedy. By gradually contracting the sphere of the poor laws; by impressing on the poor the value of independence, by teaching them that they must look not to systematic or casual charity, but to their own exertions for support, that prudence and forethought are neither unnecessary nor unprofitable virtues, we shall by degrees approach a sounder and more healthful state.

---

[1] The progress of knowledge manifested upon this subject in the House of Commons since 1796, has happily not been very small, as may be seen by contrasting the late report of the committee on the poor laws,* and the following sentiments of Mr. Pitt, in that year.

"Let us," said he, "make relief in cases where there are a number of children a matter of right and honour, instead of a ground of opprobrium and contempt. This will make a large family a blessing, and not a curse; and this will draw a proper line of distinction between those who are able to provide for themselves by their labour, and those who after having enriched their country with a number of children, have a claim upon its assistance for support." - *Hansard's Parliamentary History*, vol. 32, page 710.

*See the 'Report from the Select Committee on the Poor Laws' dated 4 July 1817 (*Parliamentary Papers*, 1817, vol vi) and cp. letter to Trower of 10 Dec. 1817, below, VII, 219.

No scheme for the amendment of the poor laws merits the least attention, which has not their abolition for its ultimate object; and he is the best friend to the poor, and to the cause of humanity, who can point out how this end can be attained with the most security, and at the same time with the least violence. It is not by raising in any manner different from the present, the fund from which the poor are supported, that the evil can be mitigated. It would not only be no improvement, but it would be an aggravation of the distress which we wish to see removed, if the fund were increased in amount, or were levied according to some late proposals,[2] as a general fund from the country at large. The present mode of its collection and application has served to mitigate its pernicious effects. Each parish raises a separate fund for the support of its own poor. Hence it becomes an object of more interest and more practicability to keep the rates low, than if one general fund were raised for the relief of the poor of the whole kingdom. A parish is much more interested in an economical collection of the rate, and a sparing distribution of relief, when the whole saving will be for its own benefit, then if hundreds of other parishes were to partake of it.

It is to this cause, that we must ascribe the fact of the poor laws not having yet absorbed all the net revenue of the country; it is to the rigour with which they are applied, that we are indebted for their not having become overwhelmingly oppressive. If by law every human being wanting support could be sure to obtain it, and obtain it in such a degree as to make life tolerably comfortable, theory would lead us to expect that all other taxes together would be light compared with the single one of poor rates. The principle of gravitation is not more certain than the tendency of such laws to change wealth and power into misery and weakness; to call away the exertions of labour from every object, except that of providing mere subsistence; to confound all intellectual

---

[2] See Curwen's speech on the Poor Laws, 21 Feb. 1817, *Hansard*, XXXV, 520-1.

distinction; to busy the mind continually in supplying the body's wants; until at last all classes should be infected with the plague of universal poverty. Happily these laws have been in operation during a period of progressive prosperity, when the funds for the maintenance of labour have regularly increased, and when an increase of population would be naturally called for. But if our progress should become more slow; if we should attain the stationary state, from which I trust we are yet far distant, then will the pernicious nature of these laws become more manifest and alarming; and then, too, will their removal be obstructed by many additional difficulties.

ADAM SMITH
1723-90

Probably no other economist has impacted the way we think about economics as Smith has. His seminal work <u>An Inquiry into the Nature and Causes of the Wealth of Nations</u> written in 1776 is still widely quoted as are his thoughts on the division of labour and laissez-faire.

THE NATURE AND CAUSES OF THE WEALTH OF NATIONS

Artificers, manufacturers and merchants, can augment the revenue and wealth of their society, by parsimony only; or, as it is expressed in this system, by privation, that is, by depriving themselves of a part of the funds destined for their own subsistence. They annually reproduce nothing but those funds. Unless, therefore, they annually save some part of them, unless they annually deprive themselves of the enjoyment of some part of them, the revenue and wealth of their society can never be in the smallest degree augmented by means of their industry. Farmers and country labourers, on the contrary, may enjoy compleatly the whole funds destined for their own subsistence, and yet augment at the same time the revenue and wealth of their society. Over and above what is[1] destined for their own subsistence, their industry annually affords a neat produce, of which the augmentation necessarily augments the revenue and wealth of their society. Nations, therefore, which, like France or England, consist in a great measure of proprietors and cultivators, can be enriched by industry and enjoyment. Nations, on the contrary, which, like Holland and Hamburgh, are composed chiefly of merchants, artificers and

---

[1] the funds

manufacturers, can grow rich only through parsimony and privation. As the interest of nations so differently circumstanced, is very different, so is likewise the common character of the people. In those of the former kind, liberality, frankness, and good fellowship, naturally make a part of that common character. In the latter, narrowness, meanness, and a selfish disposition, averse to all social pleasure and enjoyment.

The unproductive class, that of merchants, artificers, and manufacturers, is maintained and employed altogether at the expence of the two other classes, of that of proprietors, and of that of cultivators. They furnish it both with the materials of its work and with the fund of its subsistence, with the corn and cattle which it consumes while it is employed about that work. The proprietors and cultivators finally pay both the wages of all the workmen of the unproductive class, and the profits of all their employers. those workmen and their employers are properly the servants of the proprietors and cultivators. They are only servants who work without doors, as menial servants work within. Both the one and the other, however, are equally maintained at the expence of the same masters. The labour of both is equally unproductive. It adds nothing to the value of the sum total of the rude produce of the land. Instead of increasing the value of that sum total, it is a charge and expence which must be paid out of it.

The unproductive class, however, is not only useful, but greatly useful to the other two classes. By means of the industry of merchants, artificers and manufacturers, the proprietors and cultivators can purchase both the foreign goods and the manufactured produce of their own country which they have occasion for, with the produce of a much smaller quantity of their own labour, than what they would be obliged to employ, if they were to attempt, in an aukward and unskilful manner, either to import the one, or to make the other for their own use. By means of the unproductive class, the cultivators are delivered from many cares which would otherwise distract their attention from the cultivation of land. The superiority of produce, which, in consequence of this undivided attention, they are enabled to raise, is fully sufficient to pay the whole expence which the maintenance and employment of the unproductive class costs either the proprietors, or themselves. The industry of merchants, artificers, and manufacturers, though in its own nature altogether unproductive, yet contributes in this manner indirectly to increase the produce of the land. It increases the productive powers of productive labour, by leaving it at liberty to confine itself to its proper employment, the cultivation of land; and the plough goes frequently the easier and the better by means of the labour of the man whose business is most remote from the plough.

It can never be the interest of the proprietors and cultivators to restrain or to discourage in any respect the industry of merchants, artificers and manufacturers. The greater the liberty which this unproductive class enjoys, the greater will be the competition in all the different trades which compose it, and the cheaper will the other two classes be supplied, both with foreign goods and with the manufactured produce of their own country.

It can never be the interest of the unproductive class to oppress the other two classes. It is the surplus produce of the land, or what remains after deducting the maintenance, first, of the cultivators, and afterwards, of the proprietors, that maintains and employs the unproductive class. The greater this surplus, the greater must likewise be the maintenance and employment of that class. The establishment of perfect justice, of perfect liberty, and of perfect equality, is the very simple secret which most effectually secures the highest degree of prosperity to all the three classes.

The merchants, artificers, and manufacturers of those mercantile states which, like Holland and Hamburgh, consist chiefly of this unproductive class, are in the same manner maintained and employed altogether at the expence of the proprietors and cultivators of land. The only difference is, that those proprietors and cultivators are, the greater part of them, placed at a most inconvenient distance from the merchants, artificers, and manufacturers whom they supply with the materials of their work and the fund of their subsistence, are the inhabitants of other countries, and the subjects of other governments.

Such mercantile states, however, are not only useful, but greatly useful to the inhabitants of those other countries. They fill up, in some measure, a very important void, and supply the place of the merchants, artificers and manufacturers, whom the inhabitants of those countries ought to find at home, but whom, from some defect in their policy, they do not find at home.

It can never be the interest of those landed nations, if I may call them so, to discourage or distress the industry of such mercantile states, by imposing high duties upon their trade, or upon the commodities which they furnish. Such duties, by rendering those commodities dearer, could serve only to sink the real value of the surplus produce of their own land, with which, or, what comes to the same thing, with the price of which those commodities are purchased. Such duties could serve only to discourage the increase of that surplus produce, and consequently the improvement and cultivation of their own land. The most effectual expedient, on the contrary, for raising the value of that surplus produce, for encouraging its increase, and consequently the improvement and cultivation of their own land, would be to allow the most perfect freedom to the trade of all such mercantile nations.

This perfect freedom of trade would even be the most effectual expedient for supplying them, in due time, with all the artificers, manufacturers and merchants, whom they wanted at home, and for filling up in the properest and most advantageous manner that very important void which they felt there.

The continual increase of the surplus produce of their land, would, in due time, create a greater capital than what could be employed with the ordinary rate of profit in the improvement and cultivation of land; and the surplus part of it would naturally turn itself to the employment of artificers and manufacturers at home. But those artificers and manufacturers, finding at home both the materials of their work and the fund of their subsistence, might immediately, even with much less art and skill, be able to work as cheap as the like artificers and manufactures of such mercantile states, who had both to bring from a great distance. Even though from want of art and skill, they might not for some time be able to work as cheap, yet, finding a market at home, they might be able to sell their work there are cheap as that of the artificers and manufacturers of such mercantile states, which could not be brought to that market but from so great a distance; and as their art and skill improved, they would soon be able to sell it cheaper. The artificers and manufacturers of such mercantile states, therefore, would immediately be rivalled in the market of those landed nations, and soon after undersold and justled out of it altogether. The cheapness of the manufactures of those landed nations, in consequence of the gradual improvements of art and skill, would, in due time, extend their sale beyond the home market, and carry them to many foreign markets, from which they would in the same manner gradually justle out many o the manufactures of such mercantile nations.

This continual increase both of the rude and manufactured produce of those landed nations would in due time create a greater capital than could, with the ordinary rate of profit, be employed either in agriculture or in manufactures. The surplus of this capital would naturally turn itself to foreign trade, and be employed in exporting, to foreign countries, such parts of the rude and manufactured produce of its own country, as exceeded the demand of the home market. In the exportation of the produce of their own country, the merchants of a landed nation would have an advantage of the same kind over those of mercantile nations, which its artificers and manufacturers had over the artificers and manufacturers of such nations; the advantage of finding at home that cargo, and those stores and provisions, which the others were obliged to seek for at a distance. With inferior art and skill in navigation, therefore, they would be able to sell that cargo as cheap in foreign markets as the merchants of such mercantile nations; and with equal art and skill they would be able to sell it cheaper. They would soon, therefore, rival those mercantile nations in this branch of foreign trade, and in due time would justle them out of it altogether.

According to this liberal and generous system, therefore, the most advantageous method in which a landed nation can raise up artificers, manufacturers and merchants of its own, is to grant the most perfect freedom of trade to the artificers, manufacturers and merchants of all other nations. It thereby raises the value of the surplus produce of its own land, of which the continual increase gradually establishes a fund which in due time necessarily raises up all the artificers, manufacturers and merchants whom it has occasion for.

When a landed nation, on the contrary, oppresses either by high duties or by prohibitions the trade of foreign nations, it necessarily hurts its own interest in two different ways. First, by raising the price of all foreign goods and of all sorts of manufactures, it necessarily sinks the real value of the surplus produce of its own land, with which, or, what comes to the same thing, with the price of which, it purchases those foreign goods and manufactures. Secondly, by giving a sort of monopoly of the home market to its own merchants, artificers and manufacturers, it raises the rate of mercantile and manufacturing profit in proportion to that of agricultural profit, and consequently either draws from agriculture a part of the capital which had before been employed in it, or hinders from going to it a part of what would otherwise have gone to it. This policy, therefore, discourages agriculture in two different ways; first, by sinking the real value of its produce, and thereby lowering the rate of its profit; and, secondly, by raising the rate of profit in all other employments. Agriculture is rendered less advantageous, and trade and manufactures more advantageous than they otherwise would be; and every man is tempted by his own interest to turn, as much as he can, both his capital and his industry from the former to the latter employments.

Though, by this oppressive policy, a landed nation should be able to raise up artificers, manufacturers and merchants of its own, somewhat sooner than it could do by the freedom of trade; a matter, however, which is not a little doubtful; yet it would raise them up, if one may say so, prematurely, and before it was perfectly ripe for them. By raising up too hastily one species of industry, it would depress another more valuable species of industry. By raising up too hastily a species of industry which only replaces the stock which employs it, together with the ordinary profit, it would depress a species of industry which, over and above replacing that stock with its profit, affords likewise a neat produce, a free rent to the landlord. It would depress productive labour, by encouraging too hastily that labour which is altogether barren and unproductive.

J(JEAN) B(BAPTISTE) SAY
(1767-1832)

This French economist was a great admirer of Adam Smith who re-organized and popularized Smith's writings especially his thoughts about laissez-faire.

A TREATISE ON POLITICAL ECONOMY
OR
THE PRODUCTION, DISTRIBUTION & CONSUMPTION OF WEALTH

It may, perhaps be alleged, that, were all occupations quite free a large proportion of those who engaged in them would fall a sacrifice to the eagerness of competition. Possibly they might, in some few instances, although it is not very likely there should be a great excess of candidates in a line, that held out but little prospect of gain; yet, admitting the casual occurrence of this evil, it would be of infinitely less magnitude, than permanently keeping up the prices of produce at a rate that must limit its consumption, and abridge the power of purchasing in the great body of consumers.

If the measures of authority, levelled against the free disposition of each man's respective talents and capital, are criminal in the eye of sound policy, it is still more difficult to justify them upon the principles of natural right. "The patrimony of a poor man," says the author of the Wealth of nations, "lies in the strength and dexterity of his hands: and to hinder him from employing this strength and dexterity in what manner he thinks proper, without injury to his neighbour, is a plain violation of his most sacred property."

However, as society is possessed of a natural right to regulate the exercise of any class of industry, that without regulation might prejudice the rest of the community, physicians, surgeons, and apothecaries, are with perfect justice subjected to an examination into their professional ability. The lives of their fellow-citizens are dependent upon their skill, and a test of that skill may fairly be established; but it does not seem advisable to limit the number of practitioners nor the plan of their education. Society has no interest further than to ascertain their qualification.

On the same grounds, regulation is useful and proper, when aimed at the prevention of fraud or contrivance, manifestly injurious to other kinds of production, or to the public safety, and not at prescribing the nature of the products and the methods of fabrication. Thus, a manufacturer must not be allowed to advertise his goods to the public as of better than their actual quality: the home consumer is entitled to the public protection against such a breach of faith; and so, indeed, is the mercantile character of the nation, which must suffer in the estimation and demand of foreign customers from such practices. And this is an exception to the general rule, that the best of all guarantees is the personal interest of the manufacturer. For, possibly, when about to give up business, he may find it answer to increase his profit by a breach of faith, and sacrifice a future object he is about to relinquish for a present benefit. A fraud of this kind ruined the French cloths in the Levant market, about the year 1783; since when the German and British have entirely supplanted them.[1] We may go still further. An article often derives a value from the name, or from the place of its manufacture. When we judge from long experience, that cloths of such a denomination, and made at such a place, will be of a certain breadth and substance, it is a fraud to fabricate, under the same name and at the same place, a commodity of inferior substance and quality to the ordinary standard, and thus to send it into the world under a false certificate.

Hence we may form an opinion of the extent to which

---

[1] The loss of this trade has been erroneously imputed to the library of commerce, consequent upon the revolution. But *Felix Beajour*, in his *Tableau du Commerce de la Grece*, has shown that it must be referred to an earlier period, when restrictions were still in force.

government may carry its interference with benefit. The correspondence with the sample of conditions, express or implied, must be rigidly enforced, and government should meddle with production no further. I would wish to impress upon my readers, that the mere interference is itself an evil, even where it is of use:[2] first, because it harasses and distresses individuals; and secondly, because it costs money, either to the nation, if it be defrayed by government, that is to say, charged upon the public purse, or to the consumer, if it be charged upon the specific article; in the latter case, the charge must of course enhance the price, thereby laying an additional tax upon the home consumer, and *pro tanto* discouraging the foreign demand.

If interference be an evil, a paternal government will be most sparing of its exercise. It will not trouble itself about the certification of such commodities, as the purchaser must understand better than itself; or of such as cannot well be certified by its agents; for, unfortunately, a government must always reckon upon the negligence, incapacity, and misconduct of its retainers. But some articles may well admit of certification; as gold and silver, the standard of which can only be ascertained by a complex operation of chemistry, which few purchasers know how to execute, and which, if they did, would cost them infinitely more than it can be executed for by the government in their stead.

In Great Britain, the individual inventor of a new product or of a new process may obtain the exclusive right to it, by obtaining what is called a patent. While the patent remains in force, the absence of competitors enables him to raise his price far above the ordinary return of his outlay with interest, and the wages of his own industry. Thus he receives a premium from the government, charged upon the consumers of the new article; and this premium is often very large, as may be supposed in a country so immediately

---

[2]"Every restraint, imposed by legislation, upon the freedom of human action must inevitably extinguish a portion of the energies of the community, and abridge its annual produce." -*Verri. Refl. sur l'Econ. Pol. c. 12.*

productive as Great Britain, where there are consequently abundance of affluent individuals, ever on the look-out for some new object of enjoyment. Some years ago a man invented a spiral or worm spring for insertion between the leather braces of carriages, to ease their motion, and made his fortune by the patent for so trifling an invention.

Privileges of this kind no one can reasonably object to; for they neither interfere with, nor cramp any branch of industry, previously in operation. Moreover, the expense incurred is purely voluntary; and those who choose to incur it, are not obliged to renounce the satisfaction of any previous wants, either of necessity or of amusement.

MAX WEBER
(1864-1920)

This German sociologist developed the idea that the work ethic, individualism and protestant faith were inter-related.

THE PROTESTANT ETHNIC AND THE SPIRIT OF CAPITALISM

Benjamin Franklin was filled with the spirit of capitalism at a time when his printing business did not differ in form from any handicraft enterprise. And we shall see that at the beginning of modern times it was by no means the capitalistic entrepreneurs of the commercial aristocracy, who were either the sole or the predominant bearers of the attitude we have here called the spirit of capitalism. It was much more the rising strata of the lower industrial middle classes. Even in the nineteenth century its classical representatives were not the elegant gentlemen of Liverpool and Hamburg, with their commercial fortunes handed down for generations, but the self-made parvenus of Manchester and Westphalia, who often rose from very modest circumstances. As early as the sixteenth century the situation was similar; the industries which arose at that time were mostly created by parvenus.

The management, for instance, of a bank, a wholesale export business, a large retail establishment, or of a large putting-out enterprise dealing with goods produced in homes, is certainly only possible in the form of a capitalistic enterprise. Nevertheless, they may all be carried on in a traditionalistic spirit. In fact, the business of a large bank of issue cannot be carried on in any other way. The foreign trade of whole epochs has rested on the basis of monopolies and legal privileges of strictly traditional character. In retail trade-and we are not here talking of the small men without capital who are continually crying out for Government aid-the revolution which is making an end of the old traditionalism is still in full swing. It is the same development which broke up the old putting-out system, to which modern domestic labour is related only in form. How this revolution takes place and what is its significance may, in spite of the fact these things are so familiar, be again brought out by a concrete example.

Until about the middle of the past century the life of a putter-out was, at least in many of the branches of the Continental textile industry, what we should to-day consider very comfortable. We may imagine its routine somewhat as follows: The peasants came with their cloth often (in the case of linen) principally or entirely made from raw material which the peasant himself had produced, to the town in which the putter-out lived, and after a careful, often official, appraisal of the quality, received the customary price for it. The putter-out's customers, for markets any appreciable distance away, were middlemen, who also came to him, generally not yet following samples, but seeking traditional qualities, and bought from his warehouse, or, long before delivery, placed orders which were probably in turn passed on to the peasants. Personal canvassing of customers took place, if at all, only at long intervals. Otherwise correspondence sufficed, though the sending of samples slowly gained ground. The number of business hours was very moderate, perhaps five to six a day, sometimes considerably less; in the rush season, where there was one, more. Earnings were moderate; enough to lead a respectable life and good times to put away a little. On the whole, relations among competitors were relatively good, with a large degree of agreement on the fundamentals of business. A long daily visit to the tavern, with often plenty to drink, and a congenial circle of friends, made life comfortable and leisurely.

The form of organization was in every respect capitalistic; the entrepreneur's activity was of a purely business character; the use of capital, turned over in the business, was indispensable; and finally, the objective aspect of the economic process, the bookkeeping, was rational. But it was traditionalistic business, if one considers the spirit which animated the entrepreneur: the traditional manner life, the traditional rate of profit, the traditional amount of work, the traditional manner of regulating the relationships with labour, and the essentially traditional circle of customers and the manner of attracting new ones. All these dominated the conduct of the business, were at the basis, one may say, of the *ethos* of this group of business men.

Now at some time this leisureliness was suddenly destroyed, and often entirely without any essential change in the form of organization, such as the transition to a unified factory, to mechanical weaving, et. What happened was, on the contrary, often no more than this: some young man from one of the putting-out families went out into the country, carefully chose weavers for his employ, greatly increased the rigour of his supervision of their work, and thus turned them from peasants into labourers. On the other hand, he would begin to change his marketing methods by so far as possible going directly to the final consumer, would take the details into his own hands, would personally solicit customers, visiting them every year, and above all would adapt the quality of the product directly to their needs and wishes. At the same time he began to introduce the principle of low prices and large turnover. There was repeated what everywhere and always is the result of such a process of rationalization: those who would not follow suit had to go out of business. The idyllic state collapsed under the pressure of a bitter competitive struggle, respectable fortunes were made, and not lent out at interest, but always reinvested in the business. The old leisurely and comfortable attitude toward life gave way to a hard frugality in which some participated and came to the top, because they did not wish to consume but to earn, while others who wished to keep on with the old ways were forced to curtail their consumption.

And, what is most important in this connection, it was not generally in such cases a stream of new money invested in the industry which brought about this revolution-in several cases known to me the whole revolutionary process was set in motion with a few thousands of capital borrowed from relations-but the new spirit, the spirit of modern capitalism, had set to work. The question of the motive forces in the expansion of modern capitalism is not in the first instance a question of the origin of the capital sums which were available for capitalistic uses, but, above all, of the development of the spirit of capitalism. Where it appears and is able to work itself out, it produces its own capital and monetary supplies as the means to its ends, but the reverse is not true. Its entry on the scene was not generally peaceful. A flood of mistrust, sometimes of hatred, above all of moral indignation, regularly opposed itself to the first innovator. Often-I know of several cases of the sort-regular legends of mysterious shady spots in his previous life have been produced. It is very easy not to recognize that only an unusually strong character could save an entrepreneur of this new type from the loss of his temperate self-control and from both moral and economic shipwreck. Furthermore, along with clarity of vision and ability to act, it is only by virtue of very definite and highly developed ethical qualities that it has been possible for him to command the absolutely indispensable confidence of his customers and workmen. Nothing else could have given him the strength to overcome the innumerable obstacles, above all the infinitely more intensive work which is demanded of the modern entrepreneur. But these are ethical qualities of quite a different sort from those adapted to the traditionalism of the past.

And, as a rule it has been neither dare-devil and unscrupulous speculators, economic adventurers such as we meet at all periods of economic history, nor simply great financiers who have carried through this change, outwardly so inconspicuous, but nevertheless so decisive for the penetration of economic life with the new spirit. On the contrary, they were men who had grown up in the hard school of life, calculating and daring at the same time, above all temperate and reliable, shrewd and completely devoted to their business, with strictly bourgeois opinions and principles.

One is tempted to think that these personal moral

qualities have not the slightest relation to any ethical maxims, to say nothing of religious ideas, but that the essential relation between them is negative. The ability to free oneself from the common tradition, a sort of liberal enlightenment, seems likely to be the most suitable basis for such a business man's success. And today that is generally precisely the case. Any relationship between religious beliefs and conduct is generally absent, and where any exists, at least in German, it tends to be of the negative sort. The people filled with the spirit of capitalism today tend to be indifferent, if not hostile, to the Church. The thought of the pious boredom of paradise has little attraction for their active natures; religion appears to them as a means of drawing people away from labour in this world. If you ask them what is the meaning of their restless activity, why they are never satisfied with what they have, thus appearing so senseless to any purely worldly view of life, they would perhaps give the answer, if they know any at all: "to provide for any children and grandchildren". But more often and, since that motive is not peculiar to them, but was just as effective for the traditionalist, more correctly, simply: that business with its continuous work has become a necessary part of their lives. That is in fact the only possible motivation, but it at the same time expresses what is, seen from the view-point of personal happiness, so irrational about this sort of life, where a man exists for the sake of his business, instead of the reverse.

Of course, the desire for the power and recognition which the mere fact of wealth brings plays its part. When the imagination of a whole people has once been turned toward purely quantitative bigness, as in the United States, this romanticism of numbers exercises and irresistible appeal to the poets among business men. Otherwise it is in general not the real leaders, and especially not the permanently successful entrepreneurs, who are taken in by it. In particular, the resort to entailed estates and the nobility, with sons whose conduct at the university and in the officer's corps tries to cover up their social origin, as has been the typical history of German capitalistic parvenu families, is a product of later decadence. The ideal type of the capitalistic entrepreneur, as it has been represented even in Germany by occasional outstanding examples, has no relation to such more or less refined climbers. He avoids ostentation and unnecessary expenditure, as well as conscious enjoyment of his power, and is embarrassed by the outward signs of the social recognition which he receives. His manner of life is, in other words, often, and we shall have to investigate the historical significance of just this important fact, distinguished by a certain ascetic tendency, as appears clearly enough in the sermon of Franklin which we have quoted. It is, namely, by no means exceptional, but rather the rule, for him to have a sort of modesty which is essentially more honest than the reserve which Franklin so shrewdly recommends. He gets nothing out of his wealth for himself, except the irrational sense of having done his job well.

JOHN STUART MILL
(1806-73)

He believed that empirical studies were of primary importance with regard to seeking the source of knowledge. He combined utilitarianism with touches of humanism and socialism while continually calling for social reform.

ON LIBERTY

Liberty of the Individual

There is a sphere of action in which society, as distinguished from the individual, has, if any only an indirect interest; comprehending all that portion of a person's life and conduct which affects only himself or if it also affects others, only with their free, voluntary, and undeceived consent and participation. When I say only himself, I mean directly, and in the first instance: for whatever affects himself may affect others through himself; and the objection which may be grounded in this contingency, will receive consideration in the sequel. This, then, is the appropriate region of human liberty. It comprises, first, the inward domain of consciousness; demanding liberty of conscience, in the most comprehensive sense; liberty of thought and feeling; absolute freedom of opinion and sentiment on all subjects, practical or speculative, scientific, moral, or theological. The liberty of expressing and publishing opinions may seem to fall under a different principle, since it belongs to that part of the conduct of an individual which concerns other people; but, being almost of as much importance as the liberty of thought itself, and resting in great part on the same reasons, is practically inseparable from it. Secondly, the principle requires liberty of tastes and pursuits; of framing the plan of our life to suit our own character; of doing as we like, subject to such consequences as may follow: without impediment from our fellow creatures, so long as what we do does not harm, even though they should think our conduct foolish, perverse, or wrong. Thirdly, from this liberty of each individual, follows the liberty, within the same limits, of combination among individuals; freedom to unite, for any purpose not involving harm to others: the persons combing being supposed to be of full age, and not forced or deceived.

No society in which these liberties are not, on the whole, respected, is free, whatever may be its form of government; and never is completely free in which they do not exist absolute and unqualified.

The Triumph of Truth

The dictum that truth always triumphs over persecution, is one of those pleasant falsehoods which men repeat after one another till they pass into commonplaces, but which all experience refutes. History teems with instances of truth put down by persecution. If not suppressed forever, it may be thrown back for centuries. To speak only of religious opinions: the Reformation broke out at least twenty times before Luther, and was put down...Even after the era of Luther, wherever persecution was persisted in, it was successful. In Spain, Italy, Flanders, the Austrian Empire, Protestantism was rooted out; and most likely, would have been so in England, had Queen Mary lived, or Queen Elizabeth died. Persecution has always succeeded, save where the heretics were too strong a party to be effectually persecuted. No reasonable person can doubt that Christianity might have been extirpated in the Roman Empire. It spread, and became predominant, because the persecutions were only occasional, lasting but a short time, and separated by long intervals of almost undisturbed propagandism. It is a piece of idle sentimentality that truth, merely as truth, has any inherent power denied to error, of prevailing against the dungeon and the stake. Men are not zealous for truth than they often are for error, and sufficient application of legal or even of social penalties will generally succeed in stopping the propagation of either. The real advantage which truth has, consists in this, that when an opinion is true, it may be extinguished once, twice, or many times, but in the course of ages there will generally be found persons to rediscover it, until some one of its reappearances falls on a time when from favorable circumstances it escapes persecution until it has made such head as to withstand all subsequent attempts to suppress it.

Individual and State

The worth of a State, in the long run, is the worth of the individuals composing it; and a State which postpones the interests of *their* mental expansion and elevation, to a little more of administrative skill, or that semblance of it which practice gives, in the details of business; a State which dwarfs its men, in order that they may be more docile instruments in its hands even for beneficial purposes, will find that with small men no great thing can really be accomplished; and that the perfection of machinery to which it has sacrificed everything, will in the end avail it nothing, for want of the vital power which, in order that the machine might work more smoothly it has preferred to banish.

The Purest of Wisdom

When we consider either the history of opinion, or the ordinary conduct of human life, to what is to be ascribed that the one and the others are no worse than they are? Not certainly to the inherent force of the human understanding; for, on any matter not self-evident, there are ninety-nine persons totally incapable of judging it, for one who is capable; and the capacity of the hundredth person is only comparative; for the majority of the eminent men of every past generation held many opinions now known to be erroneous, and did or approved numerous things which no one will now justify. Why is it, then, that there is on the whole a preponderance among mankind of rational opinions and rational conduct? If there really is this preponderance - which there must be, unless human affairs are, and have always been, in an almost desperate state - it is owing to a quality of the human mind, the source of everything respectable in man either as an intellectual or as a moral being, namely that his errors are corrigible. He is capable of rectifying his mistakes, by discussion and experience. Not by experience alone. There must be discussion, to show how experience is to be interpreted. Wrong opinions and practices gradually yield to fact and argument: but facts and arguments, to produce any effect on the mind, must be brought before it. Very few facts are able to tell their own story, without comments to bring out their meaning. The whole strength and value, then, of human judgment, depending on the one property, that it can be set right when it is wrong, reliance can be placed on it only when the means of setting it right are kept constantly at hand. In the case of any person whose judgement is really deserving of confidence how has it become so? Because he has kept his mind open to criticism of his opinions and conduct. Because it has been his practice to listen to all that could be said against him; to profit by as much of it as was just, and expound to himself, and upon occasion to others, the fallacy of what was fallacious. Because he has felt, that the only way in which a human being can make some approach to knowing the whole of a subject, is by hearing what can be said about it by persons of every variety of opinion, and studying all modes in which it can be looked at by every character of mind. No wise man ever acquired his wisdom in any other manner.

Man the Individual

He who lets the world, or his own portion of it, choose his plan of life for him, has no need of any other faculty than the ape-like one of imitation. He who chooses his plan for himself employs all his faculties. He must use observation to see, reasoning and judgment to foresee, activity to gather materials for decision, discrimination to decide, and when he has decided, firmness and self-control to hold to his deliberate decision. And these qualities he requires and exercises exactly in proportion as the part of his conduct which he determines according to his own judgment and feelings is a large one. It is possible that he might be guided in some good path, and kept out of harm's way, without any of these things. But what will be his comparative worth as a human being? It really is of importance, not only what men do, but what manner of men they are that do it. Among the works of man, which human life is rightly employed in perfecting and beautifying, the first in importance is surely man himself. Supposing it were possible to get houses built, corn grown, battles fought, causes tried, and even churches erected and prayers said, by machinery - by automatons in human form - it would be a considerable loss to exchange for automatons even the men and women who at present inhabit the more civilized parts of the world, and who assuredly are but starved specimens of what nature can and will produce. Human nature is not a machine to be built after a model, and set to do exactly the work prescribed for it, but a tree, which requires to grow and develop itself on all sides, according to the tendency of the inward forces which make it a living thing.

JEREMY BENTHAM
(1748-1832)

The founder of utilitarianism believed that the goal of social movements, such as the American and French revolutions, should achieve the greatest good for the greatest number. His call for political equality but not economic equality serves as the cornerstone of liberalism.

PLEASURE AND PAIN

The happiness of the individuals, of whom a community is composed, that is their pleasures and their security, is the end and the sole end which the legislator ought to have in view: the sole standard, in conformity to which each individual ought, as far as depends upon the legislator, to be *made* to fashion his behaviour. But whether it be this or any thing else that is to be *done*, there is nothing by which a man can ultimately be *made* to do it, but either pain or pleasure. Having taken a general view of these two grand objects (*viz.* pain) in the character of *final* causes; it will be necessary to take a view of pleasure and pain itself, in the character of efficient causes or means.

There are four distinguishable sources from which pleasure and pain are in use to flow: considered separately, they may be termed the *physical*, the *political*, the *moral*, and the *religious*: and inasmuch as the pleasures and pains belonging to each of them are capable of giving a binding force to any law or rule of conduct, they may all of them be termed *sanctions*.

If it be in the present life, and from the ordinary course of nature, not purposely modified by the interposition of the will of any human being, nor by any extraordinary interposition of any superior invisible being, that the pleasure or the pain takes place or is expected, it may be said to issue from or to belong to the *physical sanction*.

If at the hands of a *particular* person or set of persons in the community, who under names correspondent to that of *judge*, are chosen for the particular purpose of dispensing it, according to the will of the sovereign or supreme ruling power in the state, it may be said to issue from the *political sanction*.

If at the hands of such *chance* persons in the community, as the party in question may happen in the course of his life to have concerns with, according to each man's spontaneous disposition, and not according to any settled or concerted rule, it may be said to issue from the *moral* or *popular sanction*.

If from the immediate hand of a superior invisible being, either in the present life, or in a future, it may be said to issue from the *religious sanction*.

Pleasures or pains which may be expected to issue from the *physical, political* or *moral* sanctions, must all of them be experienced, if ever, in the *present* life: those which may be expected to issue from the *religious* sanction, may be expected to be experienced either in the *present* life or in a *future*.

I. Pleasures then, and the avoidance of pains, are the "ends" which the legislator has in view: it behoves him therefore to understand their "value." Pleasures and pains are the "instruments" he has to work with: it behoves him therefore to understand their force, which is again, in other words, their value.

II. To a person considered by "himself," the value of a pleasure or pain considered by "itself," will be greater or less, according to the four following circumstances:

    1. Its "intensity."
    2. Its "duration."
    3. Its "certainty" or "uncertainty."
    4. Its "propinquity" or "remoteness."

III. These are the circumstances which are to be considered in estimating a pleasure or a pain considered each of them by itself. But when the value of any pleasure or pain is considered for the purpose of estimating the tendency of any "act" by which it is produced, there are two other circumstances to be taken into account: these are,

    4.   Its "fecundity," or the chance it has of being followed by sensations of the "same" kind: that is, pleasures, if it be a pleasure: pains, if it be a pain.

    5.   Its "purity," or the chance it has of "not" being followed by sensations of the "opposite" kind: that is, pains, if it be a pleasure: pleasures, if it be a pain.

These last two, however, are in strictness scarcely to be deemed properties of the pleasure or the pain itself; they are not, therefore, in strictness to be taken into the account of the value of that pleasure or that pain. They are in strictness to be deemed properties only of the act, or other event, by which such pleasure or pain has been produced; and accordingly are only to be taken into the account of the tendency of such act or such event.

IV. To a "number" of persons, with reference to each of whom the value of a pleasure or a pain is considered, it will be greater or less, according to seven circumstances: to wit, the six preceding ones; via.

    1.   Its "intensity."
    2.   Its "duration."
    3.   Its "certainty" or "uncertainty."
    4.   Its "propinquity" or "remoteness."
    5.   Its "fecundity."
    6.   Its "purity."

And one other; to wit:

    7.   Its "extent": that is, the number of persons to whom it "extends"; or [in other words] who are affected by it.

ROBERT OWEN
(1771-1858)

This self made millionaire and utopian socialist established a hugely successful cotton mill in New Larnack, Scotland. Visitors from around the world flocked to see how his co-operative community functioned.

MAN'S CHARACTER IS FORMED FOR HIM

From the earliest ages it has been the practice of the world to act on the supposition that each individual man forms his own character, and that therefore he is accountable for all his sentiments and habits, and consequently merits reward for some and punishment for others. Every system which has been established among men has been founded on these erroneous principles. When, however, they shall be brought to the test of fair examination, they will be found not only unsupported, but in direct opposition to all experience, and to the evidence of our senses.

This is not a slight mistake, which involves only trivial consequences; it is a fundamental error of the highest possible magnitude, it enters into all our proceedings regarding man from his infancy; and it will be found to be the true and sole origin of evil. It generates and perpetuates ignorance, hatred and revenge, where, without such error, only intelligence, confidence, and kindness would exist. It has hitherto been the Evil Genius of the world. It severs man from man throughout the various regions of the earth; and it makes enemies of those who, but for this gross error, would have enjoyed each other's kind offices and sincere friendship. It is, in short, an error which carries misery in all its consequences.

This error cannot much longer exist; for every day will make it more evident *that the character of man is, without a single exception, always formed for him; and that it may be, and is, chiefly created by his predecessors that they give him, or may give him, his ideas and habits, which are the powers that govern and direct his conduct. Man, therefore, never did, nor is it possible that be ever can, form his own character.*

The knowledge of this important fact has not been derived from any o the wild and heated speculations of an ardent and ungoverned imagination; on the contrary, it proceeds from a long and patient study of the theory and practice of human nature, under many varied circumstances; and it will be found to be a deduction drawn from such multiplicity of facts, as to afford the most complete demonstration.

True and False Principles

Every society which now exists, as well as every society history records, has been formed and governed on a belief in the notions, assumed as *first principles*:

First - That it is in the power of every individual to form his own character.

Hence the various systems called by the name of religion, codes of law and punishments. Hence also the angry passions entertained by individuals and nations towards each other.

Second - That the affections are at the command of the individual.

Hence insincerity and degradation of character. Hence the miseries of domestic life, and more than one half of the crimes of mankind.

Third - That it is necessary that a large portion of mankind should exist in ignorance and poverty, in order to secure the remaining part such a degree of happiness as they now enjoy.

Hence a system of counteraction in the pursuits of man, a general opposition among individuals to the interests of each other, and the necessary effects of such a system - ignorance, poverty, and vice.

Facts prove, however -

First - that character is universally formed *for*, and not *by* the individual.
Second - That *any* habits and sentiments may be given to mankind.
Third - That the affections are *not* under the control of the individual.
Fourth - That every individual may be trained to produce far more than he can consume, while there is a sufficiency of soil left for him to cultivate.
Fifth - That nature has provided means by which populations may be at all times maintained in the proper state to give the greatest happiness to every individual, without one check of vice or misery.
Sixth - That any community may be arranged, on a due combination of the foregoing principles, in such a manner, as not only to withdraw vice, poverty, and, in a great degree, misery, from the world, but also to place *every* individual under such circumstances in which he shall enjoy more permanent happiness than can be given to *any* individual under the principles which have hitherto regulated society.
Seventh - That all the assumed fundamental principles on which society has hitherto been founded are erroneous, and may be demonstrated to be contrary to fact. And -
Eighth - That the change which would follow the abandonment of these erroneous maxims which bring misery to the world, and the adoption of principles of truth, unfolding a system which shall remove and for ever exclude that misery, may be effected without the slightest injury to any human being.

PROUDHON
(1809-65)

<u>What is Property?</u> but theft concludes Proudhon in his famous pamphlet. He preached for a society of loosely connected mutual aid federations. A vehement opponent of communism, he believed in individual responsibility rather than authoritarian class rule.

WHAT IS PROPERTY? (1840)

Property is Theft

If I were asked to answer the following question: "What is slavery?" and I should answer in one work, "It is murder," my meaning would be understood at once. No extended argument would be required to show that the power to take from a man his thought, his will, his personality, is a power of life and death; and that to enslave a man is to kill him. Why, then, to this other question: "What is property?" may I not likewise answer, "It is robbery," without the certainty of being misunderstood; the second proposition being no other than a transformation of the first?

I undertake to discuss the vital principle of our government and our institutions, property: I am in my right. I may be mistaken in the conclusion which shall result from my investigations: I am in my right. I think best to place the last thought of my book first: still am I in my right.

Such an author teaches that property is a civil right, born of occupation and sanctioned by law; another maintains that it is a natural right, originating in labor, - and both of these doctrines, totally opposed as they may seem, are encouraged and applauded. I contend that neither labor, nor occupation, nor law, can create property; that it is an effect without a cause: am I censurable?

But murmurs arise!

"Property is robbery!" That is the war-cry of '93! That

is the signal of revolutions!

Reader, calm yourself. I am no agent of discord, no firebrand of sedition. I anticipate history by a few days; I disclose a truth whose development we may try in vain to arrest; I write the preamble of our future constitution. This proposition which seems to you blasphemous - "property is robbery" - would, if our prejudices allowed us to consider it, be recognised as the lightening-rod to shield us from the coming thunderbolt; but too many interests stand in the way! ... Alas! philosophy will not change the course of events: destiny will fulfil itself regardless of prophecy. Besides, must not justice be done and our education be finished?

"Property is robbery!"...What a revolution in human ideas! "Proprietary" and "robber" have been at all times expressions as contradictory as the beings whom they designate are hostile; all languages have perpetuated this opposition. On what authority, then, do you venture to attack universal consent, and give the lie to the human race? Who are you, that you should question the judgment of the nations and the ages?...

Disregard, reader, my title and my character, and attend only to my arguments. It is in accordance with universal consent that I undertake to correct universal error, from the "opinion" of the human race I appeal to its "faith." Have the courage to follow me; and, if your will is untrammelled, if your conscience is free, if your mind can unite two propositions and deduce a third therefrom, my ideas will inevitably become yours. In beginning by giving you my last word, it was my purpose to warn you, not to defy you; for I am certain that, if you read me, you will be compelled to assent. The things of which I am to speak are so simple and clear that you will be astonished at not having perceived them before, and you will say: "I have neglected to think." Others offer you the spectacle of genius wrestling Nature's secrets from her, and unfolding before you her sublime messages; you will find here only a series of experiments upon "justice" and "right," a sort of verification of the weights and measures of your conscience. The operations shall be conducted under your very eyes; and you shall weigh the result.

    Nevertheless, I build no system. I ask an end to privilege, the abolition of slavery, equality of rights, and the reign of law. Justice, nothing else; that is the alpha and omega of my argument: to others I leave the business of governing the world...

THE NEW POOR LAW OF 1834

An English commentator in 1764 said "Almost every proposal which hath been made for the reformation of the poor laws hath been tried in former ages, and found ineffectual." One would not be severely out of place to make such a comment about today or indeed the New Poor Law of 1834. What made the New Poor Law of 1834 such an abysmal failure was it's righteous sense of individualism and almost total belief in the power of positive thinking. Disraeli was a long time critic of the Poor Law and his Reform Bill of 1867 had much to do with his revulsion of the Poor Law.

CLASSIFICATION OF THE PAUPERS

Article 9: The paupers, so far as the workhouse admits thereof, shall be classed as follows, subject nevertheless to such arrangements as the Board of Guardians may deem necessary with regard to persons labouring under any disease of body or mind, or for the further subdivision of any such classes:

Class 1.	Men infirm through age or any other cause.
Class 2.	Able-bodied men, and youths above the age of 15 years.
Class 3.	Boys above the age of 7 years, and under that of 15.
Class 4.	Women infirm through age or any other cause.
Class 5.	Able-bodied women, and girls above the age of 15 years.
Class 6.	Girls above the age of 7 years, and under that of 15.
Class 7.	Children under 7 years of age.

To each class shall be assigned that ward or separate building and yard which may be best fitted for the reception of such class, and each class of paupers shall remain therein, without communication with those of any other class.

DISCIPLINE AND DIET OF THE PAUPERS

Article 13: All the paupers in the workhouse, except the sick and insane, and the paupers of the first, fourth, and seventh classes shall rise, be set to work, leave off work, and go to bed at the times mentioned in the Form marked A, hereunto annexed, and shall be allowed such intervals for their meals as are therein stated; and those several times shall be notified by the ringing of a bell; provided always that the Guardians may, with the consent of the Poor Law Commissioners, make such alternations in any of the said times or intervals as the Guardians may deem fit.

Article 14: Half an hour after the bell shall have been rung for rising, the names of the paupers shall be called over by the master and matron respectively in the several wards provided for the second, third, fifth, and sixth classes, when every pauper, belonging to the respective wards, must be present and must answer to his name, and be inspected by the master and matron respectively.

Article 15: The meals shall be taken by all the paupers except the sick, the children, persons of unsound mind, wayfarers, and vagrants, and the paupers of the first and fourth classes, in the dining-hall, or day-room, and in no other place whatever, and during the time of meals, order an decorum shall be maintained, and no pauper of the second, third, fifth, or sixth classes shall go to or remain in his sleeping-room, either in the time hereby appointed for work, or in the intervals allowed for meals, except by permission of the master or matron.

Article 16: The master and matron of the workhouse shall (subject to the directions of the Board of Guardians) fix the hours of rising and going to bed for the paupers of the first, fourth, and seventh classes, and determine the occupation and employment of which they may be capable; and the meals for such paupers shall be provided at such times and in such manner as the Board of Guardians may direct.

Article 17: The paupers of the respective sexes shall be dieted with the food and in the manner described in the dietary table which may be prescribed for the use of the workhouse, and in no other manner.

Provided, however, that the medical officer for the workhouse may direct in writing such diet for any individual pauper as he shall deem necessary, and the master shall obey such direction until the next ordinary meeting of the Board of Guardians, when he shall report the same in writing to the Guardians. And if the medical officer for the workhouse shall at any time certify that he deems a temporary change in the diet essential to the health of the paupers in the workhouse, or of any class or classes thereof, the Guardians shall cause a copy of such certificate to be entered on the minutes of their proceedings, and shall be empowered forthwith to order, by a resolution, the said diet to be temporarily changed according to the recommendation of the medical officer, and shall forthwith transmit a copy of such certificate and resolution to the Poor Law Commissioners.

Article 18: If any pauper shall require the master or matron to weigh the allowance of provisions served out at any meal, the master or matron shall forthwith weigh such allowance in the presence of the pauper complaining, and of two other persons.

Article 19: No pauper shall have or consume any liquor, or any food or provision other than is allowed in the said dietary table, unless by the direction in writing of the medical officer; such direction to be obeyed and reported by the master, as in Article 17.

Article 20: The clothing to be work by the paupers in the workhouse shall be made of such materials as the Board of Guardians may determine.

Article 21: The paupers of the several classes shall be kept employed according to their capacity and ability; and no pauper shall receive any compensation for his labour. Provided always that the Guardians may, without any direction of the medical officer, make such allowance of food as may be necessary to paupers employed as nurses, or in the household work; but they shall not allow to such paupers any fermented or spirituous liquors.

Article 22: The boys and girls who are inmates of the workhouse shall, for three of the working hours at least every day, be respectively instructed in reading, writing, arithmetic, and the principles of the Christian religion, and such other instruction shall be imparted to them as shall fit them for serve, and train them to habits of usefulness, industry, and virtue.

Article 23: Any pauper may quit the workhouse upon giving to the master, or (during his absence or inability to act) to the matron, a reasonable notice of his wish to do so: and in the event of any able-bodied pauper, having a family so quitting the house, the whole of such family shall be sent with him unless the Board of Guardians shall for any special reason otherwise direct, and such directions shall be in conformity with the regulations of the said Commissioners with respect to out-door relief in force for the time being.

Article 24: Provided nevertheless that the Board of Guardians shall make such regulations as they may deem fit, subject to the approval of the Poor Law Commissioners, to enable the master of the workhouse to allow any pauper to quit the workhouse, for some urgent or special reason, without giving any such notice as is required in Article 23, and to return after a temporary absence only; every such allowance shall be reported by the master to the Board of Guardians at their next ordinary meeting.

Provided also that nothing herein contained shall prevent the master of the workhouse from allowing the paupers of each sex under the age of 15, subject to such restrictions as the Board of Guardians may impose, to quit the workhouse under the care and guidance of himself, or the matron, schoolmaster, schoolmistress, porter, or some one of the assistants and servants of the workhouse, for the purpose of exercise.

Article 25: Any person may visit any pauper in the workhouse by permission of the master, or (in his absence) of the matron, subject to such conditions and restrictions as the Board of Guardians may prescribe; such interview to take place, except where a sick pauper is visited, in a room separate from the other inmates of the workhouse, in the presence of the master, matron, or porter.

Article 26: No written or printed paper of an improper tendency, or which may be likely to produce insubordination, shall be allowed to circulate, or be read aloud among the inmates of the workhouse.

Article 27: No pauper shall play at cards, or at any game of chance in the workhouse; and it shall be lawful for the master to take from any pauper, and keep until his departure from the workhouse, any cards, dice, or other articles relating to games of chance, which may be in his possession.

Article 28: No pauper shall smoke in any room of the workhouse, except by the special direction of the medical officer, or shall have any matches or other articles of a highly combustible nature in his possession.

Article 29: Any licensed minister of the religious persuasion of any inmate of the workhouse who shall at any time in the day, on the request of any inmate, enter the workhouse for the purpose of affording religious assistance to him, or for the purpose of instructing his child or children in the principles of his religion, shall give such assistance or instruction so as not to interfere with the good order and discipline of the other inmates of the workhouse; and such religious assistance or instruction shall be strictly confined to inmates who are of the religious persuasion of such minister, and to the children of such inmates, except in the cases in which the Board of Guardians may lawfully permit religious assistance and instruction to be given to any paupers who are Protestant dissenters by licensed ministers who are Protestant dissenters.

Article 30: No work, except the necessary household work and cooking, shall be performed by the paupers on Sunday, Good Friday, and Christmas-day.

Article 31: Prayers shall be read before breakfast and after supper every day, and Divine Service shall be performed every Sunday in the workhouse (unless the Guardians, with the consent of the Poor Law Commissioners shall otherwise direct), at which all the paupers shall attend, except the sick, persons of unsound mind, the young children, and such as are too infirm to do so; provided that those paupers who may object so to attend, on account of their professing religious principles differing from those of the Church of England, shall also be exempt from such attendance.

Article 32: The Guardians may make such regulations as they deem expedient to authorise any inmate of the workhouse, being a member of the established church, and not being an able-bodied female pauper having an illegitimate child, to attend public worship at a parish church or chapel, on every Sunday, Christmas-day, and Good Friday, under the control and inspection of the master or porter of the workhouse, or other officer.

Article 33: The Guardians may also make such regulations as they deem expedient to authorise any inmate of the workhouse, being a dissenter from the established church, and not being an able-bodied female pauper having an illegitimate child, to attend public worship at any dissenting chapel in the neighbourhood of the workhouse, on every Sunday, Christmas-day, and Good Friday.

PUNISHMENTS FOR MISBEHAVIOUR OF THE PAUPERS

Article 34: Any pauper who shall neglect to observe such of the regulations herein contained as are applicable to and binding on him; -

> Or who shall make any noise when silence is ordered to be kept;
> Or shall use obscene or profane language;
> Or shall by word or deed insult or revile any person;
> Or shall not duly cleanse his person;
> Or shall refuse or neglect to work, after having been required to do so;
> Or shall pretend sickness;
> Or shall play at cards or other game of chance;
> Or shall enter or attempt to enter, without permission, the ward or yard appropriated to any class of paupers other than that to which he belongs;
> Or shall misbehave in going to, at, or returning from public worship out of the workhouse, or at prayers in the workhouse;
> Or shall return after the appointed time of absence, when allowed to quit the workhouse temporarily;
> Or shall wilfully disobey any lawful order of any officer of the workhouse;

Shall be deemed DISORDERLY.

Article 35: Any pauper who shall, within seven days, repeat any one or commit more than one of the offences specified in Article 34;

> Or who shall by word or deed insult or revile the master or matron, or any other officer of the workhouse, or any of the Guardians;
> Or shall wilfully disobey any lawful order of the master or matron after such order shall have been repeated;

Or shall unlawfully strike or otherwise unlawfully assault any person;
Or shall wilfully or mischievously damage or soil any property whatsoever belonging to the Guardians;
Or shall be drunk;
Or shall commit any act of indecency;
Or shall wilfully disturb the other inmates during prayers or divine worship;

Shall be deemed REFRACTORY.

Article 36: It shall be lawful for the master of the workhouse, with or without the direction of the Board of Guardians, to punish any disorderly pauper by substituting, during a time not greater than forty-eight hours, for his or her dinner, as prescribed by the dietary, a meal consisting of eight ounces of bread, or one pound of cooked potatoes, and also by withholding from him during the same period, all butter, cheese, tea, sugar, or broth, which such pauper would otherwise receive, at any meal during the time aforesaid.

Article 37: *It shall be lawful for the Board of Guardians, by a special direction to be entered on their minutes, to order any refractory* pauper to be punished by confinement in a separate room, with or without an alteration of diet, similar in kind and duration to that prescribed in Article 36 for *disorderly* paupers; but no pauper shall be so confined for a longer period than twenty-four hours, or, if it be deemed right that such pauper should be carried before a justice of the peace, and if such period of twenty-four hours should be insufficient for that purpose, then for such further time as may be necessary for such purpose.

BENJAMIN DISRAELI
(1804-81)

A radical conservative and proponent of social imperialism he combined the rare talents of orator, politician and novelist. His book popular novel <u>Sybil: or the Two Nations</u> firmly established him as a friend of the poor.

SYBIL: OR THE TWO NATIONS

'You lean against an ancient trunk,' said Egremont, carelessly advancing to the stranger, who looked up at him without any expression of surprise, and then replied, 'They say 'tis the trunk beneath whose branches the monks encamped when they came to this valley to raise their building. It was their house, till with the wood and stone around them, their labour and their fine art, they piled up their abbey. And then they were driven out of it, and it came to this. Poor men! poor men!'

'They would hardly have forfeited their resting-place had they deserved to retain it,' said Egremont.

'They were very rich. I thought it was poverty that was a crime,' replied the stranger, in a tone of simplicity.

'But they had committed other crimes.'

'It may be so; we are very frail. But their history has been written by their enemies; they were condemned without a hearing; the people rose oftentimes in their behalf; and their property was divided among those on whose reports it was forfeited.'

'At any rate, it was a forfeiture which gave life to the community,' said Egremont; 'the lands are held by active men and not by drones.'

'A drone is one who does not labour,' said the stranger; 'whether he wear a cowl or a coronet, 'tis the same to me. Somebody I suppose must own the land; though I have heard say that this individual tenure is not a necessity; but, however this may be, I am not one who would object to the lord, provided he were a gentle one. All agree that the Monastics were easy landlords; their rents were low; they granted leases in those days. Their tenants, too, might renew their term before their tenure ran out: so they were men of spirit and property. There were yeomen then, sir: the country was not divided into two classes, masters and slaves; there was some resting-place between luxury and misery. Comfort was an English habit then, not merely an English word.'

'And do you really think they were easier landlords than our present ones?' said Egremont, inquiringly.

'Human nature would tell us that, even if history did not confess it. The Monastics could possess no private property; they could save no money; they could bequeath nothing. They lived, received, and expended in common. The monastery, too, was a proprietor that never died and never wasted. The farmer had a deathless landlord then; not a harsh guardian, or a grinding mortgagee, or a dilatory master in chancery: all was certain; the manor had not to dread a change of lords, or the oaks to tremble at the axe of the squandering heir. How proud we are still in England of an old family, though, God knows, 'tis rare to see one now. Yet the people like to say. We held under him, and his father and his grandfather before him: they know that such a tenure is a benefit. The abbot was ever the same. The monks were, in short, in every district a point of refuge for all who needed succour, counsel, and protection; a body of individuals having no cares of their own, with wisdom to guide the inexperienced, with wealth to relieve the suffering, and often with power to protect the oppressed.'

'You plead their cause with feeling,' said Egremont, not unmoved.

'It is my own; they were the sons of the people, like myself.'

'I had thought rather these monasteries were the resort of the younger branches of the aristocracy,' said Egremont.

'Instead of the pension list,' replied his companion, smiling, but not with bitterness. 'Well, if we must have an aristocracy, I would rather that its younger branches should be monks and nuns than colonels without regiments, or housekeepers of royal palaces that exist only in name. Besides, see what advantage to a minister if the unendowed aristocracy were thus provided for now. He need not, like a minister in these days, entrust the conduct of public affairs to individuals notoriously incompetent, appoint to the command of expeditions generals who never saw a field, make governors of colonies out of men who never could govern themselves, or find an ambassador in a broken dandy or a blasted favourite. It is true that many of the monks and nuns were persons of noble birth. Why should they not have been? The aristocracy had their share; no more. They, like all other classes, were benefited by the monasteries: but the list of the mitred abbots, when they were suppressed, shows that the great majority of the heads of houses were of the people.'

'Well, whatever difference of opinion may exist on these points,' said Egremont, 'there is one on which there can be no controversy: the monks were great architects.'

'Ah! there it is,' said the stranger, in a tone of plaintiveness; 'if the world but only knew what they had lost! I am sure that not the faintest idea is generally prevalent of the appearance of England before and since the dissolution. Why, sir, in England and Wales alone, there were of these institutions of different sizes, I mean monasteries, and chantries and chapels, and great hospitals, considerably upwards of three thousand; all of them fair buildings, many of them of exquisite beauty. There were on an average in every shire at least twenty structures such as this was; in this great country double that number: establishments that were as vast and as magnificent and as beautiful as your Belvoirs and your Chatsworths, your Wentworths and your Stowes. Try to imagine the effect of thirty or forty Chatsworths in this country, the proprietors of which were never absent. You complain enough now of absentees. The monks were never non-resident. They expended their revenue among those whose labour had produced it. These holy men, too, built and planted, as they did everything else, for posterity: their churches were cathedrals; their schools colleges; their halls and libraries the muniment rooms of kingdoms; their woods and waters, their farms and gardens, were laid out and disposed on a scale and in a spirit that are now extinct; they made the country beautiful, and the people proud of their country.'

'Yet if the monks were such public benefactors, why did not the people rise in their favour?'

'They did, but too late. They struggled for a century, but they struggled against property, and they were beat. As long as the monks existed, the people, when aggrieved, had property on their side. And now 'tis all over,' said the stranger; 'and travellers come and stare at these ruins, and think themselves very wise to moralise over time. They are the children of violence, not of time. It is war that created these ruins, civil war, of all our civil wars the most inhuman, for it was waged with the unresisting. The monasteries were taken by storm, they were sacked, gutted, battered with warlike instruments, blown up with gunpowder; you may see the marks of the blast against the new tower here. Never was such a plunder. The whole face of the country for a century was that of a land recently invaded by a ruthless enemy; it was worse than the Norman conquest; nor has England ever lost this character of ravage. I don't know whether the union workhouses will remove it. They are building something for the people at last. After an experiment of three centuries, your gaols being full, and your treadmills losing something of their virtue, you have given us a substitute for the monasteries.'

'You lament of the old faith,' said Egremont, in a tone of respect.

'I am not viewing the question as one of faith,' said the stranger. 'It is not as a matter of religion, but as a matter of right, that I am considering it: as a matter, I should say, of private right and public happiness. You might have changed, if you thought fit, the religion of the abbots as you changed the religion of the bishops: but you had no right to deprive men of their property, and property moreover which, under their administration, so mainly contributed to the welfare of the community.'

'As for community,' said a voice which proceeded neither from Egremont nor the stranger, 'with the monasteries expired the only type that we ever had in England of such a intercourse. There is no community in England; there is aggregation, but aggregation under circumstances which make it rather a dissociating than a uniting principle.'

It was a still voice that uttered these words, yet one of a peculiar character; one of those voices that instantly arrest attention: gentle and yet solemn, earnest yet unimpassioned. With a step as whispering as his tone; the man who had been kneeling by the tomb had unobserved joined his associate and Egremont. He hardly reached the middle height; his form slender, but well-proportioned; his pale countenance, slightly marked with the small-pox, was redeemed from absolute ugliness by a highly intellectual brown, and large dark eyes that indicated deep sensibility and great quickness of apprehension. Though young, he was already a little bald; he was dressed entirely in black; the fairness of his linen, the neatness of his beard, his gloves much worn, yet carefully mended, intimated that his faded garments were the result of necessity rather than of negligence.

'You also lament the dissolution of these bodies,' said Egremont.

'There is so much to lament in the world in which we live,' said the younger of the strangers, 'that I can spare no pang for the past.'

'Yet you approve of the principle of their society; you prefer it, you say, to our existing life.'

'Yes; I prefer association to gregariousness.'

'That is a distinction,' said Egremont, musingly.

'It is a community of purpose that constitutes society,' continued the younger stranger; 'without that, men may be drawn into contiguity, but they still continue virtually isolated.'

'And is that their condition in cities?

'It is their condition everywhere; but in cities that condition is aggravated. A density of population implies a severer struggle for existence, and a consequent repulsion of elements brought into too close contact. In great cities men are brought together by the desire of gain. They are not in a state of cooperation, but of isolation, as to the makings of fortunes; and for all the rest they are careless of neighbours. Christianity teaches us to love our neighbour as ourself; modern society acknowledges no neighbour.'

'Well, we live in strange times,' said Egremont, struck by the observation of his companion, and relieving a perplexed spirit by an ordinary exclamation, which often denotes that the mind is more stirred than it cares to acknowledge, or at the moment is able to express.

'When the infant begins to walk, it also thinks that it lives in strange times,' said his companion.

'Your inference?' asked Egremont.

'That society, still in its infancy, is beginning to feel its way.'

'This is a new reign,' said Egremont, 'perhaps it is a new era.'

'I think so,' said the younger stranger.

'I hope so,' said the elder one.

'Well, society may be in its infancy,' said Egremont, slightly smiling, 'but, say what you like, our Queen reigns over the greatest nation that ever existed.'

'Which nation?' asked the younger stranger, 'for she reigns over two.;

The stranger paused; Egremont was silent, but looked inquiringly.

'Yes,' resumed the younger stranger after a moment's interval. 'Two nations; between whom there is no intercourse and no sympathy; who are as ignorant of each other's habits, thoughts, and feelings, as if they were dwellers in different zones, or inhabitants of different planets; who are formed by a different breeding, are fed by a different food, are ordered by different manners, and are not governed by the same laws.'

'You speak of -' said Egremont, hesitatingly.
'THE RICH AND THE POOR.'

CLAUDE HENRI DE ROUVROY COMTE DE SAINT-SIMON
(1760-1825)

His writings formed the bases of modern socialism and positivism. He fought in the American revolution, returned to his native France and supported the revoluntion there calling for the public control of production, the abolition of inheritance rights and the emancipation of women.

THE ORGANIZER (1819)

The Unjust Society

Suppose that France suddenly lost fifty of her best physicists, chemists, physiologists, mathematicians, poets, painters, sculptors, musicians, writers; fifty of her best mechanical engineers, civil and military engineers, artillery experts, architects, doctors, surgeons, apothecaries, seamen, clockmakers; fifty of her best bankers, two hundred of her best business men, two hundred of her best farmers, fifty of her best ironmasters, arms manufacturers, tanners, dyers, miners, cloth-makers, cotton manufacturers, silk-makers, linen-makers, manufacturers of hardware, of pottery and china, or crystal and glass, ship chandlers, carriers, printers, engravers, goldsmiths, and other metal-workers; her fifty best masons, carpenters, joiners, farriers, locksmiths, cutlers, smelters, and a hundred other persons of various unspecified occupations, eminent in the sciences, fine arts, and professions; making in all the three thousand leading scientists, artists, and artisans of France.

These men are the Frenchmen who are the most essential producers, those who make the most important products, those who direct the enterprises most useful to the nation, those who contribute to its achievements in the sciences, fine arts and professions. They are in the most real sense the flower of French society; they are, above all Frenchmen, the most useful to their country, contribute most to its glory, increasing its civilization and prosperity. The nation would become a lifeless corpse as soon as it lost them. It would immediately fall into a position of inferiority compared with the nations which it now rivals, and would continue to be inferior until this loss has been replaced, until it had grown another head. It would require at least a generation for France to repair this misfortune; for men who are distinguished in work of positive ability are exceptions, and nature is not prodigal of exceptions, particularly in this species.

Let us pass on to another assumption. Suppose that France preserves all the men of genius that she possesses in the sciences, fine arts and professions, but has the misfortune to lose in the same day ...at the same time all the great officers of the royal household, all the ministers (with or without portfolio), all the councillors of state, all the chief magistrates, marshals, cardinals, archbishops, bishops, vicars-general, and canons, all the prefects and sub-prefects, all the civil servants, and judges, and, in addition, ten thousand of the richest proprietors who live in the style of nobles.

This mischance would certainly distress the French, because they are kind-hearted, and could not see with indifference the sudden disappearance of such a large number of their compatriots. But this loss of thirty-thousand individuals, considered to be the most important in the State, would only grieve them for purely sentimental reasons...

The prosperity of France can only exist through the effects of the progress of the sciences, fine arts and professions. The Princes, the great household officials, the Bishops, Marshals of France, prefects and idle landowners contribute nothing directly to the progress of the sciences, fine arts and professions. Far from contributing they only hinder, since they strive to prolong the supremacy existing to this day of conjectural ideas over positive science. They inevitably harm the prosperity of the nation by depriving, as they do, the scientists, artists, and artisans of the high esteem to which they are properly entitled. They are harmful because they expend their wealth in a way which is of no direct use to the sciences, fine arts, and professions: they are harmful because they are a charge on the national taxation, to the amount of three or four hundred millions under the heading of appointments, pensions, gift, compensations, for the upkeep of their activities which are useless to the nation.

These suppositions underline the most important fact of present politics: they provide a point of view from which we can see this fact in a flash in all its extent; they show clearly, though indirectly, that our social organization is seriously defective: that men still allow themselves to be governed by violence and ruse, and that the human race (politically speaking) is still sunk in immorality.

The scientists, artists, and artisans, the only men whose work is of positive utility to society, and cost it practically nothing, are kept down by the princes and other rulers who are simply more or less incapable bureaucrats.

These suppositions show that society is a world which is upside down...

Ignorance, superstition, idleness and costly dissipation are the privilege of the leaders of society, and men of ability, hard-working and thrifty, are employed only as inferiors and instruments.

To sum up, in every sphere men of greater ability are subject to the control of men who are incapable. From the point of view of morality, the most immoral men have the responsibility of leading the citizens towards virtue; from the point of view of distributive justice, the most guilty men are appointed to punish minor delinquents.

PRINCE PETER KROPOTKIN
(1842-1921)

A prince who became an anarchist. Kropotkin renounced his title and dedicated his life to the elmination of governmental institutions in favour of mutual aid and cooperation. For his efforts he was imprisoned, in his native Russia, but managed to escape to France. jailed again, he served a three year term and upon his release, he moved to England where he lived and wrote much of his work in French and English. He returned to Soviet Russia despite his dislike of Bolshevism.

ANARCHISM

Anarchism, the no-government system of socialism, has a double origin. It is an outgrowth of the two great movements of thought in the economic and the political fields which characterize the nineteenth century, and especially its second part. In common with all socialists, the anarchists hold that the private ownership of land, capital, and machinery has had its time; that it is condemned to disappear; and that all requisites for production must, and will, become the common property of society, and be managed in common by the producers of wealth. And in common with the most advanced representatives of political radicalism, they maintain that the ideal of the political organization of society is a condition of things where the functions of government are reduced to a minimum, and the individual recovers his full liberty of initiative and action for satisfying, by means of free groups and federations - freely constituted - all the infinitely varied needs of the human being.

As regards socialism, most of the anarchists arrive at its ultimate conclusion, that is, at a complete negation of the wage-system and at communism. And with reference to political organization, by giving a further development to the above-mentioned part of the radical program, they arrive at the conclusion that the ultimate aim of society is the reduction of the functions of government to *nil* - that is, to a society without government, to an-archy. The anarchists maintain, moreover, that such being the ideal of social and political organization, they must not remit it to future centuries, but that only those changes in our social organization which are in accordance with the above double ideal, and constitute an approach to it, will have a chance of life and be beneficial for the commonwealth.

As to the method followed by the anarchist thinker, it entirely differs from that followed by the utopists. The anarchist thinker does not resort to metaphysical conceptions (like "natural rights," the "duties of the State," and so on) to establish what are, in his opinion, the best conditions for realizing the greatest happiness of humanity. He follows, on the contrary, the course traced by the modern philosophy of evolution. He studies human society as it is now and was in the past; and without either endowing humanity as a whole, or separate individuals, with superior qualities which they do not possess, he merely considers society as an aggregation of organisms trying to find out the best ways of combining the wants of the individual with those of cooperation for the welfare of the species. He studies society and tries to discover its *tendencies*, past and present, its growing needs, intellectual and economic, and in his ideal he merely points out in which direction evolution goes. He distinguishes between the real wants and tendencies of human aggregations and the accidents (want of knowledge, migrations, wars, conquests) which have prevented these tendencies from being satisfied. And he concludes that the two most prominent, although often unconscious, tendencies throughout our history have been: first, a tendency towards integrating labor for the production of all riches in common, so as finally to render it impossible to discriminate the part of the common production due to the separate individual and second, a tendency towards the fullest freedom of the individual in the prosecution of all aims, beneficial both for himself and for society at large. The idea of the anarchist is thus a mere summing-up of what he considers to be the next phase of evolution. It is no longer a matter of faith; it is a matter for scientific discussion.

ARTHUR SCHOPENHAUER
(1788-1860)

Schopenhauer believed that only pain established our worth as human beings and that the only way to rescue ourselves, constructively, from this pain was to temporarily submerge outselves in art or science and to sumpathize with the plight of others.

STUDIES IN PESSIMISM

On the Sufferings of the World

Unless suffering is the direct and immediate object of life, our existence must entirely fail of its aim. It is absurd to look upon the enormous amount of pain that abounds everywhere in the world, and originates in needs and necessities inseparable from life itself, as serving no purpose at all and the result of mere chance. Each separate misfortune, as it comes, seems, no doubt, to be something exceptional; but misfortune in general is the rule.

The best consolation in misfortune or affliction of any kind will be thought of other people who are in a still worse plight than yourself; and this is a form of consolation open to every one. But what an awful fate this means for mankind as a whole!

We are like lambs in a field, disporting themselves under the eye of the butcher, who chooses out first one and then another for his prey. So it is that in our good days we are all unconscious of the evil fate may have presently in store for us - sickness, poverty, mutilation, loss of sight or reason.

No little part of the torment of existence lies in this, that Time is continually pressing upon us, never letting us take breath, but always coming after us, like a taskmaster with a whip. If at any moment Time stays his hand, it is only when we are delivered over to the misery of boredom.

But misfortune has its uses; for, as our bodily frame

would burst asunder if the pressure of the atmosphere were removed, so, if the lives of men were relieved of all need, hardship and adversity; if everything they took in hand were successful, they would be so swollen with arrogance that, though they might not burst, they would present the spectacle of unbridled folly - nay, they would go mad. And I may say, further, that a certain amount of care or pain or trouble is necessary for every man at all times. A ship without ballast is unstable and will not go straight.

Certain it is that work, worry, labor and trouble, form the lot of almost all men their whole life long. But if all wishes were fulfilled as soon as they arose, how would men occupy their lives? what would they do with their time? If the world were a paradise of luxury and ease, a land flowing with milk and honey, where every Jack obtained his Jill at once and without any difficulty, men would either die or boredom or hang themselves; or there would be wars, massacres, and murders; so that in the end mankind would inflict more suffering on itself than it has now to accept at the hands of Nature.

If children were brought into the world by an act of pure reason alone, would the human race continue to exist. Would not a man rather have so much sympathy with the coming generation as to spare it the burden of existence? or at any rate not take it upon himself to impose that burden upon it in cold blood.

I shall be told, I suppose, that my philosophy is comfortless - because I speak the truth; and people prefer to be assured that everything the Lord has made is good. Go to the priests, then, and leave philosophers in peace. At any rate, do not ask us to accommodate our doctrines to the lessons you have been taught. This is what those rascals of sham philosophers will do for you. Ask them for any doctrine you please, and you will get it. Your University professors are bound to preach optimism; and it is an easy and agreeable task to upset their theories.

I have reminded the reader that every state of welfare, every feeling of satisfaction, is negative in its character, that is to say, it consists in freedom from pain, which is the positive element of existence. It follows, therefore, that the happiness of any given life is to be measured, not by its joys and pleasures, but by the extent to which it has been free from suffering - from positive evil. If this is the true standpoint, the lower animals appear to enjoy a happier destiny than man.

There are two things which make it impossible to believe that this world is the successful work of an all-wise, all-good, and, at the same time, all-powerful being; firstly, the misery which abounds in it everywhere; and secondly the obvious imperfection of its highest product, man, who is a burlesque of what he should be. These things cannot be reconciled with any such belief. On the contrary, they are just the facts which support what I have been saying; they are our authority for viewing the world as the outcome of our own misdeeds, and therefore, as something that had better not have been. While, under the former hypothesis, they amount to a bitter accusation against the Creator, and supply material for sarcasm; under the latter they form an indictment against our own nature, our own will, and teach us a lesson of humility. They lead us to see that like the children of a libertine, we come into the world with the burden of sin upon us; and that it is only through having continually to atone for this sin that our existence is so miserable, and that its end is death.

If you accustom yourself to this view of life you will regulate your expectations accordingly, and cease to look upon all its disagreeable incidents, great and small, its sufferings, its worries, its misery, as anything unusual or irregular; nay, you will find that everything is as it should be, in a world where each of us pays the penalty of existence in his own peculiar way. Among the evils of a penal colony is the society of those who form it; and if the reader is worthy of better company, he will need no words from me to remind him of what he has to put up with at present. If he has a soul above the common, or if he is a man of genius, he will occasionally feel like some noble prisoner of state, condemned to work in the galleys with common criminals;

and he will follow his example and try to isolate himself.

In general, however, it should be said that this view of life will enable us to contemplate the so-called imperfections of the great majority of men, their moral and intellectual deficiencies, and the resulting base type of countenance, without any surprise, to say nothing of indignation; for we shall never cease to reflect where we are, and that the men bout us are beings conceived and born in sin, and living to atone for it. That is what Christianity means in speaking of the sinful nature of men.

KARL MARX
(1818-83)
&
FRIEDRICH ENGELS
(1820-95)

One of the most quoted and least read economic theorists, Marx adapted Hegel's dialectical method to his own view of materialism. He spent the last thirty-three years of his life in England where he established a lifelong association with Friedrich Engels; together they formed the International. (International Workingmen's Association).

MANIFESTO OF THE COMMUNIST PARTY

A spectre is haunting Europe - the spectre of Communism. All the powers of old Europe have entered into a holy alliance to exorcise this spectre: Pope and Czar, Metternich and Guizot, French Radicals and German police-spies.

Where is the party in opposition that has not been decried as communistic by its opponents in power? Where the Opposition that has not hurled back the branding reproach of Communism, against the more advanced opposition parties, as well as against its reactionary adversaries?

Two things result from this fact: Communism is already acknowledged by all European powers to be power.

Modern industry has established the world market, for which the discovery of America paved the way. This market has given an immense development to commerce, to navigation, to communication by land. This development has, in turn, reacted on the extension of industry; and in proportion as industry, commerce, navigation, railways extended, in the same proportion the bourgeoisie developed, increased its capital, and pushed into the background every class handed down from the Middle Ages.

We see, therefore, how the modern bourgeoisie is itself the product of a long course of development, of a series of revolutions in the modes of production and of exchange.

Each step in the development of the bourgeoisie was accompanied by a corresponding political advance of that class. An oppressed class under the sway of the feudal nobility, it became an armed and self-governing association in the medieval commune; here independent urban republic (as in Italy and Germany), there taxable "third estate" of the monarchy (as in France); afterwards, in the period of manufacture proper, serving either the semi-feudal or the absolute monarchy as a counterpoise against the nobility, and, in fact, corner-stone of the great monarchies in general - the bourgeoisie has at last, since the establishment of modern industry and of the world market, conquered for itself, in the modern representative state, exclusive political sway. The executive of the modern state is but a committee for managing the common affairs of the whole bourgeoisie.

The bourgeoisie has played a most revolutionary role in history.

The bourgeoisie, wherever it has got the upper hand, has put an end to all feudal, patriarchal, idyllic relations. It has pitilessly torn asunder the motley feudal ties that bound man to his "natural superiors," and has left no other bond between man and man than naked self-interest, than callous "cash payment." It has drowned the most heavenly ecstasies of religious fervour, of chivalrous enthusiasm, of philistine sentimentalism, in the city water of egotistical calculation. It has resolved personal worth into exchange value, and in place of the numberless indefeasible chartered freedoms, has et up that single, unconscionable freedom - Free Trade. In one word, for exploitation, veiled by religious and political illusions, it has substituted naked, shameless, direct, brutal exploitation.

The bourgeoisie has stripped of its halo every occupation

hitherto honoured and looked up to with reverent awe. It has converted the physician, the lawyer, the priest, the poet, the man of science, into its paid wage-labourers.

The bourgeoisie has torn away from the family its sentimental veil, and has reduced the family relation to a mere money relation.

The bourgeoisie has disclosed how it came to pass that the brutal display of vigour in the Middle Ages, which reactionaries so much admire, found its fitting complement in the most slothful indolence. It has been the first to show what man's activity can bring about. It has accomplished wonders far surpassing Egyptian pyramids, Roman aqueducts, and Gothic cathedrals; it has conducted expeditions that put in the shade all former migrations of nations and crusades.

The bourgeoisie cannot exist without constantly revolutionising the instruments of production, and thereby the relations of production, and with them the whole relations of society. Conservation of the old modes of production in unaltered form, was, on the contrary, the first condition of existence for all earlier industrial classes. Constant revolutionising of production, uninterrupted disturbance of all social conditions, everlasting uncertainty and agitation distinguish the bourgeois epoch from all earlier ones. All fixed, fast-frozen relations, with their train of ancient and venerable prejudices and opinions, are swept away, all new-formed ones become antiquated before they can ossify. All that is solid melts into air, all that is holy is profaned, and man is at last compelled to face with sober senses his real conditions of life and his relations with his kind.

The need of a constantly expanding market for its products chases the bourgeoisie over the whole surface of the globe. It must nestle everywhere, settle everywhere, establish connections everywhere.

The bourgeoisie has through its exploitation of the world market given a cosmopolitan character to production and consumption in every country. To the great chagrin of reactionaries, it has drawn from under the feet of industry

the national ground on which it stood. All old-established national industries have been destroyed or are daily being destroyed. They are dislodged by new industries, whose introduction becomes a life and death question for all civilised nations, by industries that no longer work up indigenous raw material, but raw material drawn from the remotest zones; industries whose products are consumed, not only at home, but in every quarter of the globe. In place of the old wants, satisfied by the production of the country, we find new wants, requiring for their satisfaction the products of distant lands and climes. In place of the old local and national seclusion and self-sufficiency, we have intercourse in every direction, universal interdependence of nations. And as in material, so also in intellectual production. The intellectual creations of individual nations become common property. National one-sidedness and narrow-mindedness become more and more impossible, and from the numerous national and local literatures there arises a world literature.

The bourgeoisie, by the rapid improvement of all instruments of production, by the immensely facilitated means of communication, draws all nations, even the most barbarian, into civilisation. The cheap prices of its commodities are the heavy artillery with which it batters down all Chinese walls, with which it forces the barbarians' intensely obstinate hatred of foreigners to capitulate. It compels all nations, on pain of extinction, to adopt the bourgeois mode of production; it compels them to introduce what it calls civilisation into their midst, ie., to become bourgeois themselves. In a word, it creates a world after its own image.

The bourgeoisie has subjected the country to the rule of the towns. It has created enormous cities, has greatly increased the urban population as compared with the rural, and has thus rescued a considerable part of the population from the idiocy of rural life. Just as it has made the country dependent on the towns, so it has made barbarian and semi-barbarian countries dependent on the civilised ones, nations of peasants on nations of bourgeois, the East on the West.

More and more the bourgeoisie keeps doing away with the scattered state of the population, of the means of production, and of property. It has agglomerated population, centralised means of production, and has concentrated property in a few hands. The necessary consequence of this was political centralisation. Independent, or but loosely connected provinces, with separate interests, laws, governments and systems of taxation, become lumped together into one nation, with one government, one code of laws, one national class interest, one frontier and one customs tariff.

The bourgeoisie, during its rule of scarce one hundred years, has created more massive and more colossal productive forces than have all preceding generations together. Subjection of nature's forces to man, machinery, application of chemistry to industry and agriculture, steam-navigation, railways, electric telegraphs, clearing of whole continents for cultivation, canalisation of rivers, whole populations conjured out of the ground - what earlier century had even a presentiment that such productive forces slumbered in the lap of social labour?

We see then that the means of production and of exchange, which served as the foundation for the growth of the bourgeoisie were generated ....cally, they have over the great mass of the proletariat the advantage of clearly understanding the lien of march, the conditions, and the ultimate general results of the proletarian movement.

The immediate aim of the Communists is the same as that of all the other proletarian parties: Formation of the proletariat into a class, overthrow of bourgeois supremacy, conquest of political power by the proletariat.

***

Abolition of the family! Even the most radical flare up at this infamous proposal of the Communists.

On what foundation is the present family, the bourgeois family, based? On capital, on private gain. In its completely developed form this family exists only among the bourgeoisie. But this state of things finds its complement in the practical absence of the family among the proletarians, and in public prostitution.

The bourgeois family will vanish as a matter of course when its complement vanishes, and both will vanish with the vanishing of capital.

Do you charge us with wanting to stop the exploitation of children by their parents? To this crime we pleas guilty.

But, you will say, we destroy the most hallowed or relations, when we replace home education by social.

And your education! Is not that also social, and determined by the social conditions under which you educate, by the intervention of society, direct or indirect, by means of schools, etc.? The Communists have not invented the intervention of society in education; they do but seek to alter the character of that intervention, and to rescue education from the influence of the ruling class.

The bourgeois claptrap about the family and education, about the hallowed co-relation of parent and child, becomes all the more disgusting, the more, by the action of modern industry, all family ties among the proletarians are torn asunder, and their children transformed into simple articles of commerce and instruments of labour.

But you Communists would introduce community of women, screams the whole bourgeoisie in chorus.

The bourgeois sees in his wife a mere instrument of production. He hears that the instruments of production are to be exploited in common, and, naturally, can come to no other conclusion than that the lot of being common to all will likewise fall to the women.

He has not even a suspicion that the real point aimed at is to do away with the status of women as mere instruments of production.

For the rest, nothing is more ridiculous than the virtuous indignation of our bourgeois at the community of women which, they pretend, is to be openly and officially established by the Communists. The Communists have no need to introduce community of women; it has existed almost from time immemorial.

Our bourgeois, not content with having the wives and daughters of their proletarians at their disposal, not to speak of common prostitutes, take the greatest pleasure in seducing each other's wives.

Bourgeois marriage is in reality a system of wives in common and thus, at the most, what the Communists might possibly be reproached with is that they desire to introduce, in substitution for a hypocritically concealed, an openly legalised community of women. For the rest, it is self-evident, that the abolition of the present system of production must bring with it the abolition of the community of women springing from that system, ie., of prostitution both public and private.

The Communists are further reproached with desiring to abolish countries and nationality.

The working men have no country. We cannot take from them what they have not got. Since the proletariat must first of all acquire political supremacy, must rise to be the leading class of the nation, must constitute itself *the* nation, it is, so far, itself national, though not in the bourgeois sense of the word.

National differences and antagonisms between peoples are vanishing gradually from day to day, owing to the development of the bourgeoisie, to freedom of commerce, to the world market, to uniformity in the mode of production and in the conditions of life corresponding thereto.

The supremacy of the proletariat will cause them to vanish still faster. United action, of the leading civilised countries at least, is one of the first conditions for the emancipation of the proletariat.

In proportion as the exploitation of one individual by another is put an end to, the exploitation of one nation by another will also be put an end to. In proportion as the antagonism between classes within the nation vanishes, the hostility of one nation to another will come to an end.

The charges against Communism made from a religious,

a philosophical, and, generally, from an ideological standpoint, are not deserving of serious examination.

Does it require deep intuition to comprehend that man's ideas, views, and conceptions, in one word, man's consciousness, changes with every change in the conditions of his material existence, in his social relations and in his social life?

What else does the history of ideas prove than that intellectual production changes its character in proportion as material production is changed? The ruling ideas of each age have ever been the ideas of its ruling class.

When people speak of ideas that revolutionise society, they do but express the fact that within the old society the elements of a new one have been created, and that the dissolution of the old ideas keeps even pace with the dissolution of the old conditions of existence.

When the ancient world was in its last throes, the ancient religions were overcome by Christianity. When Christian ideas succumbed in the 18th century to rationalist ideas, feudal society fought its death-battle with the then revolutionary bourgeoisie. The ideas of religious liberty and freedom of conscience merely gave expression to the sway of free competition within the domain of knowledge.

"Undoubtedly," it will be said, "religion, moral, philosophical and juridical ideas have been modified in the course of historical development. But religion, morality, philosophy, political science, and law, constantly survived this change."

"There are, besides, eternal truths, such as Freedom, Justice, etc., that are common to all states of society. But Communism abolishes eternal truths, it abolishes all religion, and all morality, instead of constituting them on a new basis; it therefore acts in contradiction to all past historical experience."

What does this accusation reduce itself to? The history of all past society has consisted in the development of class antagonisms, antagonisms that assumed different forms at different epochs.

But whatever form they may have taken, one fact is common to all past ages, *viz.*, the exploitation of one part of society by the other. No wonder, then, that the social consciousness of past ages, despite all the multiplicity and variety it displays, moves within certain common forms, or general ideas, which cannot completely vanish except with the total disappearance of class antagonisms.

The Communist revolution is the most radical rupture with traditional property relations; no wonder that its development involves the most radical rupture with traditional ideas.

But let us have done with the bourgeois objections to Communism.

We have seen above, that the first step in the revolution by the working class is to raise the proletariat to the position of ruling class, to establish democracy.

The proletariat will use its political supremacy to wrest, by degrees, all capital from the bourgeoisie, to centralise all instruments of production in the hands of the state, *ie.*, of the proletariat organised as the ruling class; and to increase the total of productive forces as rapidly as possible....

When, in the course of development, class distinctions have disappears, and all production has been concentrated in the hands of a vast association of the whole nation, the public power will lose its political character. Political power, properly so called, is merely the organised power of one class for oppressing another. If the proletariat during its contest with the bourgeoisie is compelled, by the force of circumstances, to organise itself as a class; if, by means of a revolution, it makes itself the ruling class, and, as such sweeps away by force the old conditions of production, then it will, along with these conditions, have swept away the conditions for the existence of class antagonisms, and of classes generally, and will thereby have abolished its own supremacy as a class.

In place of the old bourgeois society, with its classes and class antagonisms, we shall have an association, in which the free development of each is the condition for the free development of all.

OTTO VON BISMARCK
(1815-98)

The "iron chancellor" and creator of the German empire introduced a whole series of pioneering social legislation in the 1880's such as health, accident and unemployment insurance which were designed to weaken socialist appeal and strengthen German nationalism.

A SPEECH ON STATE SOCIALISM, (1884)
GIVEN BEFORE THE GERMAN PARLIAMENT

I take this opportunity immediately to bring under discussion the question of competition of private insurance companies.... I want to express here in the name of the Imperial Government, the principle that we do not regard accidents and misfortunes in general, suitable subjects for the extraction of higher interest or dividends (Bravo! on the right), that we want to provide the worker with cheap insurance against these and other evils if that is at all possible, and that we regard it as our duty to hold down the cost of insurance so far as possible in the interest of the worker and of industry, of the employer, as well as the employee. Now, I believe that there is no one who can establish such a low price as can be possible through the state.... I do not regard it as immoral for somebody to set up a private insurance company and I do regard it as human and entirely natural that in this business he strives for a return on his capital, if that can be, even a considerable surplus and the highest dividend possible....

It is another question, however, whether the state has the right...to leave the performance of a public duty, namely that of protecting the worker from accident and from need if he is injured or if he is old, to the chance that for the purpose private companies will be formed, which will charge workers and employers the highest rates they can.... As soon, however, as the state takes this matter in hand - and I believe this is its duty - it must seek the cheapest form and must make no profit from it, but rather concentrate on the welfare of the poor and the needy. Otherwise one could more justly relinquish certain state duties...such as education and defense to private companies,asking oneself who could do it most cheaply and efficiently. If provision for the needy on a level higher than the current law provides is a public duty then the state must assume it; the state cannot console itself that a private company will assume it.... The whole matter is rooted in the question: Has the state the duty of caring for its helpless fellow-citizens, or not? I maintain it has this duty.... It is folly for a community or local government to take up those tasks that individuals can perform. Those functions which the [*local*] community can fulfil with justice and advantage may be left to the community. But there are functions which only the state as a whole can perform.... To this last group belongs defense of the country.... Also to it belongs aid to the needy and prevention of such justified complaints as in fact offer really useful material for exploitation by the Social Democrats. This is the task of the state, and the sate cannot long escape it.

If someone objects that this is socialism, I do not shrink from it in the least. The question is, where is the permissible limit of state socialism? Without it we cannot conduct our economy at all. Any poor law is socialism. There are indeed states which keep themselves so far from socialism that they have no poor laws at all - I remind you of France. These French conditions quite naturally explain the interpretation of the distinguished social thinker, Leon Say...; there is expressed the French interpretation that every citizen has the right to starve, and that the state has no obligation to prevent the exercise of this right. (Hear, hear! from the right)....

The honorable Deputy [*who spoke previously*] characterizes it as something entirely new that we want to introduce a socialist element into the legislation. I have previously shown that the socialist element is nothing new and that the state cannot exist without a certain amount of socialism.... I believe that political parties - groups defined in terms of political ideals and programs - have outlived their day. They will gradually be forced, if they do not do it voluntarily, to take positions on economic questions and more than previously promote policies of [*social*] interest. This is called for by the spirit of the times.... In my opinion, a chief reason for the successes that the Social Democratic leaders have had...is that the state does not carry on enough state socialism; where it should be active it leaves a vacuum, and this is filled by others, by agitators who meddle with the state's business. The means of power in this field fall into other hands than the state's and we certainly cannot await with calm composure how they will be used....

CHARLES B.P. BONSANQUET
(Article written in 1868)

Bonsanquet a lawyer, wrote a how-to book for those well-to-do people who were interested in assisting the poor in London. The earnest, if somewhat patronizing, attitude is of special note to the reader.

LONDON: SOME ACCOUNT OF ITS GROWTH, CHARITABLE AGENCIES AND WANTS

The whole question of the temporal relief of the poor in London urgently demands consideration. Things are in a bad state and are getting worse. Statistics show that pauperism is increasing,[1] and there is an increasing mass of poverty and wretchedness (in some parts of the town at least) which is only prevented from coming on the rates by having gradually learnt to be content with a mode of life more like that of brute beasts than of men.

Our poor-law system is merely repressive; it aims..."at driving the poor into economy by terror." It is an improvement on the system that went before it, but it is quite insufficient by itself. The guardians are volunteers, and so far they deserve credit for their work, but from the nature of their position, and especially from the extent of their duties, they are necessarily guardians of the rates rather than guardians of the poor. No one goes to the metropolitan guardians for advice about any charitable scheme, or looks on them as specially interested in the welfare of individual poor persons. They have good schools for the children who have been actually received into the workhouse, and some pains are taken to get them a good start in life, but they take no

---

[1] Pauperism has increased 50 per cent in seven years, and nearly 400,000 persons now receive relief in the metropolitan district during the twelve months. Of course the numbers at any one time are much less than this.

charge of the education of the children of those who are receiving out-door relief, and do nothing to put them in the way of earning a livelihood. If we except their schools, they do little or nothing to *prevent* pauperism, or to raise up those who have fallen into it.

Under the present system it is not possible to pay sufficient attention to the peculiarities of different cases. Look at the duties of a relieving officer in a London union. The union contains several thousand poor families, and hundreds of persons come to him during the week to ask for out-door relief, - many on the very morning of the day which the Board of Guardians meets. He gives bread or other relief to urgent cases at once; in some unions all out-door cases are left to his discretion, in others all cases come before the Board, but the Guardians are everywhere in great measure guided by his advice in their grants, and sometimes dispose of the applications made to them at the rate of two or three a minute.[2] He knows very little of the character and antecedents of many of the applicants, and has but a superficial knowledge of their present circumstances, but he knows the character of the different parts of his district well, and has had much experience of the poor. Under these circumstances, however conscientious a man may be, he will necessarily go too much by general rules. He will refuse a deserving applicant, or at most will only allow her two or three loaves a week (which she may have to come some distance to fetch), because she lives in a poor neighbourhood, and he fears that if he did more for her he would be persecuted by her neighbours; whilst he will give money to another, upon whom, as those who had known her longer could tell him, such relief would be thrown away. Of course it is no part of his duty to seek out deserving cases, and yet it is not at all uncommon for respectable people to let themselves be driven into a course of borrowing and pawning which must end in parish relief, when a little timely help at the beginning of their distress might have kept them straight.

---

[2] Dr. Stallard's *London Pauperism*, p. 51

Nor can he be expected to give the case of each applicant much attention or thought, yet the advice and assistance of an experienced man might often be the means of relieving the poor-rates of the burden of a family. In such cases, it will be said, private charity comes in. It ought to do so, and it often does, but its intervention cannot be relied on, till there is more co-operation between it and the Poor Law.

Dr. Arnold thought, in 1839, "that the Poor Law should be accompanied by an organized system of church charity."[3] An actual combination of voluntary agency with a system like that of our Poor Laws has been found possible in some places, and it is to be observed that both benefit by the alliance. A system of State relief is likely to trust too much to general rules, private charity is equally likely to be impulsive and irregular. Volunteers should, it seems to me, dispense the relief, whilst the State should furnish a part at least of the funds, and should exercise the right it thus acquires of imposing rules and restrictions on the visitors. But I am not recommending any attempt at such combination in London. The suggestion would, at least, be premature. *Co-operation* between the poor-law authorities and volunteers we may reasonably hope to have soon in some form or other. *The Times* has repeatedly urged the expediency of this, pointing out how well it answered during the cotton famine in Lancashire, and the experience of this last winter (1867-8) in the East of London, has shown how much it is needed here. The discussions that have taken place, and the temporary union of relief societies that has been brought about, may prepare the way for permanent co-operation.

One point to which attention has been called is especially worthy of notice. Mr. Corbett, the Poor-Law Inspector for the Metropolitan District, strongly recommended that charitable societies should not supplement poor-law relief, but that each agency should take entire charge of its own class of cases. This is an excellent principle, but the practice in London has hitherto been directly contrary to it. The out-

---

[3] Life of Dr. Arnold, p. 468.

relief given by the guardians in the richest parishes is seldom more than enough to pay the recipient's room-rent, and is rarely, if ever, increased in winter, though the cost of living increases. The district visitor or the curate supplements this every now and then by an order for a shilling's worth of groceries; and this again is supplemented by help from the Society for the Relief of Distress, or from some local Society, or possibly from the Police Court. If Mr. Corbett's plan is to be adopted, guardians and visitors alike must take as their standard the minimum relief on which a person can live, and must give that in each case, subject to deduction on account of anything which the recipient may still be expected to earn, or which he ought to receive from any other source, such as a grown-up son or daughter. One bad result of the present want of system is, that no one feels responsible for the cases he assists; he gives a shilling or two from time to time; it is gratefully received, but so small a sum may be quite out of proportion to the needs of the family; on the other hand, when self-respect has been lost, importunity, and, still more, imposition, may make a very comfortable livelihood by drawing upon different sources.

It would not be difficult to classify cases as between the poor-law and voluntary charity; the former would take the ordinary chronic cases, the latter, perhaps, some of the more deserving chronic cases, but, especially, those temporary cases, which, it might be hoped, judicious help would save from sinking into pauperism. It would be more difficult to apportion out the work amongst our different charitable societies; and yet it is most desirable that temporal relief should come through one hand, or, if this is not possible, that the different persons relieving should at least act in concert.

It may be said that there are three principal classes of Societies engaged in distributing temporal relief in London. First there is a class, of which the Strangers' Friend Society is the most important, in which religious consolation and instruction are brought prominently forward. Similar societies, on a smaller scale, are attached, I believe, to several of the chief Nonconformist chapels. Generally speaking these societies are not "territorial." They make a point of relieving persons at their homes, and of finding out the real merits of cases; but they do not attempt to hunt out all cases of distress in a given area; and their agents rather pride themselves on being willing to help any deserving person, wherever he or she may live. The Metropolitan Visiting and Relief Association, and the parochial District Visiting Societies, form the second class. These Societies aim at thorough supervision of certain areas; but the clergymen and ladies, who are their principal agents, require to be reinforced in numbers, and to get more help from laymen and than they have hitherto received; at any rate, at times and in places in which the work of temporal relief becomes really heavy. A third class is represented by the Society for the Relief of Distress, and some of the so-called "Philanthropic" Societies. This class adopts a secular basis, and deals with physical distress mainly from the business-like and practical point of view.

I have before urged residents in London to make friends with six or eight poor families; where several persons do this in the same district, and intend to look after their temporal relief, I would suggest that they should form themselves into small knots, each with its Chairman or superintendent, and should meet occasionally. This will afford each visitor an opportunity of comparing notes with others, and will also give him some one to fall back on in case of absence or illness. Where a neighbourhood is already sufficiently visited by ladies, it will cost a man but little time to undertake the supervision of a much larger number, as sub-almoner of the Society for the Relief of Distress, or visitor for any local society. For this purpose he will not attempt to make acquaintance with the one or two hundred families on his beat, but will only visit those whose cases lady-visitors or subscribers ask him to investigate and relieve. The funds at the disposal of District Visiting Societies are generally insufficient to meet the temporary distress, from want of work and illness, which the first three months of the year always bring with them. It is just these cases that the almoner will invite them to pass on to him. He will have little or nothing to do, excepting during these months, and not more then than he can attend to on his way home in the late afternoon. He should make it a positive rule never to relieve people till he has seen them in their own houses.

If charitable people generally would only obtain and verify the addresses of street-applicants for relief before assisting them, it would at once put an end to a great deal of fraud. Probably few, who have not made a practice of doing this, are aware how often they are false. Of course, it is not necessary that the person appealed to should himself go to the address. The applicant often takes care to name a place at some distance off. The Society for the Relief of Distress will investigate a case for a subscriber in any part of London. The Notting Hill Philanthropic Society will do the same through its visitors in any part of the Notting Hill Ward; and no doubt in other parts of London.

FERDINAND LASSALLE
(1825-64)

Lasalle favored state run co-operatives; unlike Marx he believed that the state should play a major role in a socialist society. He established the first German Workers Party in 1863.

THE LAW OF WAGES

Under free competition the relation of an employer to the employed is the same as to any other merchandise. The worker is work, and work is the cost of its production. This is the leading feature of the present age. In former times the relations were those of man to man: after all, the relations of the slaveowner to the slave, and of the feudal lord to the serf, were human. The relations in former times were human, for they were those of rulers to the ruled; they were relations between one man and another man. Even the ill-treatment of the slaves and serfs proves this; for anger and love are human passions; and those ill-treated in anger were still treated as men. The cold, impersonal relation of the employer to the employed, as to a thing which is produced like any other ware on the market, is the specific and thoroughly inhuman feature of the Middle Class Age.

The Middle Class hate the idea of a State; they would replace the State by a Middle Class society permeated with free competition; for in a State, workers are still treated as men, while under the Middle Class regime the workers are like any other merchandise, and are only taken into consideration according to the cost of production.

Ancient civilization is shown by what Plutarch wrote of Marcus Crassus and his slaves: "He (Crassus) used to attend to their education and often gave them lessons himself; esteeming it the principal part of the business of a master to inspect and take care of his servants, whom he considered as the living instruments of economy. In this he was certainly right if he thought, as he frequently said, that other matters should be managed by servants, but the servants by the master." Contrast this with the words of a Liberal professor: "Swiss manufacturers boast that they can manufacture at less cost than the Germans because the Swiss have no compulsory education."

Wages, on the average, are reduced to the necessary mean of subsistence. But if this be the reward of labor, what becomes of the excess of the prices paid for the articles produced over the cost of subsistence of the workers whilst the articles are being made? This excess is divided between the employer and other capitalists, pure and simple, such as the holders of land, bankers, etc.

...There is not a single drop of the sweat of the workers that is not paid back to capital in the price of produce. Every pound in the hands of the employers produces another pound. With this increase the power of capital increases, so that every effort of the workers enables the capitalist to compel the workers to further toil. And when it is possible to reduce the prices of the products and thus cheapen the means of subsistence, then the increase of the workers does not increase with the increased produce of labor, but the power of capital does.

Take all those who have worked together in the production of some article - those who have worked with their brains as well as those who have worked with their hands; add together what they have received for their work, and they will not be able to recover the product of their labor! And when machinery is employed, thus causing a greater production with the same amount of labor, then it becomes more and more impossible for the workers to buy back with their wages the product of their work, and they become poorer and poorer.

EDUARD BERNSTEIN
(1850-1932)

Exiled in 1878 by Bismarck, this Socialist, returned to this native Germany in 1901 and became the chief spokesperson for revisionism. He refuted the need for an intensivified class struggle and prolatarian revoltion.

THE CASE FOR REFORM

My proposition, "To me that which is generally called the ultimate aim of socialism is nothing, but the movement is everything," has often been conceived as a denial of every definite aim of the socialist movement, and Mr. George Plekhanov has even discovered that I have quoted this "famous sentence" from the book *To Social Peace,* by Gerhard von Schulze-Gavernitz. There, indeed, a passage reads that it is certainly indispensable for revolutionary socialism to take as its ultimate aim the nationalization of all the means of production, but not for practical political socialism which places near aims in front of distant ones. Because as ultimate aim is here regarded as being dispensable for practical objects, and as I also have professed but little interest for ultimate aims, I am an "undiscriminating follower" of Schulze-Gavernitz. One must confess that such demonstration bears witness to a striking wealth of thought.

When eight years ago I reviewed the Schulze-Gavernitz book in *Neue Zeit,* although my criticism was strongly influenced by assumptions which I now no longer hold, yet I put on one side as immaterial that opposition of ultimate aim and practical activity in reform, and admitted -- without encountering a protest -- that for England a further peaceful development, such as Schulze-Gavernitz places in prospect before her, was not improbable. I expressed the conviction that with the continuance of free development, the English working classes would certainly increase their demands, but would desire nothing that could not be shown each time to be necessary and attainable beyond all doubt. That is at the bottom nothing else than what I say today. And if anyone wishes to bring up against me the advances in social democracy made since then in England, I answer that with this extension a development of the English social democracy has gone hand in hand from the Utopian, revolutionary sect, as Engels repeatedly represented it to be, to the party of political reform which we now know. No socialist capable of thinking, dreams today in England of an imminent victory for socialism by means of a violent revolution -- none dreams of a quick conquest of Parliament by a revolutionary proletariat. But they rely more and more on work in the municipalities and other self-governing bodies. The early contempt for the trade union movement has been given up; a closer sympathy has been won for it and, here and there also, for the co-operative movement.

And the ultimate aim? Well, that just remains an ultimate aim. "The working classes have no fixed and perfect Utopias to introduce by means of a vote of the nation. They know that in order to work out their own emancipation -- and with it that higher form of life which the present form of society irresistibly makes for by its own economic development -- they, the working classes, have to pass through long struggles, a whole series of historical processes, by means of which men and circumstances will be completely transformed. They have no ideals to realize, they have only to set at liberty the elements of the new society which have already been developed in the womb of the collapsing bourgeois society." So writes Marx in *Civil War in France*. I was thinking of this utterance, not in every point, but in its fundamental thought in writing down the sentence about the ultimate aim. For after all what does it say but that the movement, the series of processes, is everything, whilst every aim fixed beforehand in its details is immaterial to it. I have declared already that I willingly abandon the form of the sentence about the ultimate aim as far as it admits the interpretation that every general aim of the working class movement formulated as a principle should be declared valueless. But the preconceived theories about the drift of the movement which go beyond such a generally expressed aim, which try to determine the direction of the movement and its character without an ever-vigilant eye upon facts and experience, must necessarily always pass into Utopianism, and at some time or other stand in the way, and hinder the real theoretical and practical progress of the movement.

* * *

Constitutional legislation works more slowly in this respect as a rule. Its path is usually that of compromise, not the prohibition, but the buying out of acquired rights. But it is stronger than the revolution scheme where prejudice and the limited horizon of the great mass of the people appear as hindrances to social progress, and it offers greater advantages where it is a question of the creation of permanent economic arrangements capable of lasting; in other words, it is best adapted to positive social-political work.

In legislation, intellect dominates over emotion in quiet times; during a revolution emotion dominates over intellect. But it emotion is often an imperfect leader, the intellect is a slow motive force. Where a revolution sins by over-haste, the every-day legislator sins by procrastination. Legislation works as a systemic force, revolution as an elementary force.

As soon as a nation has attained a position where the rights of the propertied minority have ceased to be a serious obstacle to social progress where the negative tasks of political action are less pressing than the positive, then the appeal to a revolution by force becomes a meaningless phrase. One can overturn a government or a privileged minority, but not a nation. When the working classes do not possess very strong economic organizations of their own, and have not attained, by means of education on self-governing bodies, a high degree of mental independence, the dictatorship of the proletariat means the dictatorship of club orators and writers. I would not wish that those who see in the oppression and tricking of the working men's organizations and in the exclusion of working men from the legislature and government the highest point of the art of political policy should experience their error in practice. Just as little would I desire it for the working class movement itself.

One has not overcome Utopianism if one assumes that there is in the present, or ascribes to the present, what is to be in the future. We have to take working men as they are. And they are neither so university pauperized as was set out in the *Communist Manifesto*, nor so free from prejudices and weakness as their courtiers wish to make us believe. They have the virtues and failings of the economic and social conditions under which they live. And neither these conditions nor their effects can be put on one side from one day to another.

Have we attained the required degree of development of the productive forces for the abolition of classes? In face of the fantastic figures which were formerly set up in proof of this and which rested on generalizations based on the development of particularly favored industries, socialist writers in modern times have endeavoured to reach by carefully detailed calculations, appropriate estimates of the possibilities of production in a socialist society, and their results are very different from those figures. Of a general reduction of hours of labor to five, four, or even three or two hours, such as was formerly accepted, there can be no hope at any time within sight, unless the general standard of life is much reduced. Even under a collective organization of work, labor must begin very young and only cease at a rather advanced age, if it is to be reduced considerably below an eight-hours' day. Those persons ought to understand this first of all who indulge in the most extreme exaggerations regarding the ratio of the number of the non-propertied classes to that of the propertied. But he who thinks irrationally on one point does so usually on another.

But he who surveys the actual workers' movement will also find that the freedom from those qualities which appeared Philistine to a person born in the bourgeoisie, is very little valued by the workers, that they in no way support the morale of proletarianism, but, on the contrary, tend to make a "Philistine" out of a proletarian. With the roving proletarian without a family and home, no lasting, firm trade union movement would be possible. It is no bourgeois prejudice, but a conviction gained through decades of labor organization, which has made so many of the English labor leaders -- socialists and non-socialists -- into zealous adherents of the temperance movement. The working class socialists know the faults of their class, and the most conscientious among them, far from glorifying these faults, seek to overcome them with all their power.

ROSA LUXEMBURG
(1870-1919)

A Russian born German revolutionary this outstanding orator and writer was a founding member of the Spartacus Party which eventually became the German Communist Party. She was arrested and subsequently murdered by soldiers during the Spartacus uprising of 1919.

REFORM OR REVOLUTION

If it is true that theories are only the images of the phenomena of the exterior world in the human consciousness, it must be added, concerning Eduard Bernstein's system, that theories are sometimes inverted images. Think of a theory of instituting socialism by means of social reforms in the face of the complete stagnation of the reform movement in Germany. Think of a theory of trade union control over production in face of the defeat of the metal workers in England. Consider the theory of winning a majority in Parliament, after the revision of the constitution of Saxony and in view of the most recent attempts against universal suffrage. However, the pivotal point of Bernstein's system is not located in his conception of the practical tasks of the Social-Democracy. It is found in his stand on the course of the objective development of capitalist society, which, in turn, is closely bound to his conception of the practical tasks of the Social-Democracy.

According to Bernstein, a general decline of capitalism seems to be increasingly improbable because, on the one hand, capitalism shows a greater capacity of adaptation, and on the other hand, capitalist production becomes more and more varied.

The capacity of capitalism to adapt itself, says Bernstein, is manifested first in the disappearance of general crises, resulting from the development of the credit system, employers' organization, wider means of communication and informational services. It shows itself secondly, in the tenacity of the middle classes, which hails from the growing differentiation of the branches of production and the elevation of vast layers of the proletariat to the level of the middle class. It is furthermore proved, argues Bernstein, by the amelioration of the economic and political situation of the proletariat as a result of its trade union activity.

From this theoretic stand is derived the following general conclusion about the practical work of the Social-Democracy. The latter must not direct its daily activity toward the conquest of political power, but toward the betterment of the condition of the working class within the existing order. It must not expect to institute socialism as a result of a political and social crisis, but should build socialism by means of the progressive extension of social control and the gradual application of the principle of co-operation.

Bernstein himself sees nothing new in his theories. On the contrary, he believes them to be in agreement with certain declarations of Marx and Engels. Nevertheless, it seems to us that it is difficult to deny that they are in formal contradiction with the conceptions of scientific socialism.

If Bernstein's revisionism merely consisted in affirming that the march of capitalist development is slower than was thought before, he would merely be presenting an argument for adjourning the conquest of power by the proletariat, on which everybody agreed up to now. Its only consequence would be a slowing up of the pace of the struggle.

But that is not the case. What Bernstein questions is not the rapidity of the development of capitalist society, but the march of the development itself and, consequently, the very possibility of a change to socialism.

Socialist theory up to now declared that the point of departure for a transformation to socialism would be a general and catastrophic crisis. We must distinguish in this out-look two things: the fundamental idea and its exterior form.

The fundamental idea consists of the affirmation that

capitalism, as a result of its own inner contradictions, moves toward a point when it will be unbalanced, when it will simply become impossible. There were good reasons for conceiving that juncture in the form of a catastrophic general commercial crisis. But that is of secondary importance when the fundamental idea is considered.

The scientific basis of socialism rests, as is well known, on three principal results of capitalist development. First, on the growing anarchy of capitalist economy, leading inevitably to its ruin. Second, on the progressive socialization of the process of production, which creates the germs of the future social order. And third, on the increased organization and consciousness of the proletarian class, which constitutes the active factor in the coming revolution.

Bernstein pulls away the first of the three fundamental supports of scientific socialism. He says that capitalist development does not lead to a general economic collapse.

He does not merely reject a certain form of the collapse. He rejects the very possibility of collapse. He says textually: "One could claim that by collapse of the present society is meant something else than a general commercial crisis, worse than all others, that is a complete collapse of the capitalist system brought about as a result of its own contradictions." And to this he replies: "With the growing development of society a complete and almost general collapse of the present system of production becomes more and improbable, because capitalist development increases on the one hand the capacity of adaptation and, on the other, -- that is at the same time, the differentiation of industry."

But then the question arises: "Why and how, in that case, shall we attain the final goal? According to scientific socialism, the historic necessity of the socialist revolution manifests itself above all in the growing anarchy of capitalism, which drives the system into an impasse. But if one admits with Bernstein that capitalist development does not move in the direction of its own ruin, then socialism ceases to be objectively necessary.

* * *

It is not true that socialism will arise automatically from the daily struggle of the working class. Socialism will be the consequence of (1), the growing contradictions of capitalist economy and (2), of the comprehension by the working class of the unavoidability of the suppression of these contradictions through a social transformation. When, in the manner of revisionism, the first condition is denied and the second rejected, the labor movement finds itself reduced to a simple corporative and reformist movement. We move here in a straight line toward the total abandonment of the class viewpoint.

This consequence also becomes evident when we investigate the general character of revisionism. It is obvious that revisionism does not wish to concede that its standpoint is that of the capitalist apologist. It does not join the bourgeois economists in denying the existence of the contradictions of capitalism. But, on the other hand, what precisely constitutes the fundamental point of revisionism and distinguishes it from the attitude taken by the Social-Democracy up to now, is that it does not base its theory on the belief that the contradictions of capitalism will be suppressed as a result of the logical inner development of the present economic system.

We may say that the theory of revisionism occupies an intermediate place between two extreme. Revisionism does not expect to see the contradictions of capitalism mature. It does not propose to suppress these contradictions through a revolutionary transformation. It wants to lessen, to attenuate, the capitalist contradictions. So that the antagonism existing between production and exchange is to be mollified by the cessation of crises and the formation of capitalist combines. The antagonism between Capital and Labor is to be adjusted by bettering the situation of the workers and by the conversation of the middle classes. And the contradiction between the class State and society is to be liquidated through increased State control and the progress of democracy.

It is true that the present procedure of the Social-

Democracy does not consist in waiting for the antagonisms of capitalism to develop and in passing on, only then, to the task of suppressing them. On the contrary, the essence of revolutionary procedure is to be guided by the direction of this development, once it is ascertained, and inferring from this direction what consequences are necessary for the political struggle. Thus the Social-Democracy has combated tariff wars and militarism without waiting for their reactionary character to become fully evident. Bernstein's procedure is not guided by a consideration of the development of capitalism, by the prospect of the aggravation of its contradictions. It is guided by the prospect of the attenuation of these contradictions. He shows this when he speaks of the "adaption" of capitalist economy.

* * *

Revisionism is nothing else than a theoretic generalization made from the angle of the isolated capitalist. Where does this viewpoint belong theoretically if not in vulgar bourgeois economics?

HERBERT SPENCER
(1820-1903)

He attempted to mold the natural sciences and psychology and philosophy within Darwin's theory of evolution. The term social darwinism should more accurately be termed "social spencerism."

THE STUDY OF SOCIETY

Besides an habitual neglect of the fact that the quality of a society is physically lowered by the artificial preservation of its feeblest members, there is an habitual neglect of the fact that the quality of a society is lowered morally and intellectually, by the artificial preservation of those who are least able to take care of themselves.

If anyone denies that children bear likenesses to the progenitors in character and capacity - if he holds that men whose parents and grandparents were habitual criminals, have tendencies as good as those of men whose parents and grandparents were industrious and upright, he may consistently hold that it matters not from what families in a society the successive generations descend. He may think it just as well if the most active, and capable, and prudent, and conscientious people die without issue; while many children are left by the reckless and dishonest. But whoever does not espouse so insane a proposition, must admit that social arrangements which retard the multiplication of the mentally-best, and facilitate the multiplication of the mentally-worst, must be extremely injurious.

For if the unworthy are helped to increase, by shielding them from that mortality which their unworthiness would naturally entail, the effect is to produce, generation after generation, a greater unworthiness. From diminished use of self-conserving faculties already deficient, there must result, in posterity, still smaller amounts of self-conserving faculties. The general law which we traced above in its bodily applications, may be traced here in its mental applications. Removal of certain difficulties and dangers which have to be met by intelligence and activity, is followed by a decreased ability to meet difficulties and dangers. Among children born to the more capable who marry with the less capable, thus artificially preserved, there is not simply a lower average power of self-preservation than would else have existed, but the incapacity reaches in some cases a greater extreme....For such members of a population as do not take care of themselves, but are taken care of by the rest, inevitably bring on the rest extra exertion; either in supplying them with the necessaries of life, or in maintaining over them the required supervision, or in both. That is to say, in addition to self-conservation and conservation of their own offspring, the best, having to undertake the conservation of the worst, and of their offspring, are subject to an overdraw upon their energies. In some cases this stops them from marrying; in other cases it diminishes the numbers of their children; in other cases it brings their children to orphanhood - in every way tending to arrest the increase of the best, to deteriorate their constitutions, and to pull them down towards the level of the worst.

Fostering the good-for-nothing at the expense of the good, is an extremely cruelty. It is a deliberate storing-up of miseries for future generation. There is no greater curse to posterity than that of bequeathing them an increasing population of imbeciles and idlers and criminals. To aid the bad in multiplying, is, in effect, the same as maliciously providing for our descendants a multitude of enemies. It may be doubted whether the maudlin philanthropy which, looking only at direct mitigations, persistently ignores indirect mischiefs, does not inflict a greater total of misery than the extremist selfishness inflicts. Refusing to consider the remote influences of his incontinent generosity, the thoughtless giver stands but a degree above the drunkard who thinks only of today's pleasure and ignores to-morrow's pain, or the spendthrift who seeks immediate delights at the cost of ultimate poverty. In one respect, indeed, he is worse; since, while getting the present pleasure produced in giving pleasure, he leaves the future miseries to be borne by others - escaping them himself.

How far the mentally-superior may, with a balance of benefit to society, shield the mentally-inferior from the evil results of their inferiority, is a question too involved to be here discussed at length. Doubtless it is in the order of things that parental affection, and regard of relatives, and the spontaneous sympathy of friends and even of strangers, should mitigate the pains which incapacity has to bear, and the penalties which unfit impulses bring around. Doubtless, in many cases the reactive influence of this sympathetic care which the better take of the worse, is morally beneficial, and in a degree compensates by good in one direction for evil in another. It may be fully admitted that individual altruism, left to itself, will work advantageously - wherever, at least, it does not go to the extent of helping the unworthy to multiply. But an unquestionable injury is done by agencies which undertake in a wholesale way to foster good-for-nothings: putting a stop to that natural process of eliminations by which society continually purifies itself. For not only by such agencies is this preservation of the worst and destruction of the best carried further than it would else be, but there is scarcely any of that compensating advantage which individual altruism implies. A mechanically-working State-apparatus, distributing money drawn from grumbling ratepayers, produces little or no moralizing effect on the capables to make up for multiplication of the incapables. Here, however, it is needless to dwell on the perplexing questions hence arising. My purpose is simply to show that a rational policy must recognize certain general truths of Biology; and to insist that only when study of these general truths, as illustrated throughout the living world, has woven them into the conceptions of things, is there gained a strong conviction that disregard of them must cause enormous mischiefs...

Pervading all nature we may see at work a stern discipline, which is a little cruel that it may be very kind. That state of universal welfare maintained throughout the lower creation, to the great perplexity of many worthy people, is at bottom the most merciful provision which the circumstances admit of. It is much better than the ruminant animal, when deprived by age of the vigor which made its existence a pleasure, should be killed by some beast of prey than that it should linger out a life made painful by infirmities, and eventually die of starvation. By the destruction of all such, not only is existence ended before it becomes burdensome, but room is made for a younger generation capable of the fullest enjoyment; and, moreover, out of the very act of substitution happiness is derived for a tribe of predatory creatures. Note further, that their carnivorous enemies not only remove from herbivorous herds individuals past their prime, but also weed out the sickly, the malformed, and the least fleet or powerful. By the aid of which purifying process, as well as by the fighting, so universal in the pairing season, all vitiation of the race through the multiplication of its inferior samples is prevented; and the maintenance of a constitution completely adapted to surrounding conditions, and therefore most productive of happiness, is insured.

The development of the higher creation is a progress toward a form of being capable of a happiness undiminished by these drawbacks. It is in the human race that the consummation is to be accomplished. Civilization is the last stage of its accomplishment. And the ideal man is the man in whom all the conditions of that accomplishment are fulfilled. Meanwhile the well-being of existing humanity and the unfolding of it into this ultimate perfection, are both secured by that same beneficent, though severe, discipline to which the animate creation at large is subject: a discipline which is pitiless in the working out of good: a felicity-pursuing law which never swerves for the avoidance of partial and temporary suffering. The poverty of the incapable, the distresses that come upon the imprudent, the starvation of the idle, and those shoulderings aside of the weak by the strong, which leave so many "in shallows and in miseries," are the decrees of a large, far-seeing benevolence. It seems hard that an unskilfulness which with all his efforts he cannot overcome, should entail hunger upon the artisan. It seems hard that a laborer incapacitated by ...

FRIEDRICH WILHELM NIETZSCHE
(1844-1900)

Contrary to popular belief his famous statement "God is Dead" was not a source of joy to Nietzsche but a profound calamity. He was not so much opposed to Christ but rather to the institutions that took his name. He believed that only through the transformation of humans into some higher form of animal could we possibly survive our suicidal tendencies.

THE WILL TO POWER AS SOCIETY AND INDIVIDUAL

Society and State
716 (March-June 1888)

Basic principle: only individuals feel themselves responsible. Multiplicities are invented in order to do things for which the individual lacks the courage. It is for just this reason that all communalities and societies are a hundred times more upright and instructive about the nature of man than is the individual, who is too weak to have the courage for his own desires -

The whole of "altruism" reveals itself as the prudence of the private man: societies are not "altruistic" towards one another - The commandment to love one's neighbor has never yet been extended to include one's actual neighbor. That relationship is still governed by the words of Manu: "We must consider all countries that have common borders with us, and their allies, too, as our enemies. For the same reason, we must count all *their* neighbors as being well-disposed toward us."

The study of society is so invaluable because man as society is much more naive than man as a "unit." "Society" has never regarded virtue as anything but a means to strength, power, and order.

How simple and dignified is Man when he says: "Virtue could scarcely endure by its own strength. Fundamentally it is only the fear of punishment that keeps men within bounds and leaves everyone in peaceful possession of his own.

717 (Nov. 1887-March 1888)

The state organized immorality - *internally*: as police, penal law, classes, commerce, family; *externally*: as will to power, to war, to conquest, to revenge.

How does it happen that the state will do a host of things that the individual would never countenance? - Through division of responsibility, of command, and of execution. Through the interposition of the virtues of obedience, duty, patriotism, and loyalty. Through upholding pride, severity, strength, hatred, revenge - in short, all typical characteristics that contradict the herd type.

718 (Nov. 1887-March 1888)

None of you has the courage to kill a man, or even to whip him, or even to - but the tremendous machine of the state overpowers the individual, so he repudiates responsibility for what he does (obedience, oath, etc.)

- Everything a man does in the service of the state is contrary to his nature.

- in the same way, everything he learns with a view to future state service is contrary to his nature.

This is achieved through division of labor (so that no one any longer possesses the full responsibility):

the lawgiver - and he who enacts the law;

the teacher of discipline - and those who have grown hard and severe under discipline.

728 (March-June 1888)

It is part of the concept of the living that it must grow - that it must extend its power and consequently incorporate alien forces. Intoxicated by moral narcotics, one speaks of the right of the individual to *defend* himself; in the same sense one might also speak of his right to attack: for both - and the second even more than the first - are necessities for every living thing: - aggressive and defensive egoism are not matters of choice, to say nothing of "free will," but the fatality of life itself.

In this case it is all the same whether one has in view an individual or a living body, an aspiring "society." The right to punish (or the self-defense of society) is at bottom called a "right" owing to a misuse of the word. A right is acquired through treaties - but self-protection and self-defense do not rest on the basis of a treaty. At least a people might just as well designate as a right its need to conquer, its lust for power, whether by means of arms or by trade, commerce and colonization - the right to growth, perhaps. A society that definitely and *instinctively* gives up war and conquest is in decline: it is ripe for democracy and the rule of shopkeepers - In most cases, to be sure, assurances of peace are merely narcotics.

750 (1884)

The rotted ruling classes have ruined the image of the ruler. The "state" as a court of law is a piece of cowardice, because the great human being is lacking to provide a standard of measurement. Finally, the sense of insecurity grows so great that men cower in the dust before *any* forceful will that commands.

751 (March-June 1888)

"The will to power" is so hated in democratic ages that their entire psychology seems directed toward belittling and defaming it. The type of the great ambitious man who thirsts after honor is supposed to be Napoleon! And Caesar! And Alexander! - As if these were not precisely the great *despisers* of honor!

And Helvetius demonstrates to us that men strive after power so as to possess the enjoyments available to the powerful: he understands this striving for power as will to enjoyment! as hedonism!

752 (1884)

According to whether a people feels "right, vision, the gift of leadership, etc., belong to the few" or "to the many" - there will be an oligarchic or a democratic government.

Monarchy represents the belief in one man who is utterly superior, a leader, savior, demigod.

Aristocracy represents the belief in an elite humanity and higher caste.

Democracy represents the disbelief in great human beings and an elite society: "Everyone is equal to everyone else." "At bottom we are one and all self-seeking cattle and mob."

753 (1885)

I am opposed to 1. socialism, because it dreams quite naively of "the good, true, and beautiful" and of "equal rights" (- anarchism also desires the same ideal, but in a more brutal fashion); 2. parliamentary government and the press, because these are the means by which the herd animal becomes master.

754 (1884)

The arming of the people - is ultimately the arming of the mob.

755 (1884)

How ludicrous I find the socialists, with their nonsensical optimism concerning the "good man," who is waiting to appear from behind the scenes if only one would abolish the old "order" and set all the "natural drives" free.

And the party opposed to them is just as ludicrous, because it does not admit the element of violence in the law, the severity and egoism in every kind of authority. " "I and my kind" want to rule and survive; whoever degenerates will be expelled or destroyed" - this is the basic feeling behind every ancient legislation.

The idea of a higher kind of man is hated more than monarchs. Anti-aristocratic: that assumes hatred of monarchy only as a mask -

756 (1885-1886)

How treacherous all parties are! - they bring to light something about their leaders which the latter have perhaps always taken great care to hide under a bushel.

757 (1884)

Modern socialism wants to create the secular counterpart to Jesuitism: *everyone* a perfect instrument. But the purpose, the wherefore? has not yet been ascertained.

758 (Summer-Fall 1883)

Slavery today: a piece of barbarism! Where are those *for whom* they work? One must not always expect the contemporaneity of the two complementary castes.

Utility and pleasure are *slave theories* of life: the "blessing of work" is the self=glorification of slaves. - Incapacity for *otium*.

759 (Nov. 1887-March 1888)

One has no right to existence or to work, to say nothing of a right to "happiness": the individual human being is in precisely the same case as the lowest worm.

760 (Fall 1888)

We must think of the masses as unsentimentally as we think of nature: they preserve the species.

761 (1885-1886)

To look upon the distress of the masses with an ironic melancholy: they want something *we* are capable of - ah!

762 (1885)

European democracy represents a release of forces only to a very small degree. It is above all a release of laziness, of weariness, of *weakness*.

763 (Spring-Fall 1887)

From the future of the worker. - Workers should learn to feel like soldiers. An honorarium, an income, but no pay!
No relation between payment and achievement! But the individual, each according to his kind, should be so placed that he can achieve the highest that lies in his power.

764 (1882)

The workers shall live one day as the bourgeois do now - but *above* them, distinguished by their freedom from wants, the *higher caste*: that is to say, poorer and simpler, but in possession of power.
For *lower* men the reverse valuation obtains; it is a question of implanting "virtues" in them. Absolute

commands; terrible means of compulsion; to tear them away from the easy life. The others may *obey*; and their vanity demands that they appear to be dependent, not on great men, but on *"principles."*

The Individual
766 (1886-1887)

Basic error: to place the goal in the herd and not in single individual! The herd is a means, no more! But now one is attempting to understand the herd as an individual and to ascribe to it a higher rank than to the individual - profound misunderstandings! ! ! Also to characterize that which makes herdlike, sympathy, as the more valuable side of our nature!

767 (1883-1888)

The individual is something quite new which creates new things, something absolute; all his acts are entirely his own.
Ultimately, the individual derives the values of his acts from himself; because he has to interpret in a quite individual way even the words he has inherited. His interpretation of a formula at least is personal, even if he does not create a formula: as an interpreter he is still creative.

768 (1882)

The "ego" subdues and kills: it operates like an organic cell: it is a robber and violent. It wants to regenerate itself - pregnancy. It wants to give birth to its god and see all mankind at his feet.

HENRY GEORGE
(1839-97)

An outspoken American economist who first proposed a single tax on property. This tax, he believed would cover all expenses of government. Although he has been much ignored; his ideas about a single tax are resurfacing a century later, especially in April when people are completing their income tax forms!

SOCIAL PROBLEMS

Shooting Rubbish

This gulf-stream of humanity that is setting on our shores with increasing volume is in all respects worthy of more attention than we give it. In many ways one of the most important phenomena of our time, it is one which forcibly brings to the mind the fact that we are living under conditions which must soon begin to rapidly change. But there is one part of the immigration coming to us this year which is specially suggestive. A number of large steamers of the transatlantic liners are calling, under contract with the British Government, at small ports on the west coast of Ireland, filling up with men, women and children, whose passages are paid by their government, and then, ferrying them across the ocean, are landing them on the wharves of New York and Boston with a few dollars apiece in their pockets to begin life in the New World.

The strength of a nation is in its men. It is its people that make a country great and strong, produce its wealth, and give it rank among other countries. Yet here is a civilized and Christian government, or one that passes for such, shipping off its people, to be dumped upon another continent, as refuse is shipped off from New York to be shot into the Atlantic Ocean. Nor are these people undesirable material for the making of a nation. Whatever they may sometimes become here, when cooped up in tenement-houses and exposed to the corruption of our politics, and to the temptation of a life greatly differing from that to which they have been accustomed, they are in their own country, as any one who has been among them there can testify, a peaceable, industrious, and, in some important respects, a peculiarly moral people, who lack intellectual and political education, and the robust virtues that personal independence along can give, simply because of the poverty to which they are condemned. Mr. Trevelyan, the Chief Secretary for Ireland, has declared in the House of Commons that they are physically and morally healthy, well capable of making a living, and yet the Government of which he is a member is shipping them away at public expense as New York ships its rubbish!

These people are well capable of making a living, Mr. Trevelyan says, yet if they remain at home they will only be able to make the poorest of poor livings in the best of times, and when seasons are not of the best, taxes must be raised and alms begged to keep them alive; and so as the cheapest way of getting rid of them, they are shipped away at public expense.

What is the reason of this? Why is it that people, in themselves well capable of making a living, cannot make a living for themselves in their own country? Simply that the natural, equal, and unalienable rights of man, with which, as asserted by our Declaration of Independence, these human beings have been endowed by their Creator, are denied them. The famine, the pauperism, the misgovernment, and turbulence of Ireland, the bitter wrongs which keep aglow the fire of Irish "sedition," and the difficulties with regard to Ireland which perplex English statesmen, all spring from what the National Assembly of France, in 1789 declared to be the cause of public misfortunes and corruptions of government - the contempt of human rights. The Irish peasant is forced to starve, to beg, or to emigrate; he becomes in the eyes of those who rule him mere human refuse, to be shipped off anywhere, because, like the English peasant, who, after a slave's life, dies a pauper's death, his natural rights in his native soil are denied him; because his unalienable right to procure wealth by his own exertions and to retain it for his own uses is refused him.

The country from which these people are shipped - and the Government-aided emigration is as nothing compared to the voluntary emigration - is abundantly capable of maintaining in comfort a very much larger population than it has ever had. There is no natural reason why in it people themselves capable of making a living should suffer want and starvation. The reason that they do is simply that they are denied natural opportunities for the employment of their labour, and that the laws permit others to extort from them the proceeds of such labour as they are permitted to do. Of these people who are now being sent across the Atlantic by the English government, and sot on our wharves with a few dollars in their pockets, there are probably none of mature years who have not by their labour produced wealth enough not only to have supported them hitherto in a much higher degree of comfort than that in which they have lived, but to have enabled them to pay their own passage across the Atlantic, if they wanted to come, and to have given them on landing here a capital sufficient for a comfortable start. They are penniless only because they have been systematically robbed from the day of their birth to the day they left their native shores.

A year ago I travelled through that part of Ireland from which these Government-aided emigrants come. What surprises an American at first, even in Connaught, is the apparent spareness of population, and he wonders if this can indeed be that over-populated Ireland of which he has heard so much. There is plenty of good land, but on it are only fat beasts, and sheep so clear and white that you at first think that they must be washed and combed every morning. Once this soil was tilled and was populous, but now you will find only traces of ruined hamlets, and here and there the miserable hut of a herd, who lives in a way no Tierra del Fuegan could envy. For the "owners" of this land, who live in

London and Paris, many of them never having seen their estates, find cattle more profitable than men, and so the men have been driven off. It is only when you reach the bog and the rocks, in the mountains and by the sea-shore, that you find a dense population. Here they are crowded together on land on which Nature never intended men to live. It is too poor for grazing, so the people who have been driven from the better land are allowed to live upon it - as long as they pay their rent. If it were not too pathetic, the patches they call fields would make you laugh. Originally the surface of the ground must have been about as susceptible of cultivation as the surface of Broadway. But at the cost of enormous labour the small stones have been picked off and piled up, though the great boulders remain, so that it is impossible to use a plough; and the surface of the bog has been cut away, and manured by seaweed brought from the shore on the backs of men and women, till it can be made to grow something.

For such patches of rock and bog - soil it could not be called, save by courtesy - which has been made to produce anything only b y their unremitting toil - these people are compelled to pay their absentee landlords rents varying from a pound to four pounds per acre, and then they must pay another rent for the seaweed, which the surf of the wild Atlantic throws upon the shore, before they are permitted to take it for manure, and another rent still for the bog from which they cut their turf. As a matter of fact, these people have to pay more for the land than they can get out of the land. They are really forced to pay not merely for the use of the land and for the use of the ocean, but for the use of the air. Their rents are made up, and the manage to live in good times, by the shillings earned by the women, who knot socks as they carry their creels to and from the market or sea-shore; by the earnings of the men, who go over to England every year to work as harvesters, or by remittances sent home by husbands or children who have managed to get to America. In spite of their painful industry the poverty of these people is appalling. In good times they just manage to keep above the starvation line. In bad times, when a blight strikes their potatoes, they must eat seaweed, or beg relief rom the poor-rates, or from the charitable contributions of the world. When so rich as to have a few chickens or a pig, they no more think of eating them than Vanderbilt thinks of eating his $50,000 race-horses. They are sold to help pay the rent. In the loughs you may see fat salmon swimming in from the sea; but, if every one of them were marked by nature with the inscription, "Lord So-and-So, London, with the compliments of God Almighty," they could not be more out of the reach of these people. The best shops to be found in the villages will have for stock a few pounds of sugar and tea weighed out into ounce and half-ounce papers, a little flour, two or three red petticoats, a little coarse cloth, a few yards of flannel, and a few of cotton, some buttons and thread, a little pig-tail tobacco, and, perhaps, a bottle or two of "the native" hid away in the ground some distance from the cabin, so that if the police do capture it the shopkeeper cannot be put in jail. For the Queen must live and the army must be supported, and the great distillers of Dublin and Belfast and Cork, who find such a comfortable monopoly in the excise, have churches to build and cathedrals to renovate. So poor are these people, so little is there in their miserable cabins, that sub-sheriff who, in 1882, superintended the eviction of near one hundred families in one place, declared that the effects of the whole lot were not worth £3.

But the landlords - ah! the landlords! - they live differently. Every now and again in travelling through this country you come across some landlord's palatial home mansion, its magnificent grounds inclosed with high walls. Pass inside these walls and it is almost like entering another world. Wide stretches of rich velvety lawn, beds of bright flowers, noble avenues of arching trees, and a spacious mansion rich with every appointment of luxury, with its great stables, kennels, and appurtenances of every kind. But though they may have these luxurious home places, the large landlords, with few exceptions, live in London or Paris, or pass part of the year in the great cities and the rest in

Switzerland or Italy or along the shores of the Mediterranean; and occasionally one of them takes a trip over here to see our new country, with its magnificent opportunities for investing in wild lands which will soon be as valuable as English or Irish estates. They have not to work; their incomes come without work on their part - all they have to do is to spend. Some collect galleries of the most valuable paintings, some are fanciers of old books, and give fabulous prices for rare editions. Some of them gamble, some keep studs of racers and costly yachts, and some get rid of their money in ways worse than these. Even their agents, whose business it is to extort the rent from the Irishmen who do work, live luxuriously. But it all comes out of the earnings of just such people as are now being shot penniless on our wharves - out of their earnings, or out of what is sent them by relatives in America, or by charitable contributions.

It is to maintain such a system of robbery as this that Ireland is filled with policemen and troops and spies and informers, and a people who might be an integral part of the British nation are made to that nation a difficulty, a weakness and a danger. Economically, the Irish landlords are of no more use than so many great, ravenous, destructive beasts - packs of wolves, herds of wild elephants, or such dragons as St. George is reputed to have killed. They produce nothing; they only consume and destroy. And what they destroy is more even than what they consume. For, not merely is Ireland turned into a camp of military police and red-coated soldiery to hold down the people while they are robbed; but the wealth producers, stripped of capital by this robbery of their earnings, and condemned by it to poverty and ignorance, are unable to produce the wealth which they could and would produce did labour get its full earnings, and were wealth left to hose who make it. Surely true statesmanship would suggest that if any one is to be shovelled out of a country it should be those who merely consume and destroy; not those who produce wealth.

But English statesmen think otherwise, and these surplus Irish men and women; these refuse Irish men and women and little children - surplus and refuse because the landlords of Ireland have no use for them, *are* shovelled out of their own country and shot upon our wharves. They have reached "the land of the free and the home of the brave" just in time for the fourth of July, when they may hear the Declaration of Independence, with its ringing assertion of unalienable rights, read again in our annual national celebration.

Have they, then, escaped from the system which in their own country made them serfs and human rubbish? Not at all. They have not even escaped the power of their old landlords to take from them the proceeds of their toil.

For we are not merely getting these surplus tenants of English, Scotch, and irish landlords - we are getting the landlords, too. Simultaneously with this emigration is going on a movement which is making the landlords and capitalists of Great Britain owners of vast tracts of American soil. There is even now scarcely a large landowning family in Great Britain that does not own even larger American estates, and American land is becoming with them a more and more favourite investment. These American estates of "their graces" and "my lords" are not as yet as valuable as their home estates, but the natural increase in our population, augmented by emigration, will soon make them so.

Every "surplus" Irishman, Englishman, or Scotchman sent over here assists directly in sending up the value of land and the rent of land. The stimulation of emigration from the Old Country to this is a bright idea on the part of these landlords of two continents. They get rid of people who, at home, in hard times, they might have to support in some sort of fashion, and lessen, as they think, the forces of disaffection, while at the same time they augment the value of their American estates.

It is not improbable that some of these evicted tenants may find themselves over here paying rent to the very same landlords to swell whose incomes they have so long toiled in their old country; but whether this be so or no, their mere coming here, by its effect in increasing the demand for land, helps to enable those landlords to compel some others of the people of the United States to give up to them a portion of their earnings in return for the privilege of living upon American soil. It is merely with this view, and for this purpose, that the landlords of the Old World are buying so much land in the New. They do not want it to live upon; they prefer to live in London or Paris, as many of the privileged classes of America are now learning to prefer to live. They do not want to work it; they do not propose to work at all. All they want with it is the power, which, as soon as our population increases a little, its ownership will give, of demanding the earnings of other people. And under present conditions it is a matter, not of a generation or two, but only of a few years, before they will be able to draw form their American estates sums even greater than from their Irish estates. That is to say, they will virtually own more Americans than they now own Irishmen.

So far from these Irish immigrants having escaped from the system that has impoverished and pauperized the masses of the Irish people for the benefit of a few of their number, that system has really more unrestricted sway here than in Ireland. In spite of the fact that we read the Declaration of Independence every Fourth of July, make a great noise and have a great jubilation, that first of the unalienable rights with which every man is endowed by his Creator - the equal right to the use of the natural elements without which wealth cannot be produced, nor even life maintained - is no better acknowledged with us than it is in Ireland.

There is much said of "Irish landlordism," as though it were a peculiar kind of landlordism, or a peculiarly bad kind of landlordism. This is not so. Irish landlordism is in nothing worse than English landlordism, or Scotch landlordism, or American landlordism, nor are the Irish landlords harder than any similar class. Being generally men of education and culture, accustomed to an easy life, they are, as a whole, less grasping towards their tenants than the farmers who rent of them are to the labourers to whom they sublet. They regard the land as their own, that is all, and expect to get an income from it; and the agent who sends them the best income they naturally regard as the best agent.

Such popular Irish leaders as Mr. Parnell and Mr. Sullivan, when they come over here and make speeches, have a good deal or say about the "feudal landlordism" of Ireland. This is all humbug - an attempt to convey the impression that Irish landlordism is something different from American landlordism, so that American landowners will not take offence, while Irish landowners are denounced. There is in Ireland nothing that can be called feudal landlordism. All the power which the Irish landlord has, all the tyranny which he exercises, springs from his ownership of the soil, from the legal recognition that it is *his* property. If landlordism in Ireland seems more hateful than in England, it is only because the industrial organization is more primitive, and there are fewer intermediaries between the man who is robbed and the man who gets the plunder. And if either Irish or English landlordism seems more hateful than the same system in America, it is only because this is a new country, not yet quite fenced in. But, as a matter of law, these "my lords" and "your graces," who are now getting themselves far greater estates in the United States than they have in their own country, have more power as landlords here than there.

In Ireland, especially, the tendency of legislation for a series of years has been to restrain the power of the landlord in dealing with the tenant. In the United States he has in all its fullness the unrestricted power of doing as he pleases with his own. Rack-renting is with us the common, almost the exclusive, form of renting. There is no long process to be gone through with to secure an eviction, no serving notice upon the relieving officer of the district. The tenant whom the landlord wants to get rid of can be expelled with the minimum of cost and expense.

Says the New York *Tribune's* "Broadway Lounger" incidentally in his chatter:

> "Judge Gedney tells me that on the first of this month he signed no less than two hundred and fifty warrants of dispossession

against poor tenants. His district includes many blocks of the most squalid variety of tenement-houses, and he has fully as much unpleasant work of this kind as any of his judicial brethren. The first of May is, of course, the heaviest field-day of the year for such business, but there are generally at the beginning of every month at least one hundred warrants granted. And to those who fret about the minor miseries of life, no more wholesome cure could be administered than an enforced attendance in a district court of such occasions. The lowest depths of misery are sounded. Judge Gedney says, too, that in the worst cases the suffering is more generally caused by misfortune than by idleness or dissipation. A man gets a felon on his hand, which keeps him at home until his savings are gone and all his effects are in the pawn-shop, and then his children fall sick or his wife dies, and the agent of the house, under instructions from the owner who is perhaps in Europe enjoying himself, won't wait for the rent, and serves him with a summons."

A while ago, when it was bitter cold, I read in the papers an item telling how, in the city of Wilkesbarre, Pennsylvania, a woman and her three children were found one night huddled in a hogshead on a vacant lot, famished and almost frozen. The story was a simple one. The man, out of work, had tried to stead, and been sent to prison. Their rent unpaid, their landlord had evicted them, and as the only shelter they knew of, they had gone to the hogshead. In Ireland, bad as it is, the relieving-officer would have had to be by to have offered them at least the shelter of the almshouse.

These Irish men and women who are being landed on our wharves with two or three dollars in their pockets, do they find access to nature any freer here than there? Far out in the West, if they know where to go, and can get there, they may for a little while yet; but through they may see even around New York plenty of unused land, they will find that it all belongs to somebody. Let them go to work at what they will, they must, here as there, give up some of their earnings for the privilege of working, and pay some other human creature for the privilege of living. On the whole their chances will be better here than there, for this is yet a new country, and a century ago our settlements only fringed the eastern seaboard of a vast continent. But from the Atlantic to the Pacific we already have our human rubbish, the volume of which some of this Irish human rubbish will certainly go to swell. Wherever you go, throughout the country the "tramp" is known; and in this metropolitan city there are already, it is stated by the Charity Organizational Society, a quarter of a million people who live on alms! What in a few years more, are we to do for a place in which to shoot our rubbish? Will it make our difficulty the less than our human refuse can vote?

GEORGES SOREL
(1847-1922)

His classic, if somewhat cumbersome book Reflections on Violence called for a triumphant virile syndalist order to supplant the mediocre capitalist order. Some of his views were incorporated much to his dispair, into Mussolini's fascism.

REFLECTIONS ON VIOLENCE

Violence and the Decadence of the Middle Classes

It is very difficult to understand proletarian violence as long as we think in terms of the ideas disseminated by middle-class philosophers; according to their philosophy, violence is a relic of barbarism which is bound to disappear under the influence of the progress of enlightenment. It is therefore quite natural that Jaures, who has been brought up on middle-class ideology, should have a profound contempt for people who favour proletarian violence; he is astonished to see educated Socialists hand in hand with the Syndicalist; he wonders by what miracle men who have proved themselves thinkers can accumulate *sophistries* in order to give a semblance of reason to the dreams of stupid people who are incapable of thought.[1] This question worries the friends of Jaures considerably, and they are only too ready to treat the representatives of the *new school* as demagogues, and accuse them of seeking the applause of the impulsive masses.

Parliamentary Socialists cannot understand the ends pursued by the *new school*; they imagine that ultimately all Socialism can be reduced to the pursuit of the means of

---

[1]This is apparently the way in which the proletarian movement is spoken of in the fashionable circles of refined Socialism.

getting into power. Is it possible that they think the followers of the *new school* wish to make a higher bid for the confidence of simple electors and cheat the Socialists of the seats provided for them? Again, the apologia of violence might have the very unfortunate result of disgusting the workers with electoral politics, and this would tend to destroy the chances of the Socialist candidates by multiplying the abstentions from voting! Do you wish to revive civil war? they ask. To our great statesmen that seems mad.

Civil war has become very difficult since the discovery of the new firearms, and since the cutting of rectilinear streets in the capital towns.[2] The recent troubles in Russia seem even to have shown that Governments can count much more than was supposed on the energy of their officers. Nearly all French politicians had prophesied the imminent fall of Czarism at the time of the Manchurian defeats, but the Russian army in the presence of rioting did not manifest the weakness shown by the French army during our revolutions; nearly everywhere repression was rapid, efficacious, and even pitiless. The discussions which took place at the congress of social democrats at Jena show that the Parliamentary Socialists no longer rely upon an armed struggle to obtain possession of the State.

Does this mean that they are utterly opposed to violence? It would not be in their interest for the people to be quite calm; a certain amount of agitation suits them, but this agitation must be contained within well-defined limits and controlled by politicians. When he considers it useful for his own interests, Jaures makes advances to the

---

[2] Cf. the reflections of Engels in the preface to the new edition of articles by Marx which he published in 1895 under the title, *Struggles of the Classes in France from 1848 to 1850*. This preface is wanting in the French translation. In the german edition a passage has been left out, the social democratic leaders considering certain phrases of Engels not politic enough.

Confederation General due Travail,[3] sometimes he instructs his peaceable clerks to fill his paper with revolutionary phrases; he is past master in the art of utilising popular anger. A cunningly conducted agitation is extremely useful to Parliamentary Socialists, who boast before the Government and the rich middle class of their ability to moderate revolution; they can thus arrange the success of the financial affairs in which they are interested, obtain minor favours for many influential electors, and get social laws voted in order to appear important in the eyes of the blockheads who imagine that these Socialists are great reformers of the law. In order that all this may come off there must always be a certain amount of movement, and the middle class must always be kept in a state of fear.

It is conceivable that a regular system of diplomacy might be established between the Socialist party and the State each time an economic conflict arose between workers and employers; the *two powers* would settle the particular difference. In Germany the Government enters into negotiations with the Church each time the clericals stand in the way of the administration. Socialists have even been urged to imitate Parnell, who so often found a means of imposing his will on England. This resemblance is all the greater in that Parnell's authority did not rest only on the number of votes at his disposal, but mainly upon the terror which every Englishman felt at the bare announcement of agrarian troubles in Ireland. A few acts of violence controlled by a Parliamentary group were exceedingly useful to the Parnellian policy, just as they are useful to the policy of Jaures. In both cases a Parliamentary group *sells peace of mind to the Conservatives*, who dare not use the force they command.

This kind of diplomacy is difficult to conduct, and the Irish after the death of Parnell do not seem to have

---

[3]According to the necessities of the moment he is for or against the general strike. According to some he voted for the general strike at the International Congress of 1900; according to others he abstained.

succeeded in carrying it on with the same success as in his time. In France it presents particular difficulty, because in no other country perhaps are the workers more difficult to manage: it is easy enough to arouse popular anger, but it is not easy to stifle it. As long as there are no very rich and strongly centralised trade unions whose leaders are in continuous relationship with political men,[4] so long will it be impossible to say exactly to what lengths violence will go. Jaures would very much like to see such associations of workers in existence, for his prestige will disappear at once when the general public perceives that he is not in a position to moderate revolution.

Everything becomes a question of valuation, accurate estimation, and opportunism; much skill, tact, and calm audacity are necessary to carry on such a diplomacy, ie., to make the workers believe that you are carrying the flag of revolution, the middle class that you are arresting the danger which threatens them, and the country that you represent an irresistible current of opinion. The great mass of the electors understands nothing of what passes in politics, and has no intelligent knowledge of economic history; they take sides with the party which seems to possess power, and you can obtain everything you wish from them when you can prove to them that you are strong enough to make the Government capitulate. But you must not go too far, because the middle class might wake up and the country might be given over to a resolutely conservative statesman. A proletarian violence which escapes all valuation, all measurement, and all opportunism, may jeopardise everything and ruin socialistic diplomacy.

This diplomacy is played both on a large and small scale; with the Government, with the heads of the groups in

---

[4]Gambetta complained because the French clergy was "acephalous"; he would have liked a select body to have been formed in its midst, with which the Government could discuss matters (Garilhe, *Le clerge seculier francais un XIXe stecle, pp. 88-89).* Syndicalism has no head with which it would be possible to carry on diplomatic relations usefully.

Parliament, and with influential electors. Politicians seek to draw the greatest possible advantage from the discordant forces existing in the political field.

Parliamentary Socialists feel a certain embarrassment from the fact that at its origin Socialism took its stand on absolute principles and appealed for a long time to the same sentiments of revolt as the most advanced Republican Party. These two circumstances prevented them from following a party policy like that which Charles Bonnier often recommended: this writer, who has long been the principal theorist of the Guesdist party, would like the Socialists to follow closely the example of Parnell, who used to negotiate with the English parties without allowing himself to become the vassal of any one of them; in the same way it might be possible to come to an agreement with the Conservatives, if the latter pledged themselves to grant better conditions to the proletariat than the Radicals (*Socialiste*, August 27, 1905). This policy seemed scandalous to many people. Bonnier was obliged to dilute his thesis. He then contented himself with asking that the party should act in the best interests of the proletariat (September 17, 1905); but how is it possible to know where these interests lie when the principle of the class war is no longer taken as your unique and absolute rule?

Parliamentary Socialists believe that they possess special faculties which enable them to take into account, not only the material and immediate advantages reaped by the working classes, but also the moral reasons which compel Socialism to form part of the great Republican family. Their congresses spend their energies in putting together formulas designed to regulate Socialist diplomacy, in settling what alliances are permitted and what forbidden, in reconciling the abstract principle of the class war (which they are anxious to retain verbally) with the reality of the agreements with politicians. Such an undertaking is madness, and therefore leads to equivocations, when it does not force deputies into attitudes of deplorable hypocrisy. Each year problems have to be rediscussed, because all diplomacy requires a flexibility which is incompatible with the existence of perfectly clear statutes.

OSCAR WILDE
(1854-1900)

Wilde was more widely known for his flamboyant lifestyle and his plays such as the Importance of Being Earnest. This essay is outside of his usual concern.

THE SOUL OF MAN

The majority of people spoil their lives by an unhealthy and exaggerated altruism - are forced, indeed, so to spoil them. They find themselves surrounded by hideous poverty, by hideous ugliness, by hideous starvation. It is inevitable that they should be strongly moved by all this. The emotions of man are stirred more quickly than man's intelligence; and, as I pointed out some time ago in an article on the function of criticism, it is much more easy to have sympathy with suffering than it is to have sympathy with thought. Accordingly, with admirable, though misdirected intentions, they very seriously and very sentimentally set themselves to the task of remedying the evils that they see. But their remedies do not cure the disease: they merely prolong it. Indeed, their remedies are part of the disease.

They try to solve the problem of poverty, for instance by keeping the poor alive; or, in the case of a very advanced school, by amusing the poor.

But this is not a solution: it is an aggravation of the difficulty. The proper aim is to try and reconstruct society on such a basis that poverty will be impossible. And the altruistic virtues have really prevented the carrying out of this aim. Just as the worst slave-owners were those who were kind to their slaves, and so prevented the horror of the system being realised by those who suffered from it, and understood by those who contemplated it, so, in the present state of things in England, the people who do most harm are the people who try to do most good; and at last we have had the spectacle of men who have really studied the problem and know the life - educated men who live in the East End - coming forward and imploring the community to restrain its altruistic impulses of charity, benevolence, and the like. They do so on the ground that such charity degrades and demoralises. They are perfectly right. Charity creates a multitude of sins.

There is also this to be said. It is immoral to use private property in order to alleviate the horrible evils that result from the institution of private property. It is both immoral and unfair.

VLADMIR ILYICH LENIN
(1870-1924)

Lenin announced that imperialism was the last stage of capitalism and called for a world-wide struggle of workers against capitalism in general. His short rule, after the Russian Revolution, was that of a dictator. His major revision of Marx was to determine that the Communist party would act as the vanguard to the promised land, not the prolotariat as Marx had stated.

"LEFT WING" COMMUNISM, AN INFANTILE DISORDER

Newspapers, pamphlets and leaflets perform a necessary work of propaganda, agitation and organization. Not a single mass movement in any at all civilized country can dispense with a journalistic apparatus. No outcries against "leaders," no solemn vows to preserve the purity of the masses from the influence of leaders will obviate the necessity of utilizing for his work people who come from a bourgeois intellectual environment or will get rid of the bourgeois-democratic, "private property" atmosphere and environment in which this work is performed under capitalism. Even two and a half years after the overthrow of the bourgeoisie, after the conquest of political power by the proletariat, we still have this atmosphere around us, this mass (peasant, artisan) environment of bourgeois-democratic private-property relations.

Parliamentarism is one form of activity, journalism is another. The content of both can be communist, and it should be communist if those engaged in both spheres are real Communists, are real members of a proletarian mass party. Yet, in neither sphere - nor *in any other sphere of activity* under capitalism and during the period of transition from capitalism to Socialism - is it possible to avoid those difficulties which the proletariat must overcome, those special problems which the proletariat must solve in order to utilize for its own purposes the services of those who have come from the ranks of the bourgeoisie, in order to gain the victory over bourgeois intellectual prejudices and influences, in order to weaken the resistance of (and, ultimately, completely to transform) the petty-bourgeois environment.

Did we not, before the war of 1914-18, witness in all countries an extraordinary abundance of instances of extreme "left" anarchists, syndicalists and others fulminating against parliamentarism, deriding bourgeois-vulgarized parliamentary Socialists, castigating their careerism, and so on and so forth, and yet themselves making the same kind of bourgeois career *through* journalism and *through* work in the syndicates (trade unions)? Are not the examples of Messrs. Jouhaux and Merrheim, to limit oneself to France typical?

The childishness of those who "repudiate" participation in parliament consists precisely in the fact that they think it possible to *"solve"* the difficult problem of combating bourgeois-democratic influences *within* the working-class movement by such a "simple," "easy," supposedly revolutionary method, when in reality they are only running away from their own shadow, only closing their eyes to difficulties and only trying to brush them aside with mere words. The most shameless careerism, bourgeois utilization of parliamentary seats, glaring reformist perversion of parliamentary activity, vulgar, petty-=bourgeois routine are all unquestionably common and prevalent characteristic features that are engendered by capitalism everywhere, not only outside but also inside the working-class movement. But then capitalism, and the bourgeois environment it creates (which disappears very slowly even after the overthrow of the bourgeoisie, for the peasantry constantly regenerates the bourgeoisie), give rise to what is also essentially bourgeois careerism, national chauvinism, petty-bourgeois vulgarity, etc., only varying insignificantly in form - in positively every sphere of activity and life.

You think, my dear boycottists and antiparliamentarians, that you are "terribly revoluntary," but in reality *you are frightened* by the comparatively small difficulties of the struggle against bourgeois influences within the working-class movement, whereas your victory - ie., the overthrow of the bourgeoisie and the conquest of political power by the proletariat - will create *these very same* difficulties on a still larger, an infinitely larger scale. Like children, you are frightened by a small difficulty which confronts you today, not understanding that tomorrow and the day after you will have to learn just the same, and learn thoroughly, to overcome the same difficulties, only on a immeasurably greater scale.

As long as the bourgeoisie has not been overthrown, and after that as long as small-scale economy and small commodity production have not entirely disappeared, the bourgeois atmosphere, proprietary habits and petty-bourgeois traditions will hamper proletarian work both outside and inside the working-class movement, not only in one field of activity, parliamentary, but inevitably in every field of social activity, in all cultural and political spheres without exception. And the attempt to brush aside, to fence oneself off from *one* of the "unpleasant" problems or difficulties in one sphere of activity is a profound mistake, which will later most certainly have to be paid for. We must study and learn how to master every sphere of work and activity without exception, to overcome all difficulties and all bourgeois habits, customs and traditions everywhere. Any other way of presenting the question is just trifling, just childishness.

JANE ADDAMS
(1860-1935)

Founder of the Hull House Settlement House in Chicago with Ellen Gates Starr. Suffragette and peace movement leader. Won the Nobel Peace Prize in 1935.

PEACE & BREAD IN TIME OF WAR

A Review of Bread Rations and Woman's Traditions

As the European war continued and new relief organizations developed for the care of the wounded and orphaned, the members of our group felt increasingly the need for the anodyne of work, although it was difficult to find our places. For instance, the American Red Cross, following the practice of the British society, had become part of the military organization as it had never done before and its humanitarian appeal for funds had fully utilized the war enthusiasms. Such a combination made it not only more difficult for pacifists to become identified with the Red Cross, but all war activities which were dependent upon public funds became very timid in regard to pacifist co-operation. This was, of course, quite natural as the newspapers constantly coupled the words traitor and pro-German with the word pacifist, as if they described one and the same person. There were in fact many examples arising from the fear of imperiling a good cause by having a pacifist identified with it, that resulted in individual pacifists withdrawing from organizations which they had themselves founded or fostered. But although our feelings were sometimes hurt at the moment when it was made obvious that one or another was *persona non grata*, I think, on the whole, we frankly recognized the instinct for practical politics as responsible for certain incidents; at any rate, we learned to take our rebuffs without a sense of grievance. Personally, I found these incidents easier to bear than the occasional persecutions which came the other way around; when enthusiastic and fanatical pacifists openly challenged the honesty and integrity of their former associates who had become convinced of the necessity for the war.

With many other Americans I, therefore, experienced a great sense of relief when Congress finally established a Department of Food Administration for the United States and when Mr. Hoover, who had spent two and a half years in Europe in intimate contact with the backwash of war, made his first appeal to his fellow countrymen in the name of the food shortage of the entire world, insisting that "the situation is more than war, it is a problem of humanity."

Certainly here was a line of activity into which we might throw ourselves with enthusiasm, and if we were not too conspicuous we might be permitted to work without challenge. The latter was perhaps too much to hope for. But although the challenge came from time to time, in my case at least it did not prove a deterrent and I was soon receiving many more invitations than I could possibly accept to speak on food conservation in relation to European needs; some of these invitations were under the auspices of the Federal Department of Food Administration, and in California, Texas, Colorado and other states under the auspices of the State. But what I cared most for was an opportunity to speak to women's organizations, because I not only believed, as I somewhat elaborately stated, that "in this great undertaking women may bear a valiant part if they but stretch their minds to comprehend what it means in this world crisis to produce food more abundantly and to conserve it with wisdom," but I also believed that we might thus break through into more primitive and compelling motives than those inducing so many women to increase the war spirit. There was
something as primitive and real about feeding the helpless as there was about the fighting and in the race history the tribal feeding of children antedated mass fighting by perhaps a million years. Anthropologists insist that war has not been in the world for more than 20,000 years. It is in fact so recent

that existing remnants of primitive people do not understand it. They may be given to individual murder but not to the collective fighting of numbers of men against other masses of men. Could not the earlier instinct and training in connection with food be aroused and would it be strong enough to overwhelm and quench the later tendency to war. Each individual within himself represented something of both strains: I used to remind myself that although I had had ancestors who fought in all the American wars since 1684, I was also the daughter, granddaughter and the great granddaughter of millers. My earliest recollection was of being held up in a pair of dusty hands to see the heavy stone mill wheels go round. The happiest occupation of my childhood was to watch the old foaming water wheel turning in the back of the mill. I could tell by the sound of the mill when the old wheel was used, which occurred occasionally long after the turbines were established. Watching the foaming water my childish mind followed the masses of hard yellow wheat through the processes of grinding and bolting into the piled drifts of white flour and sometimes further into myriad bowls of bread and milk.

Again, those two strains of War and Bread mingled in my memory of months of travel. Certainly drilling soldiers and the constant reviewing of troops were seen in all the capital cities of Europe but there were also the peasant women who, all the world over, are still doing such a large part of the work connected with the growing and preparation of foods. I recalled them everywhere in the fields of vast Russia as in the tiny pastures of Switzerland; by every roadside in Palestine they were grinding at the hand mills; in Egypt they were forever carrying the water of the Nile that the growing corn might not perish.

The newspapers daily reported the changing fortunes of war on both fronts and our souls turned sick with anxiety and foreboding because all that the modern world held dear hung upon the hazards of battle. But certainly the labor for bread, which to me was more basic and legitimate than war, was still going on everywhere. In my desire to uncover it, to make clear woman's traditional activity with something of its poetry and significance, I read endlessly in Fraser's "Golden Bough," two large volumes of which are given over to the history and interpretation of the innumerable myths dealing with the Spirits of the Corn. These spirits are always feminine and are usually represented by a Corn Mother and her daughter, vaguely corresponding to the Greek Demeter - the always fostering Earth, and her child Persephone.

At the risk of breaking into the narrative of this book, so far as there is one, I am venturing to repeat some of the material which brought a touch of comfort to me and which, so far as I was able at that moment, I handed on to other women. Fraser discovers that relics of the Corn Mother and the Corn Maiden are found in nearly all the harvest fields of Europe; among many tribes of North American Indians; the Eastern world has its Rice Mother for whom there are solemn ceremonies when the seed rice, believed to contain "soul stuff," is gathered. These deities are always feminine, as is perhaps natural from the association with fecundity and growth, and about them has gathered much of the poetry and song in the sowing of the grain and the gathering of the harvest, and those saddest plaints of all, expressing the sorrows of famine.

Myths centering about the Corn Mother but dimly foreshadowed what careful scientific researches have later verified and developed. Students of primitive society believe that women were the first agriculturists and were for a long time the only inventors and developers of its processes. The men of the tribe did little for cultivating the soil beyond clearing the space and sometimes surrounding it by a rough protection. The woman as consistently supplied all cereals and roots eaten by the tribe as the man brought in the game and fish, and in early picture writing the short hoe became as universally emblematic of woman as the spear of the hunter, or the shield and battle axe of the warrior. In some tribes it became a fixed belief that seeds would not grow if planted by a man, and apparently all primitive peoples were convinced that seeds would grow much better if planted by women. In

Central Africa to this day a woman may obtain a divorce from her husband and return to her father's tribe, if the former fails to provide her with a garden and a hoe.

It is said that every widespread myth has its counterpart in the world of morals. This is certainly true of the "fostering Mother." Students in the origin of social customs contend that the gradual change from the wasteful manner of nomadic life to a settled and much more economic mode of existence may be fairly attributed to these primitive agricultural women. Mothers in order to keep their children alive had transplanted roots from the forest or wild grains from the plains, into patches of rudely cultivated ground. We can easily imagine when the hunting was poor or when the flocks needed a new pasture, that the men of the tribe would be for moving on, but that the women might insist that they could not possibly go until their tiny crops were garnered; and that if the tribe were induced to remain in the same caves or huts until after harvest the women might even timidly hope that they could use the same fields next year, and thus avert the loss of their children sure to result from the alternation of gorging when the hunt was good and of starving when it was poor. The desire to grow food for her children led to a fixed abode and to the beginning of a home, from which our domestic morality and customs are supposed to have originated.

With such a historic background, it seemed to me that women might, in response to the food saving and food production appeals issued in one country after another, so enlarge their conception of duty that the consciousness of the world's needs for food should become the actual impulse of their daily activities.

It also presented another interesting aspect; from the time we were little children we have all of us, at moments at least, cherished overwhelming desires to be of use in the great world, to play a conscious part in its progress. The difficulty has always been in attaching our vague purposes to the routine of our daily living, in making a synthesis between our ambitions to cure the ills of the world on the one hand,

and the need to conform to household requirements on the other.

It was a very significant part of the situation, therefore, that at this world's crisis the two had become absolutely essential to each other. A great world purpose could not be achieved without woman's participation founded upon an intelligent understanding and upon the widest sympathy, at the same time the demand could be met only if it were attached to her domestic routine, its very success depending upon a conscious change and modification of her daily habits.

It was no slight undertaking to make this synthesis, it afforded probably the most compelling challenge which has been made upon woman's constructive powers for centuries. It required all her human affection and all her clarity of mind to make the kind of adjustment which the huge scale of the situation demanded.

It is quite understandable that there was no place for woman and her possible contribution in international affairs under the old diplomacy. Such things were indeed not "woman's sphere." But it was possible that as women entered into politics when clean milk and the premature labor of children became factors in political life, so they might be concerned with international affairs when these at last were dealing with such human and poignant matters as food for starving peoples who could be fed only through international activities.

I recall a great audience in Hot Springs, Arkansas, made up of all the members of the General Federation of Women's Clubs. It seemed to me that every woman there might influence her community "back home," not only to produce and to save more food, but to pour into the war torn world such compassion as would melt down its animosities and bring back into it a gregarious instinct older and more human that the motives responsible for war. I believed that a generous response to this world situation might afford an opportunity to lay over again the foundations for a wider, international morality, as woman's concern for feeding her children had made the beginnings of an orderly domestic life.

We are told that when the crops of grain and roots so painstakingly produced by primitive women began to have a commercial value their production and exchange were taken over by the men, as men later turned the manufacturing of pottery and other of woman's early industries into profit making activities. Such a history, suggested that this situation might be woman's opportunity if only because foods were, during the war, no longer considered primarily in regard to their money-making value but from the point of view of their human use. Because the production of food was, for the moment, dependent upon earlier motives, it had fallen back into woman's hands. There had developed a wide concern for the feeding of hungry people, an activity with which women were normally connected.

As I had felt the young immigrant conscripts caught up into a great world movement, which sent them out to fight, so it seemed to me the millions of American women might be caught up into a great world purpose, that of conservation of life; there might be found an antidote to war in woman's affection and all-embracing pity for helpless children.

Certainly compassion is not without its social utility. Up to the present moment the nations, in their foreign policies, have conspicuously lacked that humane quality which has come in their domestic policies through the increasing care for the poor, and the protection of children. These have been responsible for all sorts of ameliorative legislation during the later years, in one nation after another. In their relations to each other, however, nations have been without such motives of humanitarian action until the Allied nations, during the war, evolved a strikingly new foreign policy in their efforts to relieve the starvation and distress throughout widespread areas.

There are such unexpected turnings in the paths of moral evolution that it would not be without precedent that a new and powerful force might be unloosed in the world when the motive for producing and shipping food on the part of great nations was no longer a commercial one but had for the moment shifted to a desire to feed hungry people with whose governments they had entered into obligations. Such a force might in the future have to be reckoned with as a factor in international affairs.

In those dark years, so destructive of the old codes, the nations were forced back to their tribal function of producing and conserving food in contrast to the methods of modern commerce. All food supplies had long been collected and distributed through the utilization of the commercial motive. When it was commercially valuable to a man, to a firm or nation, food was shipped; when it was not commercially valuable, food was withheld or even destroyed. At that moment, however, the Allied Nations were collecting and conserving a common food supply and each nation was facing the necessity of making certain concessions to the common good that the threat of famine for all might be averted. A new internationalism was being established day by day; the making of a more reasonable world order, so cogently urged by the President of the United States, was to some extent already under way, the war itself forming its matrix.

There was a substitution of the social utility motive for that of commercial gain, energized pity for that of business enterprise. Mr. Hoover had said: "The wheat loaf has ascended in the imagination of enormous populations as the positive symbol of national survival." It seemed as if the age-long lack of organization between the nations, the dearth of human relationships in world politics, was about to be corrected, because an unspeakable disaster had forced the nations to consider together the primitive questions of famine and pestilence. It was possible that a new international ethic was arising from these humble beginnings, as the defense and feeding of the dependent members of the tribe had laid the foundations of tribal loyalty and of national existence itself. In spite of the great mass of social data accumulated in the last century, in spite of widespread intellectual training, there has been no successful attempt to reduce the chaos of human affairs into a rational world order. Society failed to make a community of nations and was at least tragically driven to the beginnings of one along the old primitive folkways, as if in six thousand years no other method could have been devised.

It seemed, therefore, a great historic achievement that there should have been devised a workable method for the collective purchase of food, to prohibit profiteering in "the precious stuff that men live by," even for the duration of the war. We had all been much impressed by the methods of food distribution in Belgium. Fifteen million dollars each month were lent to that unhappy nation by the United States, which had taken over the responsibility of feeding her beleaguered population. This amount was spent in the United States for food and its value was carefully considered by the Division of Research in Nutritive Value in the Department of Food Administration. This Division undertook to know, as well as science could tell, what were the necessary daily rations to maintain health and strength in the several occupations, and how the requirements could best be met from the stores on hand. Such words as "adequate nutrition" and "physiological values" had been made practical issues and the administrative world represented by governmental officials was then seriously considering the production of food and the feeding of human beings in the light of pure science.

As a result, the political relations at least between Belgium and her Allies had completely shifted from the commercial to the humanitarian. To quote again from a speech of Mr. Hoover's: "For three years three million bushels monthly of North American wheat, largely from the charity of the world, has been the daily bread of ten million human beings in Belgium and Northern France. To those who doled out this scant allowance, wheat became indelibly the precious symbol of life."

To transfer this concern for food into the international field was to enlarge its functions enormously as well as to increase its proportions. The Allied Nations had seriously undertaken to solve the problem of producing with the utmost economy of human labor the largest amount of food and of distributing that food to the points of greatest need, they had been forced to make international arrangements for its distribution, exactly as intelligently as they were producing war supplies.

It was easier to do this because each of the Allied Nations, in addition to feeding the soldiers and the munition makers who were directly concerned in the tragic business of "winning the war," had also become responsible for feeding its entire civilian population. The appointment of food controllers, the issuing of bread cards and the system of rationing, was undertaken quite as much in the interest of just dealing in food supplies as for food conservation itself. The British government, in the winter of 1916, when we were constantly speaking on food conservation as such, had undertaken the responsibility of providing the British Isles with all its imported food, and other belligerent and neutral nations had been obliged to pursue the same course in order to avert starvation. Commercial competition had been suppressed, not in response to any theory, but because it could not be trusted to feed the feeble and helpless. The European governments had been compelled to undertake, as the consequence of the shortage in materials, the single-handed purchase of their supplies both for civil and military purposes. There had grown up an enormous consolidation of buying for a hundred and twenty million European people - a phenomenon never before witnessed in the economic history of the world.

With this accomplishment, it seemed reasonable to hope for world order in other directions as well. Certainly some of the obstructions were giving way. An English economist had said in 1917: "The war has, so far, in Europe generally, thrown the customs tariff flat." Were they, perhaps, disappearing under this onslaught of energized pity for worldwide needs, and was a motive power, new in the relations between nations being evolved in response to hunger and dependence as the earliest domestic ethics had been? It was becoming clear that nations cannot oppose their political frontiers as an obstacle to free labor and exchange without suffering themselves and causing suffering; that the world was faced with a choice between freedom in international commerce or international conflicts of increasing severity. Under this new standard of measurement, preferential tariffs would inevitably disappear because the nation denied the open door must suffer in its food supplies; the control of strategic waterways or interstate railroad lines by any one nation which might be tempted to consider only the interest of its own commerce would become unthinkable. All that then would be necessary to secure the internationalization of the Straits of Bosphorus would be a demonstration of the need in Western Europe for Russian wheat, which had hitherto been exported so capriciously; the international building and control of a railroad into Mesopotamia would depend, not upon the ambition of rival nations, but upon the world's need of the food which could again be secured from the capacious valley of the Euphrates by the restoration of the canal system so long ago destroyed. Serbia would be assured a railroad to the sea through a strip of international territory, because ready access to sea-going ships is so necessary to a nation's food and because one of the principal causes of the economic friction that so often lies behind wars is the fear of countries that have no ports lest the neighboring country through which their export and import trade has to pass should hamper and interrupt the transit.

Certainly during the winter of 1916-17 I, personally, came to believe it possible that the more sophisticated questions of national grouping and territorial control would gradually adjust themselves if the paramount human question of food for the hungry were fearlessly and drastically treated upon an international basis. I ventured further, that the League of Nations, upon which the whole world, led by President Wilson, was fastening its hopes, might be founded not upon broken bits of international law, but upon ministrations to primitive human needs.

Much had been said during the war about primitive emotion and instinctive action, but certainly their use need not be reserved to purposes of destruction. After all, the first friendly communication between tribe and tribe came through the need of food when one or the other was starving and too weak to fight; primitive human compassion made the folkway which afterward developed into political relationships. I dared to believe that this early human instinct to come together in order to avert widespread starvation could not be forever thwarted by appeals to such later separatist instincts as nationalism and therefore urged that the gates be opened and that these primitive emotions be allowed to flood our devastated world. By all means let the beneficent tide be directed and canalized by the proposed League of Nations which was, after all, the outgrowth of century old dreams.

THORSTEIN VEBLEN
(1857-1920)

Like Sorel and Marx, Veblen thought the capitalist unsuitable to lead society and like Saint-Simon he believed that the recruitment of societal leaders should be made from the technical ranks. His principal book <u>The Theory of the Leisure Class</u>, caused a considerable stir within industrial circles with it's release in 1899, especially his thoughts about the spending patterns of the elite which he characterized as "conspicuous consumption."

THE THEORY OF THE LEISURE CLASS

Pecuniary Emulation

In the sequence of cultural evolution the emergence of a leisure class coincides with the beginning of ownership. This is necessarily the case, for these two institutions result from the same set of economic forces. In the inchoate phase of their development they are but different aspects of the same general facts of social structure.

It is as elements of social structure - convention facts - that leisure and ownership are matters of interest for the purpose in hand. An habitual neglect of work does not constitute a leisure class; neither does the mechanical fact of use and consumption constitute ownership. The present inquiry, therefore, is not concerned with the beginning of indolence, nor with the beginning of the appropriation of useful articles to individual consumption. The point in question is the origin and nature of a conventional leisure class on the one hand and the beginnings of individual ownership as a conventional right or equitable claim on the other hand.

The early differentiation out of which the distinction between a leisure and a working class arises is a division maintained between men's and women's work in the lower stages of barbarism. Likewise the earliest form of ownership is an ownership of the women by the able-bodied men of the community. The facts may be expressed in more general terms, and truer to the import of the barbarian theory of life, by saying that it is an ownership of the woman by the man.

There was undoubtedly some appropriation of useful articles before the custom of appropriating women arose. The usages of existing archaic communities in which there is no ownership of women is warrant for such a view. In all communities the members, both male and female, habitually appropriate to their individual use a variety of useful things; but these useful things are not thought of as owned by the person who appropriates and consumes them. The habitual appropriation and consumption of certain slight personal effects goes on without raising the question of ownership; that is to say, the question of a conventional, equitable claim to extraneous things.

The ownership of women begins in the lower barbarian stages of culture, apparently with the seizure of female captives. The original reason for the seizure and appropriation of women seems to have been their usefulness as trophies. The practice of seizing women from the enemy as trophies, gave rise to a form of ownership-marriage, resulting in a household with a male head. This was followed by an extension of slavery to other captives and inferiors, besides women, and by an extension of ownership-marriage to other women than those seized from the enemy. The outcome of emulation under the circumstances of a predatory life, therefore, has been on the one hand a form of marriage resting on coercion, and on the other hand the custom of ownership. The two institutions are not distinguishable in the initial phase of their development; both arise from the desire of the successful men to put their prowess in evidence by exhibiting some durable result of their exploits. Both also minister to that propensity for mastery which pervades all predatory communities. From the ownership of women the concept of ownership extends itself to include the products of their industry, and so there arises the ownership of things as well as of persons.

In this way a consistent system of property in goods is gradually installed. And although in the latest stages of the development, the serviceability of goods for consumption has come to be the most obtrusive element of their value, still, wealth has by no means yet lost its utility as a honorific evidence of the owner's prepotence.

Wherever the institution of private property is found, even in a slightly developed form, the economic process bears the character of a struggle between men for the possession of goods. It has been customary in economic theory, and especially among those economists who adhere with least faltering to the body of modernized classical doctrines, to construe this struggle for wealth as being substantially a struggle for subsistence. Such is, no doubt, its character in large part during the earlier and less efficient phases of industry. Such is also its character in all cases where the "niggardliness of nature" is so strict as to afford but a scanty livelihood to the community in return for strenuous and unremitting application to the business of getting the means of subsistence. But in all progressing communities an advance is presently made beyond this early stage of technological development. Industrial efficiency is presently carried to such a pitch as to afford something appreciably more than a bare livelihood to those engaged in the industrial process. It has not been unusual for economic theory to speak of the further struggle for wealth on this new industrial basis as a competition for an increase of the comforts of life - primarily for an increase of the physical comforts which the consumption of goods affords.

The end of acquisition and accumulation is conventionally held to be the consumption of the goods accumulated - whether it is consumption directly by the owner of the goods or by the household attached to him and for this purpose identified with him in theory. This is at least felt to be the economically legitimate end of acquisition, which alone it is incumbent on the theory to take account of.

Such consumption may of course be conceived to serve the consumer's physical wants - his physical comfort - or his so-called higher wants - spiritual, aesthetic, intellectual, or what not; the latter class of wants being served indirectly by an expenditure of goods, after the fashion familiar to all economic readers.

But it is only when taken in a sense far removed from its naive meaning that consumption of goods can be said to afford the incentive from which accumulation invariably proceeds. The motive that lies at the root of ownership is emulation; and the same motive of emulation continues active in the further development of the institution to which it has given rise and in the development of all those features of the social structure which this institution of ownership touches. the possession of wealth confers honor; it is an invidious distinction. Nothing equally cogent can be said for the consumption of goods, nor for any other conceivable incentive to acquisition, and especially not for any incentive to the accumulation of wealth.

It is of course not to be overlooked that in a community where nearly all goods are private property the necessity of earning a livelihood is a powerful and ever-present incentive for the poorer members of the community. The need of subsistence and of an increase of physical comfort may for a time be the dominant motive of acquisition for those classes who are habitually employed at manual labor, whose subsistence is on a precarious footing, who possess little and ordinarily accumulate little but it will appear in the course of the discussion that even in the case of these impecunious classes the predominance of the motive of physical want is not so decided as has sometimes been assumed. On the other hand, so far as regards those members and classes of the community who are chiefly concerned in the accumulation of wealth, the incentive of subsistence or of physical comfort never plays a considerable part. Ownership began and grew into a human institution on grounds unrelated to the subsistence minimum. The dominant incentive was from the outset the invidious distinction attaching to wealth, and, save temporarily and by exception, no other motive has usurped the primacy at any later stage of the development.

Property set out with being booty held as trophies of the successful raid. So long as the group had departed but little from the primitive communal organization, and so long as it still stood in close contact with other hostile groups, the utility of things or persons owned lay chiefly in an invidious comparison between their possessor and the enemy from whom they were taken. The habit of distinguishing between the interests of the individual and those of the group to which he belongs is apparently a later growth. Invidious comparison between the possessor of the honorific booty and his less successful neighbors within the group was no doubt present early as an element of the utility of the things possessed, though this was not at the outset the chief element of their value. The man's prowess was still primarily the group's prowess, and the possessor of the booty felt himself to be primarily the keeper of the honor of his group. This appreciation of exploit from the communal point of view is met with also at later stages of social growth, especially as regards the laurels of war.

But so soon as the custom of individual ownership begins to gain consistency, the point of view taken in making the invidious comparison on which private property rests will begin to change. Indeed, the one change is but the reflex of the other. the initial phase of ownership, the phase of acquisition by naive seizure and conversion, begins to pass into the subsequent stage of an incipient organization of industry on the basis of private property (in slaves); the horde develops into a more or less self-sufficing industrial community; possessions then come to be valued not so much as evidence of successful foray, but rather as evidence of the prepotence of the possessor of these goods over other individuals within the community. The invidious comparison now becomes primarily a comparison of the owner with the other members of the group. Property is still of the nature of trophy, but, with the cultural advance, it becomes more and more a trophy of successes scored in the game of ownership carried on between the members of the group under the quasi-peaceable methods of nomadic life.

Gradually, as industrial activity further displaces predatory activity in the community's everyday life and in men's habits of thought, accumulated property more and more replaces trophies of predatory exploit as the conventional exponent of prepotence and success. With the growth of settled industry, therefore, the possession of wealth gains in relative importance and effectiveness as a customary basis of repute and esteem. Not that esteem ceases to be awarded on the basis of other, more direct evidence of prowess; not that successful predatory aggression or warlike exploit ceases to call out the approval and admiration of the crowd, or to stir the envy of the less successful competitors; but the opportunities for gaining distinction by means of this direct manifestation of superior force growth less available both in scope and frequency. At the same time opportunities for industrial aggression, and for the accumulation of property by the quasi-peaceable methods of nomadic industry, increase in scope and availability. And it is even more to the point that property now becomes the most easily recognized evidence of a reputable degree of success as distinguished from heroic or signal achievement. It therefore becomes the conventional basis of esteem. Its possession in some amount becomes necessary in order to have any reputable standing in the community. It becomes indispensable to accumulate, to acquire property, in order to retain one's good name. When accumulated goods have in this way once become the accepted badge of efficiency, the possession of wealth presently assumes the character of an independent and definitive basis of esteem. The possession of goods, whether acquired aggressively by one's own exertion or passively by transmission through inheritance from others, becomes a conventional basis of reputability. The possession of wealth, which was at the outset valued simply as an evidence of efficiency, becomes, in popular apprehension, itself a meritorious act. Wealth is now itself intrinsically honorable and confers honor on its possessor. By a further refinement, wealth acquired passively by transmission from ancestors or other antecedents presently becomes even more honorific than wealth acquired by the possessor's own effort; but this distinction belongs at a later stage in the evolution of the pecuniary culture and will be spoken of in its place.

Prowess and exploit may still remain the basis of award of the highest popular esteem, although the possession of wealth has become the basis of commonplace reputability and of a blameless social standing. The predatory instinct and the consequent approbation of predatory efficiency are deeply ingrained in the habits of thought of those peoples who have passed under the discipline of a protracted predatory culture. According to popular award, the highest honors within human reach may, even yet, be those gained by an unfolding of extraordinary predatory efficiency in war, or by a quasi-predatory efficiency in statecraft; but for the purpose of a commonplace decent standing in the community these means of repute have been replaced by the acquisition and accumulation of goods. In order to stand well in the eyes of the community, it is necessary to come up to a certain, somewhat indefinite, conventional standard of wealth; just as in the earlier predatory stage it is necessary for the barbarian man to come up to the tribe's standard of physical endurance, cunning and skill at arms. A certain standard of wealth in one case, and of prowess in the other, is a necessary condition of reputability, and anything in excess of this normal amount is meritorious.

Those members of the community who fall short of this, somewhat indefinite, normal degree of prowess or of property suffer in the esteem of their fellowmen; and consequently they suffer also in their own esteem, since the usual basis of self-respect is the respect accorded by one's neighbors. Only individuals with an aberrant temperament can in the long run retain their self-esteem in the face of the disesteem of their fellows. Apparent exceptions to the rule are met with, especially among people with strong religious convictions. But these apparent exceptions are scarcely real exceptions, since such persons commonly fall back on the putative approbation of some supernatural witness of their deeds.

So soon as the possession of property becomes the basis of popular esteem, therefore, it becomes also a requisite to that complacency which we call self-respect. In any community where goods are held in severalty it is necessary, in order to ensure his own peace of mind, that an individual should possess as large a portion of goods as others with whom he is accustomed to class himself; and it is extremely gratifying to possess something more than others. But as fast as a person makes new acquisitions, and becomes accustomed to the resulting new standard of wealth, the new standard forthwith ceases to afford appreciably greater satisfaction than the earlier standard did. The tendency in any case is constantly to make the present pecuniary standard the point of departure for a fresh increase of wealth; and this in turn gives rise to a new standard of sufficiency and a new pecuniary classification of one's self as compared with one's neighbors. So far as concerns the present question, the end sought by accumulation is to rank high in comparison with the rest of the community in point of pecuniary strength. So long as the comparison is distinctly unfavorable to himself, the normal, average individual will live in chronic dissatisfaction with his present lot; and when he has reached what may be called the normal pecuniary standard of the community, or of his class in the community, this chronic dissatisfaction will give place to a restless straining to place a wider and ever-widening pecuniary interval between himself and this average standard. The invidious comparison can never become so favorable to the individual making it that he would not gladly rate himself still higher relatively to his competitors in the struggle for pecuniary reputability.

BENITO MUSSOLINI
(1883-1945)

The founder and leader of fascism. As dictator, in 1928, he suspended the Italian parliament replacing it with a corporate state. He included many of Sorel's ideas about the social myth in fascist ideology and some of his corporatist views have re-emerged today.

THE DOCTRINE OF FASCISM

In the Fascist theory of history, man is such only by virtue of the spiritual process to which he contributes as a member of the family, the social group, the nation, and in his relation to history to which all nations have contributed. Hence the great value of tradition in records, in language, in customs and in the rules of social life. Apart from history, man is a nonentity. Fascism is therefore opposed to all individualistic abstractions based on eighteenth-century materialism; and it is opposed to all Jacobin utopias and innovations. It does not believe in the possibility of happiness on earth as conceived by eighteenth-century economic writers, and therefore rejects the teleological notion that at some future time the human family will secure a final settlement of all its difficulties. This notion runs counter to experience which teaches that life is in continual motion and undergoing a process of evolution. In politics Fascism aims at realism: in practice it desires to deal only with those problems which are the spontaneous product of historic conditions and which find or suggest their own solution. Only by experiencing reality and getting a firm hold on the forces at work within it, may man influence other men and nature.

Being anti-individualistic, the Fascist system of life stresses the importance of the State and recognizes the individual only insofar as his interests coincide with those of the State, which stands for the consciousness and the university of man as a historic entity. It is opposed to classic

Liberalism which arose as a reaction to absolution and exhausted its historical function when the State became the expression of the consciousness and will of the people. Liberalism denied the State in the name of the individual; Fascism reasserts the rights of the State as expressing the real essence of the individual. And if liberty is to be the attribute of living men and not that of abstract dummies invented by individualistic Liberalism, then Fascism stands for liberty and for the only liberty worth having, the liberty of the State and the individual within the State. The Fascist conception of the State is all-embracing: outside of it no human or spiritual values may exist, much less have any value. Thus understood, Fascism is totalitarian and the Fascist State, as a synthesis and unit which includes all values, interprets, develops and lends additional power to the whole life of a people.

No individuals or groups, political parties, associations, economic unions, social classes are to exist apart from the State. Fascism therefore opposes Socialism which rejects unity within the State, obtained by the fusion of all classes into a single ethical and economic reality, since it sees in history nothing more than the class struggle. Fascism likewise opposes trade-unionism as a class weapon. But Fascism recognizes the real needs which gave rise to Socialism and trade-unionism, when they are brought within the orbit of the State, giving them due weight in the cooperative system through which widely different interests are coordinated and harmonized for the unity of the State.

Grouped according to their several interests, individuals form classes; they form trade unions when they are organized according to their various economic callings; but first and foremost they form the State which is no mere matter of numbers, the sum-total of Individuals forming a majority. Fascism therefore opposes the form of democracy which entrusts the nation to a majority, debasing it to the level of the largest number; but, it the Nation be considered, as it should be, from the point of view of equality instead of quantity, as an idea, it is the purest form of democracy, the mightiest, because it is the most ethical, the most coherent, the truest, the expression of a people through the conscience and will of a few, if not indeed, of a single man, tending to express itself as the consciousness and the will of the mass, as of the whole group ethnically moulded by natural and historical conditions into a nation, advancing, as a single conscience and a single will along the self-same geographically defined region, but a people, historically perpetuating itself; a multitude unified by an idea and imbued with the will to live, the will to power, a consciousness and a personality becomes a Nation. It is not the Nation which produces the State; that is an old-fashioned naturalistic idea which afforded a basis for nineteenth-century publicity in favour of national governments. It is rather the State which forms the Nation, by lending strength and power and real life to a people conscious of its own moral unity.

The right to national independence does not arise from any merely literary and idealistic form of self-consciousness; still less from a more or less passive and unconscious *de facto* situation, but from an active, conscious, political will, expressing itself in action and prepared to assert its rights. It arises, in short, from the existence at least *in fieri* of a State. Indeed, as the expression of a universal ethical will, the State itself creates the right to national independence.

A nation, as expressed in the State, is a living, ethical entity only insofar as it is progressive. Inactivity means death. Therefore the State does not only stand for Authority which governs and confers legal form and spiritual value on individual wills, but it is also Power which makes its will felt and respected beyond its own boundaries, thus affording practical evidence of the universal character of the decisions necessary to ensure its development. This implies organization and expansion, potential if not actual. Thus the State is equal to the will of a single man whose development cannot be checked by obstacles and it proves its own universality by achieving self-expression.

The Fascist State, as a higher and more powerful expression of personality, is a force, but a spiritual one. It sums up all the manifestations in the intellectual and moral life of man. Its functions cannot therefore be limited to that of enforcing law and order, as the Liberal doctrine would have it. It is no mere mechanical device for defining the sphere within which the individual may duly exercise his supposed rights. The Fascist State is an inwardly accepted standard and a rule of conduct, a discipline of the whole person; it permeates the will no less than the Intellect. It stands for a principle which becomes the central motive of man as a member of civilized society, sinking deep down into his personality; it dwells in the heart of the man of action and of the thinker, of the artist and of the man of science: soul of the soul.

Fascism, in short, is not only a lawgiver and founder of institutions, but an educator and a promoter of spiritual life. It does not merely aim at remoulding the forms of life, but also their content, man, his character and his faith. To achieve this purpose it enforces discipline and makes use of authority, entering into the mind and ruling with undisputed sway. Therefore it has chosen as its emblem the Lictors' rods, the symbol of unity, strength and justice.

As far as concerns the future development of mankind, quite apart from all present-day political considerations, Fascism does not on the whole believe in the possibility or utility of perpetual peace. Pacifism is therefore rejected as a cloak for cowardly supine renunciation as against self-sacrifice. War alone keys up all the energies of man to their greatest pitch and sets the mark of nobility on those nations which have the bravery to face it. All other tests are substitutes which never place a man face to face with himself before the alternative of life and death. Therefore all doctrines which postulate peace at any price as their premise are incompatible with Fascism. Equally foreign to the spirit of Fascism, even though they may be accepted for their utility in meeting special political situations, are all internationalist or League organizations which, as history amply proves, crumble to the ground whenever the heart of nations is stirred deeply by sentimental, idealist or practical considerations. Fascism carries this anti-pacifist attitude into the life of the individual. (I don't care). *me ne frego*, scrawled on his bandages by a wounded man became the proud motto of the storm-troopers, and it is not only an act of philosophical stoicism, it sums up a doctrine which is not merely political; it is the evidence of a fighting spirit which accepts all risks. It stands for a new mode of life of the Italians. The Fascist accepts and loves life; he rejects and despises suicide as cowardly. Life as he understands it means the fulfilment of duty, moral improvement, conquest; life must be lofty and full, it must be lived for oneself but above all for others, both nearby and far off, present and future.

The demographic policy of the Regine is a consequence of these premises. The Fascist loves his neighbour, but that word does not stand for a vague and incomprehensible idea. Love of one's neighbour does not exclude necessary educational severity; still less does it exclude differentiation and rank. Fascism will have nothing to do with universal embraces; as a member of the community of nations it looks other peoples straight in the eyes; it is vigilant, on its guard; it follows others in all their activities and takes note of any change in their interests; and it does not allow itself to be deceived by changing and deceptive appearances.

Such a conception of life makes of Fascism the resolute negation of the doctrine underlying so-called scientific and Marxist Socialism, the doctrine of historic materialism which would explain the history of mankind in terms of the class struggle and of changes in the processes and means of production, to the exclusion of all else.

That the vicissitudes of economic life, the discovery of raw materials, new technique processes, scientific inventions, have their importance nobody denies; but that they are sufficient to explain human history to the exclusion of other factors is absurd. Fascism believes now and always in sanctity and heroism, that is to say in acts wherein no economic motive, immediate or remote, is at work. Having denied historic materialism, which sees in men puppets on the fringes of history, appearing and disappearing on the crest of the waves while the real directive forces move and work in the depths, Fascism also denies the immutable and irreparable character of class struggle, which is the natural outcome of that economic conception of history; above all it denies that class struggle is the principal agent in social transformations. Having thus struck a blow at Socialism in the two main points of its doctrine, all that remains of it is the sentimental aspiration, old as humanity itself, towards social relations in which the sufferings and sorrows of the humble will be alleviated. But here again Fascism rejects the economic interpretation of happiness as something to be secured through Socialism, automatically so to say, at a given stage in social evolution, when a maximum of material comfort will be assured to all. Fascism denies the materialist conception of happiness as a possibility, and abandons it to the economists of the mid-eighteenth century. This means that Fascism denies the equation: well-being--happiness, by which men are merely considered as animals, happy when they can feed and fatten thus being reduced to a purely vegetative existence.

Besides Socialism, Fascism points its guns at the whole block of Democratic ideologies and rejects both their premises and their practical application and methods. Fascism denies that numbers, as such, may be the determining factors in human society; it denies the right of numbers to govern by means of periodical consultations; it asserts the incurable and fruitful and beneficent inequality of men, who cannot be levelled by any such mechanical and external device as universal suffrage. Democratic Regimes may be described as those under which the people are deluded from time to time into the belief that they are exercising sovereignty, while all the time real sovereignty belongs to and is exercised by other forces, sometimes irresponsible and secret. Democracy is a kingless Regime infested by many kings who are sometimes more exclusive, tyrannical and destructive than a single one, even if he is a tyrant. This explains why, although Fascism was Republican in tendency prior to 1922 owing to causes of expediency, that was abandoned before the March on Rome, considering that the form of government is no longer a matter of preeminent importance, and that the study of past and present Monarchies and past and present Republics shows that neither the Monarchy nor the Republic may be judged *sub specie aeternitatis*, but that each stands for a form of government expressing the political evolution, the history, the traditions and the psychology of a given country.

Fascism has outgrown the dilemma: Monarchy versus Republic, over which the Democratic regimes dallied too long, blaming all imperfections on the former and praising the latter as the ideal regime, while actual experience teaches us that Republics are inherently reactionary and absolutist, while some Monarchies accept the most daring social and political experiments.

THE FABIAN SOCIETY

The Fabian Society began in 1884. They rejected the class struggle of Marx and were instrumental in establishing the British Labour Party. Some of its more famous member were Beatrice and Sidney Webb, George Bernard Shaw, G.D.H. Cole and Britain's first Labour Prime Minister, Clement Attlee. They issued short party tracts calling for class co-operation and enlighten socialism.

FABIAN TRACT #19 (1938)
THE HOUSING PROBLEM

The housing problem is an evil which may be regarded as arising from under-consumption, due to maldistribution of wealth, or from the private ownership of land, according to the angle from which you examine it. With few exceptions people live in overcrowded or insanitary conditions because they cannot afford the rents commonly charged for adequate accommodation. Society can deal with this problem either:

(a) by placing increased purchasing power at the disposal of those who cannot now command a fair share of the commodities which civilization produces; or

(b) by providing them with houses at prices which their present purchasing power can afford.

A Socialist Movement must indeed have recourse to both of these methods for the consummation of its policy. It must increase purchasing power on the one hand, but, as a corollary to this, it must-by land nationalization, price-control, etc.-keep commodity prices, including rents, at a reasonable level.

But since the measures required to realize these objectives are necessarily part of a long-term programme, ranging far beyond the housing question, and since both the wider interests of the nation and political considerations require a rapid solution of this particular problem, it is imperative that the immediate housing needs of the people be supplied by a more direct approach.

A STANDARD OF OVERCROWDING

The most striking deficiency in our housing policy is the absence of a yardstick. There is in fact no common standard laid down, as part of the basis of our social organization, defining a minimum standard of housing for the individual family or citizen. It is not only as a nation that we lack such a standard; for no important political party possesses it, nor is there even one recognized in general by what are termed men and women of goodwill.

This defect the Socialist Movement must rectify without delay. Partly because without a standard our policy must be wanting in coherence and coordination, and partly because in a matter of this kind a standard is an epitome of policy instantly to be grasped by the electorate at large.

What then ought our standard to be? To answer this we must ask another question. Who in a modern civilized community should be regarded as entitled to a house or, in the technical if inelegant phrase of housing reformers, a structurally separate dwelling? Certainly every unit that can justifiably be described as a family--i.e. two or more people living together who are desirous of possessing such a home. This is not to deny that many single people have an equally good claim to a home of the same kind. But their claim is not so self-evident. Many of them prefer to be lodgers in somebody else's household, and we cannot assume--e.g. from the census--that all single people living independently require some fresh provision. But taking the two member (and over) family standard, a simple inquiry and calculation in each local government area will provide us with the number of families within that area--call it area X--who have not got such a home and for whom one must be provided.

In urban districts many of these families are now living in what were formerly good single family houses let out as tenements. These form a group by themselves.

Next to them come the families who, whilst already possessing a separate home, are overcrowded to the detriment often of their physical and nearly always of their spiritual and intellectual wellbeing. These make a second group.

To satisfy the needs of this second group justly and quickly, a national standard is even more imperative than for the first. We have to decide, therefore, what the socialist standard of over-crowding is to be. The following is suggested as a minimum standard of accommodation below which replacement becomes automatically necessary; for new homes the standard will be somewhat higher:

(a) Every family is clearly entitled to a home which possesses at least one common living-room which is not used for either cooking or sleeping purposes;

(b) It must have adequate bathroom and lavatory arrangements;

(c) The sleeping accommodation must be sufficient to provide for the separation of the sexes, after ten years of age; for giving the parents a separate room apart from the necessary association with them of very young children, and for not overcrowding the family as a whole beyond a ratio of three per room with 400 cubic feet of air space for each individual in the room.

(d) In addition to the above there must be proper provision for the storage of food, clothes and fuel; modern facilities for lighting and heating; suitable facilities for cooking; and proper ventilation, exterior lighting, etc.

Finally, there are those families who, whilst already occupying accommodation which complies with the requirements in space set out above, are illhoused in a totally different sense. They are forced to live in cellars or basements, or, most numerous of all, in dwellings which prove to be ineradicably infested with vermin. These form a third group. The test for them will, of course, be drawn up in consultation with the Royal Sanitary Institute and must be uniform throughout the country.

In order that there should not be inequalities between the claims of local authorities with varying conceptions of fitness; and also that the central authorities may from the outset be in possession of a volume of information adequate to their task, it will be necessary to obtain returns from every local authority as early as possible of the number of families in each of these groups.

Some authorities and individual members of many others, it must be remembered, are themselves owners of dubious or "borderline" property. Any rehousing scheme on a national scale designed to provide every family with a decent home will inevitably affect the value of their property and must have dangerous reactions on the minds of the landlords concerned. To prevent any danger of procrastination on the part of recalcitrant authorities a short Bill might well be prepared before the next general election, which in the event of Labour obtaining a majority could be passed at once through Parliament, requiring information to be submitted within, say, a six months' period. This would not prevent the new legislation preparing for a great house-building campaign form going forward in the meantime; but it would enable it at an early stage to have a definite objective and a precision in development without which confusion and delay might easily ensue.

Whatever form the actual organization for equipping the nation with an adequate supply of houses may take, the Medical Officers of Health and their staffs of sanitary inspectors must clearly provide the intelligence service for the enterprise. On their energy and thoroughness in collecting and classifying information, during this preliminary period, all else will depend.

But not all the families now living in unsatisfactory conditions will of necessity require new houses to be built for them. Reconditioning has for the most part been looked upon askance by Socialists. Firstly, because there was suspicion, too often justified by events, that it would mean little more than "a lick and a promise" to decaying property, in order to make something virtually uninhabitable "good enough for the lower classes". Secondly, because it has been generally believed that reconditioning is in fact an uneconomic proposition, involving a considerable capital outlay in repair and modernization on houses which even when repaired and modernized can have only an expectation of life considerably shorter than a new house. None the less, there is at the present time a considerable number of houses, still with many years of serviceable existence in front of them, which could probably be converted with greater rapidity and less cost than building new ones. At this early stage of our social transitions this opportunity can scarcely be neglected. The conditions governing such conversion will, of course, be precisely the same both as regards the family standards and the quality of the accommodation provided as those for new houses or flats. It may indeed be worth considering a system of house licensing by local authorities in accordance with provisions laid down by the central authority.

Reconditioning under these circumstances becomes a purely economic proposition. The local authority will have the duty of watching for and inspecting houses which seem suitable for the purpose. If on investigation it is proved that they will provide accommodation for a sufficient number of families to make their conversion at least as satisfactory a proposition as new building, then and then only will they be acquired.

JAKOB BURCKHARDT
(1818-1897)

This shy quiet Swiss professor believed that only through the study of history could the world rid itself of its illusions. He staunchly sided with defeated minorities because their defeats confirmed that success had little to do with merit. He equally maintained that our disapproval of results should never prevent us from studying the causes themselves.

REFLECTIONS ON HISTORY

On War

It is part of the wretchedness of life on earth that even the individual believes that he can only attain a full consciousness of his own value if he compares himself with others and, in certain circumstances, actually makes others feel it. The State, law, religion and morality are hard put to it to keep this bent within bounds, that is, to prevent its finding public expression. In the individual the open indulgence of it is regarded as ridiculous, intolerable, ill-mannered, dangerous, criminal.

On a big scale, however, nations from time to time assume that it is allowable and inevitable for them to fall upon each other on some pretext or other. The main pretext is that in international relations there is no other way of arriving at a decision, and: "If we don't, others will." We shall leave aside for the moment the highly diverse internal histories of the outbreaks of wars, which are often extremely complex.

A people actually feels its full strength as a people only in war, in the comparative contest with other peoples, because it only exists at that time. It must then endeavor to sustain its power at that level. Its whole standard has been enlarged.

In philosophic form, the dictum of Heraclitus, "war is the farther of all things," is quoted in proof of the benefits of war. Lasaulx accordingly explains that antagonism is the cause of all growth, that harmony is born only of the conflict of forces, the "discordant harmony" or the "harmonious conflict" of things. This means, however, that both sides are still in possession of some vital energy, and not that one triumphs while the other lies prostrate. Indeed, according to him, war is divine in character, a world law and present in all nature. Not without cause do the Indians worship Shiva, the god of destruction. The warrior, he says, is filled with the joy of destruction, wars clear the air like thunderstorms, they steel the nerves and restore the heroic virtues, upon which States were originally founded, in place of indolence, double-dealing and cowardice. We might here also recall H. Leo's reference to "fresh and cheerful war, which shall sweep away the scrofulous mob."

Our conclusion is - men are men in peace as in war, and the wretchedness of earthly things lies equally upon them both. In any case, we generally suffer from an optical illusion in favour of those parties and their members with whose interests our own are in any way connected.

Lasting peace not only leads to enervation; it permits the rise of a mass of precarious, fear-ridden, distressful lives which would not have survived without it and which nevertheless clamour for their "rights," cling somehow to existence, bar the way to genuine ability, thicken the air and as a whole degrade the nation's blood. War restores real ability to honour. As for these wretched lives, war may at least reduce them to silence.

Further, war, which is simply the subjection of all life and property to *one* momentary aim, is morally vastly superior to the mere violent egoism of the individual; it develops power in the service of a supreme general idea and under a discipline which nevertheless permits supreme heroic virtue to unfold. Indeed, war alone grants to mankind the magnificent spectacle of a general submission to a general aim.

And since, further, only real power can guarantee a peace and security of any duration, while war reveals where real power lies, the peace of the future lies in such a war.

Yet it should, if possible, be a just and honourable war - perhaps a war of defense such as the Persian War, which developed the powers of the Hellenes gloriously in all ways, or such as the war of the Netherlands against Spain.

Further, it must be a genuine war, with existence at stake. A permanent smouldering of small feuds, for instance, may replace war but is without value as a crisis. The German feudal heroes of the fifteenth century were highly astonished when they were confronted with an elemental power like the Hussites.

Nor did the disciplined "sport of kings" of the eighteenth century lead to much more than misery.

In quite a special sense, however, the wars of today are certainly aspects of a great general crisis, but individually they lack the significance and effect of genuine crises. Civilian life remains in its rut in spite of them, and it is precisely the pitiable existences referred to above which survive. But these wars leave behind them vast debts, ie., they bequeath the main crisis to the future. Their brevity too deprives them of their value as crises. The full forces of despair do not come into play, and hence do not remain victorious on the field of battle, and yet it is they, and they alone, which could bring about real regeneration of life, ie., reconciliation in the abolition of an old order by a really vital new one.

Finally, it is quite unnecessary - as unnecessary as in the case of the barbarian invasion - to prophesy of all destruction that regeneration will come of it. It may be that this globe is already aged (nor does it matter how old it is in the absolute sense, ie., how many times it has revolved round the sun - it may be very young for all that). We cannot imagine, in great tracts of denuded country, that new forests will ever arise to replace those which have been destroyed. And so peoples may be destroyed, and not even survive as component elements of other races.

And often it is the most righteous defense that has proved most futile, and we must be thankful that Rome went so far as to proclaim the glory of Numantia, that conquerors have a sense of the greatness of the conquered.

The thought of a higher world plan, etc., is cold comfort. Every successful act of violence is a scandal, ie., a bad example. The only lesson to be drawn from an evil deed successfully perpetrated by the stronger party is not to set a higher value on earthly life than it deserves.

RANDOLPH S. BOURNE
(1886-1918)

Bourne railed against intellectuals who supported the First World War. He believed that, to do so, would only lead to rule by the herd. Such rule would, in turn, merely be a rule of absolutes.

TWILIGHT OF IDOLS
in THE NEW REPUBLIC vol IV Sept. 4, 1915 pp. 117-119

The working-out of this American philosophy in our intellectual life then has meant an exaggerated emphasis on the mechanics of life at the expense of the quality of living. We suffer from a real shortage of spiritual values. A philosophy that worked when we were trying to get that material foundation for American life in which more impassioned living could flourish no longer works when we are faced with inexorable disaster and the hysterias of the mob. The note of complacency which we detect in the current expressions of this philosophy has a bad taste. The congruous note for the situation would seem to be, on the contrary, that of robust desperation, - a desperation that shall rage and struggle until new values come out of the travail, and we see some glimmering of our democratic way. In the creation of these new values, we may expect the old philosophy, the old radicalism, to be helpless. It has found a perfectly definite level, and there is no reason to think that it will not remain there. Its flowering appears in the technical organization of the war by an earnest group of young liberals, who direct their course by an opportunist programme of State-socialism at home and a league of benevolently-imperialistic nations abroad. At their best they can give us a government by prudent, enlightened college men instead of by politicians. At their best, they can abolish war by making everybody a partner in the booty of exploitation. That is all, and it is technically admirable. Only there is nothing in the outlook that touches in any way the happiness of the individual, the vivifying of the personality, the comprehension of social forces, the flair of art, - in other words, the quality of life. Our intellectuals have failed us as value-creators, even as value-emphasizers. The allure of the martial in war has passed only to be succeeded by the allure of the technical. The allure of fresh and true ideas, of free speculation, of artistic vigor, of cultural styles, of intelligence suffused by feeling, and feeling given fibre and outline by intelligence, has not come, and can hardly come, we see now, while our reigning philosophy is an instrumental one.

When can come this allure? Only from those who are thorough malcontents. Irritation at things as they are, disgust at the continual frustrations and aridities of American life, deep dissatisfaction with self and with the groups that give themselves forth as hopeful - out of such moods there might be hammered new values. The malcontents would be men and women who could not stomach the war, or the reactionary idealism that has followed in its train. They are quite through with the professional critics and classicists who have let cultural values die through their own personal ineptitude. Yet these malcontents have no intention of being cultural vandals, only to slay. They are not barbarians, but seek the vital and the sincere everywhere. All they want is a new orientation of the spirit that shall be modern, an orientation to accompany that technical orientation which is fast coming, and which the war accelerates. They will be harsh and often bad-tempered, and they will feel that the break-up of things is no time for mellowness. They will have a taste for spiritual adventure, and for sinister imaginative excursions. It will not be Puritanism so much as complacency that they will fight. A tang, a bitterness, an intellectual fibre, a verve, they will look for in literature, and their most virulent enemies will be those unaccountable radicals who are still morally servile, and are now trying to suppress all free speculation in the interests of nationalism. Something more mocking, more irreverent, they will constantly want. They will take institutions very lightly, indeed will never fail to be surprised at the seriousness with which good radicals take the stated offices and systems. Their own contempt will be scarcely veiled, and they will be glad if they can tease, provoke, irritate thought on any subject. These malcontents will be more or less of the American tribe of talent who used either to go immediately to Europe, or starved submissively at home. But these people will neither go to Europe, nor starve submissively. They are too much entangled emotionally in the possibilities of American life to leave it, and they have no desire whatever to starve. So they are likely to go ahead beating their heads at the wall until they are either bloody or light appears. They will give offense to their elders who cannot see what all the concern is about, and they will hurt the more middle-aged sense of adventure upon which the better integrated minds of the younger generation will have compromised. Optimism is often compensatory, and the optimistic mood in American thought may mean merely that American life is too terrible to face. A more sceptical, malicious, desperate, ironical mood may actually be the sign of more vivid and more stirring life fermenting in America today. It may be a sign of hope. That thirst for more of the intellectual "war and laughter" that we find Nietzsche calling us to may bring us satisfactions that optimism-haunted philosophies could never bring. Malcontentedness may be the beginning of promise. That is why I evoked the spirit of William James, with its gay passion for ideas, and its freedom of speculation, when I felt the slightly pedestrian gait into which the war had brought pragmatism. It is the creative desire more than the creative intelligence that we shall need if we are ever to fly.

PETER BOOTHROYD

Peter Boothroyd is an Associate Professor at the School of Community and Regional Planning in the Centre for Human Settlements at the University of British Columbia.

FROM KEYNES TO BUDDHIST ECOLOGY: RATIONALIZING AND CRITICIZING THE WELFARE STATE

Introduction

By the late 1940's, the welfare state as a societal form was beginning to mature in the industrialized world. By the late 1960's, it had reached its zenith in that world and had become the model for many poorer countries in the "Third World." By the late 1980's, even those countries that had adopted a development path outlined by Lenin building on Marx were moving away from centralized socialism and toward their own versions of the welfare state.

How sustainable is this phenomenon called the welfare state? Does it mark the pinnacle of human achievement-- is it the societal form that is so logical and of such ubiquitous appeal that its evolution effectively marks the "end of history" in the sense that the future will simply be an exercise in fine-tuning welfare state operations? Or does its apparent universality mask some underlying weaknesses that will lead to its collapsing, as many apparently universal and eternal empires have before?

The intellectual roots of the welfare state are traceable in the readings excerpted for this book. They show the manner in which the values and assumptions which underlie the welfare state have evolved. Such understanding is necessary if we are to judge the viability of the welfare state, and to replace it should we find it lacking.

This chapter presents the rationale for, and criticisms of, the Welfare State. The chapter is intended to provoke thought about the nature of the society we live in and the possibilities for its evolution. The thinking of John Maynard

Keynes (1883-1946), who in his 1936 book *The General Theory of Employment, Interest, and Money* provided the most widely referenced economic rationale for replacing pure capitalism with the welfare state, is the pivot of the chapter. The utilitarianism of John Stuart Mill is identified as providing the philosophical basis for Keynes' theory . The thinking of some contemporaries of Keynes who provided their own alternatives to feudalism, classical liberalism, and orthodox Leninism, and who led and still influence major social movements, is then briefly presented. These contemporaries were Mussolini, Mao and Gandhi. Finally, two current but radically different critiques of the Keynesian welfare state are presented. These critiques come from "monetarists" and "Buddhist ecologists." The former advocate privatizing public services, stabilizing economic growth through money supply rather than fiscal finetuning, and helping the poor through simplified transfer payments; the latter believe we have reached the limits to growth and therefore must reduce consumption and redistribute wealth and power.

Nature of the Welfare State

The welfare state is a state, i.e., a form of governance ultimately backed by military power, that protects the free market as the dominant production and distribution institution, intervening as necessary to maintain stability and to ensure its citizens enjoy decent standards of living. Welfare state governments are elected through universal franchise: one person one vote. They are more active in managing their societies' economies than are governments which oversee pure liberal laissez-faire economies (e.g., England in the 19th century or Chile in the 1980's) but they exercise less economic control than governments of socialist states (especially those based on Leninist principles). Welfare state governments permit more individual freedom in terms of personal religious and political beliefs than do conservative religion-based states (e.g., those based on fundamentalist Islamic principles) or secular military dictatorships (e.g., of Myanmar today, formerly Burma), and they permit, indeed encourage, a greater range of consumption levels and patterns than do socialist governments.

The welfare state seems to offer the ideal happy medium ("the middle way", as strongly welfare state Sweden has been called) between some fundamentally conflicting societal goals: order vs. freedom, material wealth vs. spiritual autonomy, social equity vs. individual incentive, investment vs. consumption. It holds out the promise of a continually increasing quality of life for all people: the rich will get richer and the poor will get less poor. Consumer choice will expand for all. Leisure time will expand. Government will become the province of specialized technocrats monitored by a few periodically-elected politicians. More will be provided for citizens, less demanded of them.

Intellectual Roots of the Welfare State

Liberals and Socialists: From the preceding readings in this book, the evolving intellectual roots of such a system are readily discernible. Most apparent is the continuing tension between liberals and socialists. Liberals emphasize equality of opportunity and the rights of the individual vis-a-vis the state, believe in private property as one of those rights, and argue for division of labour in a free market as the engine of growth. When liberals concerned themselves with distribution issues, they resigned themselves to a persistence of poverty or contented themselves with the notion that the fruits of growth will trickle down to the poor.

Socialists share the liberals' opposition to hereditary privilege and autocratic government and their optimism about longterm growth stimulated by technology. However, they believe a state-managed economy could overcome the inefficiency, instability, and inequality, in capitalism that they observe. Socialists have differed about means (by revolution or ballot box) and ultimate ends (full communism or social democracy.)

John Stuart Mill and the Utilitarian Basis of the Welfare State: John Stuart Mill (1806-73) began the line of thought that bridged these two basic philosophic positions. In his 1848 *Principles of Political Economy*, Mill pointed out that the state could distribute the products of capitalism without necessarily interfering in its productive processes. He showed that the laissez-faire individual freedom concerns of liberalism need not be at odds with the desire of socialists to produce more equality. In showing the logical possibility of capitalism coexisting with social welfare, Mill was ahead of his time.

Mill's views about power were more immediately influential than his views about the production and distribution of wealth. In his later works, which focused on political institutions, he developed, to completion many think, the theoretical basis for political liberalism. He spelled out the rationale for representative democracy based on a universal franchise (along with universal basic education and taxation), women included. Such is the political form of the welfare state. Mill did not consider the potential of participatory democracy as a form of government, though he did endorse voluntary co-ops and trade unions as useful organizations.

Mill wrestled with the problem of what a representative government should do with its power. He believed that given an educated electorate and a fair electoral system, a form of proportional representation, governments will preserve liberty, private property, collective minority rights, and free enterprise, and at the same time will be socially responsible in protecting people from each other and ensuring a reasonable distribution of wealth. By universalizing the franchise and basic education in the latter part of the 19th century and early part of the 20th, virtually all the industrialized countries took a major step toward Mill's ideal. Adoption of proportional representation systems in many countries on the European continent took these countries even closer.

Mill's political and economic theory was grounded in

Utilitarianism which in its basics had been developed by his father, James Mill, and Jeremy Bentham. Most generally, utilitarianism is the doctrine that society exists to enable individuals to get as much as possible of what they themselves determine is good for them. Societal good is the sum of individual satisfactions. A good political system creates the greatest happiness for the greatest number.

Mill's utilitarianism provided for social welfare to be determined both through political decisions, the quality of which being indicated by the number of votes endorsing the decisions and through market transactions, the level of welfare being indicated by numbers of dollars spent and earned. In both its political and economic dimensions, utilitarianism abstracts the individual from community, society, and history. The individual's desires are seen as being best expressed through votes and dollars. By deeming all votes and all dollars as commensurable, utilitarianism provides a quantitative basis for determining social welfare, i.e, for determining the greatest good for the greatest number. Mill's utilitarianism continues as the implicit, and therefore rarely questioned ontology of welfare state economics and politics.

Politically, welfare states assume that governments should be formed by representatives elected by the people on the basis of one vote per person. Similarly, within government, decisions should be made on the basis of one vote per representative. At neither level should account be taken of differences in knowledge among the voters: all votes should be equally weighted. To attempt to take into account differences in knowledge or wisdom would lead to the demise of democracy; persons claiming superiority as aristocrats, vanguard proletarians, or able tyrants, would forcibly take power. The only alternative to brute force as the basis for power is the universal legitimacy provided by the vote-counting calculus that quantifies the social contract, which in this age of science, is reason enough to accept it.

Economically, welfare states assume that most production and consumption decisions should be left to the market where people vote with their dollars-- not one person one vote but one dollar one vote. The market ensures maximum efficiency in production and freedom in consumption, thus making a major contribution to the greatest good for the greatest number. In the Millian tradition, the state, which is seen as the only alternative to the market, may affect income distribution but should not tell people how to spend their money. Ideally, there should be no rationing, luxury taxes, or affirmative action; sumptuary laws are beyond consideration. If the state enters the production realm, it should do so as much as possible on market principles. Hence in Canada we create Crown corporations whose boards, once appointed, are insulated from political decisions. Even the civil service is in theory guided by the market in its policies on hiring and firing, salary scales, procurements, etc. A civil servant should be paid according to her market worth, not according to her parentage, gender or need.

Utilitarianism and Liberal Economics: A narrower brand of utilitarianism than Mill's was adopted by the mainstream of liberal economics in the late 19th century. "Political economy," which had been concerned with broad questions of national productive capability and income distribution among the classes, became the technical, specialized field of "Economics" which focused on individual decision-making to maximize satisfaction or profits in the universal competitive market place and the summative implications for prices and levels of production/consumption. Mill's reflections on the social role of government and the implications of utilitarianism for public decision-making were ignored by economists in favour of his market-place utilitarianism. Society became defined as an aggregate of individual self-oriented producers and consumers. Left alone, these individuals would establish an optimal equilibrium of prices and production levels, i.e., would establish the greatest possible good for the greatest number given existing conditions of scarcity.

Contrary to Mill's argument in *The Principles of Political Economy* that production and distribution can be treated as independent domains, the economists argued that for the state to take on a distribution role would in fact interfere with production. For a free competitive market to produce the optimal equilibrium of production and consumption, optimality being a function of individual preferences, the forces of supply and demand must be free to respond to changing conditions as quickly as possible. Redistribution by the state necessarily must produce sub-optimal consumption and investment patterns.

Perhaps the most prominent economist at the turn of the century was Alfred Marshall (1842-1924). His 1890 text became a standard work. Significantly, it was entitled *Principles of Economics* rather than the favoured title of his predecessors: Principles of Political Economy. Marshall developed the concept of individual preference into the mathematical conceptions of marginal utility and marginal cost, purporting to show how optimal equilibria are achieved when the forces of aggregate supply and demand are allowed to operate freely through the agencies of individual buyers and sellers calculating marginal utilities and costs. Excess consumption would right by leading higher prices thereby reducing consumption and, as producers responded over time, to increased production. Excess production would right itself by lowering prices thereby increasing consumption and over time by lowering production. Business cycles, in short, were self-correcting.

Keynes' Utilitarianism: The utilitarian tradition in economics was carried forward in the work of John Maynard Keynes, a student of Marshall. Partly, Keynes built on the works of Marshall and other contemporary classical economists (as Keynes called them). Partly, he repudiated them and went on to provide the economics rationale for the welfare state.

By carrying on the frameworks of the recent classicists in his use of such categories as marginal propensity to consume, effective demand, and marginal efficiencies of capital, Keynes continued their utilitarian assumption that the economy functions best when it is seen as, is permitted to be, a product of individual gain-maximizers. On this assumption, his successors have developed comprehensive but reductionist indexes of wellbeing termed "national income," "gross national product" etc. which measure economic health in terms of growth in aggregate purchased consumption.

But while he maintained the classicists' utilitarian perspective on the laissez-faire economy, he saw the need to contextuate that economy in a utilitarian political system that made decisions about the distribution of income and the optimal rate of growth. He thus departed from the classicists' apolitical utilitarianism and re-established the conceptually richer but less elegant version of John Stuart Mill. It is this departure from the classicists and return to Mill's social concerns that defines Keynes' contribution to welfare state theory.

Keynes Compared to Mill: Keynes' biography is similar to Mill's. Like Mill, Keynes was a precocious but well-rounded child of an intellectual father, clerked for a time in the British civil service that ran India, was influential among academics and politicians, held an attitude of noblesse oblige toward the workers whom he regarded as inferior but educable, and argued for both logic and reality-testing in theory building.

Mill and Keynes both believed poverty could and would be eradicated by industrial society. In this view, they stood against the pessimism of the early 19th century economists Thomas Malthus and David Ricardo and were aligned with Marx and Smith. But while Smith thought poverty would naturally be eliminated as the wealth of a nation grew and wages rose, and Marx thought poverty would be eliminated once the stresses and strains of capitalism led to its replacement with socialism administered by a dictatorship of the proletariat, Mill and Keynes both believed in the state playing a redistributive role without destroying capitalism.

Both Mill and Keynes also believed that productive forces could soon grow to the point that expansion would no longer be necessary and a stationary state could ensue.

But as one would expect, because of their respective times if for no other reason, there are also important differences in the thinking and influence of Mill and Keynes. Mill, rather ahead of his time, had pointed out that the state could take on a distributist role without needing to interfere in the efficient productive processes of laissez-faire capitalism. Keynes went beyond this. Though believing in the state's role as distributor, he devoted little attention to it as a moral matter. Rather, he focused on the state as a planner of production stability with redistribution being one of the state's stabilizing tools. But like Mill, he argued that such state intervention in the economy need not work against the interests of the free market or individual entrepreneurs and property owners. In this view, Keynes was perfectly in tune with his time. His theory, which systematized the ideas of major liberal politicians such as David Lloyd George and Franklin D. Roosevelt, was immediately embraced by a rising generation of economists heading for professorships and influential positions in the burgeoning technocratic bureaucracy.

The thinking of Keynes and Mill have been complementary in the evolution of the welfare state. Mill, a holistic political economist as was typical in his century, laboured as much on theories of ethics and democracy as of economic systems and developed the political rationale for the welfare state. Keynes, as a modern economist, a specialist, did not concern himself with the workings of the political system. He accepted representative democracy as it had been worked out over the previous century as a given. He concerned himself with the workings of the capitalist economy and identified a supporting role for the state. He thus created the economic rationale for the welfare state.

Keynes' Perspective on Capitalism: As did the two most significant economists who preceded him, Adam Smith

(1723-90) and Karl Marx (1818-83), Keynes simultaneously admired and had contempt for capitalists. All three saw capitalism as a productive force capable of ending human want but also saw certain outcomes of capitalist behaviour as antithetical to the interests of society as a whole. For Smith, the problem lay in the drive of capitalists to collude in driving down wages or creating monopolies. Smith resolved his ambivalence by calling for a thoroughly individualistic laissez-faire economy vigilant against businessmen lobbying for special interests. For Marx, the problem lay in capitalism's exploitation of workers. His resolution lay in revolutionary socialism, i.e., the mass take over of factories by workers. Keynes' primary concern was with the instability of capitalism. He shared the view of Smith and Marx that in practice the economy was unfair: capitalist profits were excessive, income too unequal. His solution was neither the individualism of Smith nor the collectivism of Marx. It was a compromise in the spirit of Mill. Whereas Mill's compromise seemed illogical, Keynes' was quickly accepted.

Keynes' General Theory: Keynes' compromise was laid out in his 1936 book, *The General Theory of Employment, Interest, and Money.* It was essentially this: in the interests of stability and fairness, let the state manage the amount being produced in the economy and ensure a reasonable distribution of income; in the interests of efficiency and freedom, let capitalists freely determine their products and production processes, leaving all individuals free to compete in maximizing their earnings and owning property. By regulating the overall pace of national production, government can actually assist the market to produce steady growth and efficiently allocate resources.

Keynes showed that for the state to take on social roles of investment and redistribution was not just morally desirable but also necessary if capitalism was to survive. Unlike Mill, who saw the socially responsible state and individual freedom as contradictory and who therefore sought resolution in assigning the state and the market separate dominions of production and distribution, Keynes saw the state as potentially supportive of individual initiative and consumption. This supportive role is played not through the dialectical process Marx envisioned whereby a socialist dictatorship dissolves into an egalitarian free communist utopia, but rather is played directly, immediately, and within the context of capitalism. Keynes was right when he predicted his concepts would be seen as both radical and acceptable.

Keynes came to prominence in the 1920's, but it was not until the midst of the Great Depression of the 1930's that his magnum opus appeared. While appearing radical to the classical liberals who still controlled the economics departments of universities, as well as the business elite and their politicians, *The General Theory* offered solutions to the depression which Roosevelt since 1933 had been beginning to implement as a New Deal for the United States and which Lloyd George had proposed in the 1929 British election campaign. The book not only explained why business cycles occur but why, in the modern age and in the absence of government action, depressions might last a long time.

Against the classicists who considered as absurd the notion that there could be periods of time when people might not have enough money to purchase the goods they produce, i.e., that "effective demand," could be deficient, Keynes simply presented the empirical evidence that widespread poverty does indeed exist side-by-side with spare productive capacity when, from time to time, business slumps occur. That the productive forces of labour and factories can be unemployed not because consumers do not want what could be produced but because consumers do not have money to make their demand effective. As ordinary people not befuddled by the abstractions of classical economic theory could observe, the 1930's was one of those times.

Keynes' argument with the classical free enterprise economists, who had dominated universities and government for a century with their views that state intervention in the economy should be restricted to protecting the value of money, was not over different philosophies about human nature or morality, but over the nature of capitalism's dynamics in the real world. Up until the 1930's Keynes's own theory had been classical. With *The General Theory*, he saw himself as resurrecting to the mainstream of economic thought the issue of effective demand that haunted Malthus, Marx, and Major Douglas (the founder of Social Credit philosophy). In contrast to the classical mainstream, they and now he, were unwilling to accept unemployment as inevitable or self-correcting.

> The idea that we can safely neglect the aggregate demand function is fundamental to the Ricardian economics, which underlie what we have been taught for more than a century. Malthus, indeed, had vehemently opposed Ricardo's doctrine that it was impossible for effective demand to be deficient; but vainly. ... Ricardo conquered England as completely as the Holy Inquisition conquered Spain. Not only was his theory accepted by the city, by statesmen and by the academic world. But controversy ceased; the other view completely disappeared; it ceased to be discussed. You will not find it mentioned even once in the whole works of Marshall, Edgeworth and Professor Pigou, from whose hands the classical theory has received its most mature embodiment. It could only live on furtively, below the surface, in the underworlds of Karl Marx, Silvio Gesell or Major Douglas...
>
> The completeness of the Ricardian victory is something of a curiosity and a mystery. It must have been due to a complex of suitabilities in the doctrine to the environment into which it was projected. That it reached conclusions quite different from what the ordinary uninstructed person would expect, added, I suppose, to its intellectual prestige. That its teaching, translated into practice, was austere and often unpalatable, lent it virtue. That it was adapted to carry a vast and consistent logical superstructure, gave it beauty. That it could explain much social injustice and apparent cruelty as an inevitable accident in the scheme of progress, and the attempts to change such things as likely on the whole to do more harm than good, commended it to authority. That it afforded a measure of justification to the free activities of the individual capitalist, attracted to it the support of the dominant social force behind authority...

> The celebrated *optimism* of traditional economic theory, which has led to economists being looked upon as Candides, who, having left this world for the cultivation of their gardens, teach all is for the best in the best of all possible worlds provided we will let well alone, is also to be traced, I think, to their having neglected to take account of the drain on prosperity which can be exercised by an insufficiency of effective demand. (Keynes 1936 [1964] 32-33, emphasis in original)

The General Theory explained the onset of depressions in the modern industrial era as resulting from investors suddenly fearing that production is beginning to exceed consumption and becoming pessimistic about what the return would be from new investment.

> Let us recur to what happens at the crisis. So long as the boom was continuing, much of the new investment showed a not unsatisfactory yield. The disillusion comes because doubts suddenly arise concerning the reliability of the prospective yield, perhaps because the current yield shows signs of falling off as the stock of newly produced durable goods steadily increases. (Keynes 1936 [1964] 317)

Investor pessimism is magnified in the stockmarket by speculators and amateur investors. The "stock-minded" public reduces consumption at the very time consumption is needed in order to reduce stocks and stimulate production. Investors become even more pessimistic. Workers are laid off, and consumption falls further. The cycle of decline continues. Although interest rates fall in a depression as investors' demand for money falls, lower rates alone fail to overcome investor pessimism. The state must step in to stimulate mutually reinforcing investment and consumption by developing appropriate monetary policy (low interest rates), fiscal policy (capital works through deficit financing as necessary), and social policy (some redistribution to encourage consumption by the poor) so as to ensure that employment and consumption stabilize at high levels.

> In conditions of laissez-faire the avoidance of wide fluctuations in employment may therefore prove impossible without a far-reaching change in the psychology of investment markets such as there is no reason to expect [to occur spontaneously]. I conclude that the duty of ordering the current volume of investment cannot be safely left in private hands. (Keynes 1936 [1964] 320)

> ..it is unlikely that full employment can be maintained, whatever we may do about investment, with the existing propensity to consume. There is room, therefore for both policies to operate together;-- to promote investment and, at the same time, to promote consumption... (Keynes 1936 [1964] 325)

> ... experience suggest that in existing conditions... measures for the redistribution of incomes in a way likely to raise the propensity to consume may prove positively favourable to the growth of capital... (Keynes 1936 [1964] 372)

> The State will have to exercise a guiding influence on the propensity to consume partly through its scheme of taxation, partly by fixing the rate of interest, and partly, perhaps, in other ways. Furthermore, it seems unlikely that the influence of banking policy on the rate of interest will be sufficient by itself to determine an optimum rate of investment. I conceive, therefore, that a somewhat comprehensive socialisation of investment will prove the only means of securing an approximation to full employment; though this need not exclude all manner of compromises and of devices by which public authority will co-operate with private initiative. (Keynes 1936 [1964] 378)

In a radical departure from the common economic wisdom, Keynes' argued that investment and consumption, rather than being in a trade-off relationship, actually reinforce each other until full employment is reached: increasing consumption increases investment.

> ...we have seen that, up to the point where full employment prevails, the growth of capital depends not at all on a low propensity to consume but is, on the contrary, held back by it... (Keynes 1936 [1964] 372-3)

The positive role Keynes identified for consumption in the economic system overturned one of the classical justifications for inequality: that helping the poor will only lead to them consuming more rather than saving/investing, and that therefore it is in the long term interest of society for most income to go to the rich who invest what they do not need for consumption. Redistribution of income can in fact help increase production. Redistribution, within limits, is thus a means as well as an end in its own right.

> ... in existing conditions savings by institutions and through sinking funds is more than adequate, and that measures for the redistribution of incomes in a way likely to raise the propensity to consume may prove positively favourable to the growth of capital...
>
> Thus our argument leads towards the conclusion that in contemporary conditions the growth of wealth, so far from being dependent on the abstinence of the rich [i.e., abstinence from consumption in order to invest more], as is commonly supposed, is more likely to be impeded by it. One of the chief social justifications of great inequality of wealth is, therefore, removed. (Keynes 1936 [1964] 372-3).

While Keynes believed in some redistribution, he was no socialist. He wanted to tame capitalism, not eliminate it. He saw an important place for free enterprise in negotiating deals, organizing production processes, and determining products. With regard to production, the state's role was to be limited to managing the overall volume.

> For my own part, I believe that there is social and psychological justification for significant inequalities of incomes and wealth, but not for such large disparities as exist today. There are valuable human activities which require the motive of money-making and the environment of private wealth-ownership for their full fruition. Moreover, dangerous human proclivities can be canalized into comparatively harmless channels by the existence of opportunities for money-making and private wealth... (Keynes 1936 [1964] 374)

> ... no obvious case is made out for a system of State Socialism which would embrace most of the economic life of the community. It is not the ownership of the instruments of production which it is important for the State to assume. If the State is able to determine the aggregate amount of resources devoted to augmenting the instruments and the basic rate of reward to those who own them, it will have accomplished all that is necessary. Moreover, the necessary measures of socialisation can be introduced gradually and without a break in the general traditions of society.
>
> Our criticism of the accepted classical theory of economics has consisted not so much in finding logical flaws in its analysis as in pointing out that its tacit assumptions are seldom or never satisfied, with the result that it cannot solve the economic problems of the actual world. But if our central controls succeed in establishing an aggregate volume of output corresponding to full employment as nearly as is practicable, the classical theory comes into its own again from this point onwards. If we suppose the volume of output to be given, i.e., to be determined by forces outside the classical scheme of thought, then there is no objection to be raised against the classical analysis of the manner in which private self-interest will determine what in particular is produced, in what proportions the factors of production will be combined to produce it, and how the value of the final product will be distributed between them... It is in determining the volume, not the direction, of actual employment that the existing system has broken down. (Keynes 1936 [1964] 378-9)

Keynes' foresaw society evolving within one or two generations into a "quasi-stationary state" where growth in investment would cease as total consumer demand for material goods stabilized, "where change and progress would result only from changes in technique, taste, population and institutions (Keynes 1936 [1964] 220-1)." Rather implicitly, he indicated in *The General Theory* an assumption that slow population growth had become a permanent feature of advanced society. Somewhat more explicitly, he believed that people's wants could be sated with what would seem to be, from the vantage point of the 1990's, a relatively modest level of productive capacity.

> It is commonly urged as an objection to schemes for raising employment by investment under the auspices of public authority that it is laying up trouble for the future. "What will you do," it is asked, "when you have built all the houses and roads and town halls and electric grids and water supplies and so forth which the stationary population of the future can be expected to require?" But it is not so easily understood that the same difficulty applies to private investment and to industrial expansion; particularly to the latter, since it is much easier to see an early satiation of the demand for new factories and plant which absorb individually but little money, than of the demand for dwelling-houses. (Keynes 1936 [1964] 106)

> ... only experience can show how far...it is safe to stimulate the average propensity to consume without forgoing our aim of depriving capital of its scarcity value within one or two generations. (Keynes 1936 [1964] 377)

> If I am right in supposing it to be comparatively easy to make capital-goods so abundant that the marginal efficiency of capital is zero, this may be the most sensible way of gradually getting rid of many of the objectionable features of capitalism (Keynes 1936 [1964] 220-1)

Keynes' quasi-stationary state idea was founded in assumptions about psychology and the economy. It had no relation to today's concerns about the limits to growth posed by the natural environment. Although Keynes saw himself as continuing the Malthusian line of inquiry, he restricted himself to the aspect of Malthus' thought which was concerned with gluts and deficient demand. Malthus' more popularly known concern with the implications of the finitude of land for a growing population was virtually ignored by Keynes. In Keynes' mind, the replacement of agriculture with industry in advanced countries meant that land availability was no longer a significant issue. Industrial output was primarily responsibility for our well-being, and with industrialization came a greatly reduced rate of population growth.

Just as Keynes ignored the land-population question so did he fail to consider, explicitly at least, the finitude of the fuels and raw materials on which factories and consumers depend, and the impacts of pollution on the environment. Though perhaps in his own mind the need to study environmental limits was obviated by his assumption that in advanced nations capital growth would cease within one or two generations as the capital stock reached a level sufficient to meet human wants, his discussions, like those of his contemporaries, addressed the economy in isolation from the ecology within which all industrial and consumption processes take place. To the extent he bothered with such matters at all it was to declare sanguinely that "whilst there may be intrinsic reasons for the scarcity of land, there are no intrinsic reasons for the scarcity of capital (Keynes 1936 [1964] 376)." His General Theory was in fact quite partial. Of course, this limitation from today's environmentalist perspective was shared by virtually all his contemporaries whether liberals, socialists or fascists, and it continues to be so shared today.

Keynes' Impact: The General Theory had an immediate impact. As one biographer puts it:

> ... the *General Theory* fell amongst the economists of the day with a very big bang. Nothing for any of them was ever quite the same again. The publications of working economists over the next few years attest to the book's impact... One preliminary attempt at a bibliography ten years later uncovered some three hundred articles in major professional journals commenting on Keynes's work or largely inspired by it, not to mention numerous books and monographs... even opponents of Keynes's vision reformulated their objections within something that looked like his framework. (Moggridge 1976 108)

Keynes retooled economics. Henceforth, economists thought, they could fine-tune economic performance, i.e., ensure stable growth by alternately stimulating and cooling down the economy to counter the natural business cycles of the market. When unemployment begins to rise, government can pump money into the economy by running a budget deficit. If after the economy is righted it starts to overheat, i.e., become inflationary because consumer demand exceeds the capacity of the productive capacity of the fully employed workforce, government can take money out of the economy by paying back the deficits it incurred in slower times. No more need there arise the absurdity of workers who are willing to work being unemployed and the absurdity of factories in which they could work sitting idle, while consumers have their wants unsatisfied. The state and the market can work effectively together, the former determining how much is produced when, the latter who produces what where.

If Keynes did not single-handedly create a general turning point in mainstream Western economic thought, his *General Theory* with its extensive analysis certainly marks that point. Keynesianism provided the theoretical basis for the welfare state. While subsequent economists working within the welfare state might debate fine points amongst themselves, or in some cases even see themselves as anti-Keynesian, the fundamental principles Keynes articulated have continued to be widely supported.

The completeness and confidence with which Keynes' theory and resulting anticyclical tools have been blended into the economics profession are indicated in the following excerpts from a 1960's edition of a standard North American economics textbook.

> In recent years, 90 per cent of North American economists have stopped being 'Keynesian economists' or anti-Keynesian economists.' Modern economists are 'post-Keynesians' ...the new generation has worked toward a synthesis of whatever is valuable in older economics and in modern [Keyensian] theories of income determination. The result might be called 'neoclassical economics' and is accepted in its broad outlines by all but a few extreme left-wing and right-wing writers. (Samuelson and Scott 1968 226).

> Everywhere in the free world, governments and central banks have shown they can win the battle of the slump if people want them to. They have the weapons of fiscal policy (expenditure and taxes) and of monetary policy (open-market operations, Bank Rate policy, legal reserve ratio policy) to

shift the schedules that determine national income and employment... [T]he age-old tendencies for the system to fluctuate will still be there, but no longer will the world let them snowball into vast depressions or into galloping inflations... Economists and politicians are now hopeful that the public will understand and support the bold use of these anti-business cycle weapons. ...their very power means that they must be wielded by men of experience and understanding... (Samuelson and Scott 1968 378-79).

Keynesian theory was a crucial element in the evolution of the welfare state, not only because it legitimated government intervention in the economy but because it simultaneously enabled the market to function freely, growth to continue, and stability to replace the previous laissez-faire period of booms and busts. The Keynesian prescriptions that shape welfare state economic systems can be itemized as:

- Free market forces should determine what is produced, where, and how.

- But, business cycle booms and busts should be avoided by the state regulating the pace of industrial capitalist production through monetary, fiscal and social policy.

- Distribution of income should be primarily a market function. The inevitable inequalities that result are fair inasmuch as they reflect differential efforts, talents, and social contributions, and are necessary in that they create incentives to produce.

- But, the state should affect distribution patterns by providing safety nets for those who fall to the bottom of the market ladder and by ensuring that demand by worker-consumers stays high enough to absorb production.

- Growth is desirable; growth in current consumption and growth in investment for future consumption can and must occur simultaneously; through growth, all sectors of society can consume more without the need for redistribution.

The Keynesian welfare state model is win-win in terms of the classical antonymies of market vs. state, consumption vs. investment, rich vs. poor. All interests win in the model because it is based on the crucial assumption that there are no natural limits to growth in a modern economy. In the interpretation of this assumption, however, there is a major difference between Keynes and the mainstream economists who followed him. Although Keynes did not seem to think there are intrinsic limits to economic growth, he did think that growth would essentially come to an end in one or two generations when industrial capacity reached the point that it could meet all material wants and expansion was no longer necessary.

Subsequent welfare state economists, having become much more realistic about humans' virtually limitless capacity and desire to consume in a society where consumption has become the meaning of life, have not dared to predict the coming of such a quasi-stationary state. The closest they come to making such a prediction is to expect continuing increases in the efficiency of technology as offsets to population and consumption growth and continuing shifts in the economic base from manufacturing to services which depend on less natural resource processing.

Keynes' Role in Internationalizing the Welfare State: Though not as significant as his impact on the domestic policy of industrial countries, the role Keynes played in shaping the postwar international context for development of the poor nations is also noteworthy. The public stage for this role was the 1944 Monetary and Financial Conference, in Bretton Woods, New Hampshire. The conference was organized by the newly formed United Nations to deal with issues of postwar reconstruction and demobilization to create an international economic system that would ensure stable growth and prosperity for all nations. From the conference was born the International Bank for Development and Reconstruction (the World Bank) and the International Monetary Fund (IMF). These institutions, and the equivalent regional institutions such as the Asian Development Bank that were subsequently spawned, brought to the international level the kind of economic planning Keynes had prescribed a decade before for the governments of states. The post-colonial (some say neo-colonial) system of international aid and development was initiated. Thus, as the industrialized welfare states consolidated their internal planning and delivery systems in the post-war period, they simultaneously extended their reach to bring the poorer countries within their orbit.

The ends of the international planning were those of Keynes and the welfare state at home: to foster capital investment as a stimulus to private investment and consumption and to create a stable business climate for growth. Within this context, the market could be freed to be efficient and productive. Now at the global as well as at national levels, the contradictions between governance and free enterprise would be resolved. That the needs of the latter, including the protection of private property rights, would not be overlooked was ensured by the formulas for constituting the governing bodies of the World Bank, IMF and their regional clones. The industrialized welfare states, particularly the United States, paid most of the shots, and their representatives called the tunes. The USSR opted out in order to promote development along socialist, preferably Marxist-Leninist, lines. Multilateral as well as bilateral international development aid from the West became big business planned by technocrats who were trained, regardless of their nationalities, in Keynesian economics and Millian politics in the welfare state universities of the West.

Alternatives to the Welfare State in Keynes' Time

Of course, Keynes' political economy theory was not the only one to be advanced in the inter-war period as a solution to the troubles of the time. Nor was his the only one to be found convincing by large numbers of people. Much of the world-- including Italy, Germany, Spain, Portugal, Japan, Argentina, i.e., industrialized countries whose economies and political institutions were very weak because they had very recently industrialized, politically consolidated, lost a war -- was attracted to one or another authoritarian philosophy that combined beliefs in technological material progress with beliefs in hierarchy, service to the state, ordered collectivism in place of the socialists' class conflict and the liberals' individualism, militarism in many cases, and racism in some. For the most part these right wing authoritarian philosophies were not systematically articulated, intellectualism being seen as one of the weaknesses to be stamped out. (Mussolini's (1883-1945) *The Doctrine of Fascism* provides perhaps the clearest exposition of such philosophies.) In contrast to Keynesianism, their power lay not in the cogency of argument but in powerful emotional mythological appeals to national security, excitement, pride, or self-righteousness. The clash between these world views and those of the liberals and socialists provided on both sides the ideological justification for World War II.

The Fascist, Nazi, and Shintoist regimes that fought and lost World War II have been replaced by welfare states of varying forms. Their philosophies have been largely forgotten over the past five decades. But in some places they are slowly regaining their appeal as the welfare state fails to deliver all that is expected of it. Where social fabrics are particularly weak, military dictatorships have taken over without bothering to appeal to philosophy at all.

While the industrialized world countries outside the USSR were becoming fascist or welfare states in the inter-war period, many of the non-industrialized peoples were fighting colonialism. Of the many nationalistic philosopher activists who emerged to challenge the liberal and fascist colonial powers, as well as the remnants of indigenous feudalism, two stand out in terms of the power of their ideas and the breadth of their followings: Mohandas Gandhi (1869-1948) and Mao Tse Tung (1893-1976).

Under Mao's leadership, the liberation of China from Japanese colonialism, as well as form indigenous feudalism and liberal capitalism, was consolidated in 1949. Mao adapted the principles and practice of Lenin and Stalin to create a still more radical approach to social development. He gave a prominent place to peasants in creating the revolution and in his leadership of post-revolution China attempted to institute immediately a level of egalitarianism that leaders of the USSR thought would be possible only after complete industrialization. Mao's successfully direct approach encouraged peoples round the world who were, from a liberal and Marxist point of view, at a low level of development, i.e. at a low level of industrialization. For a time, his promotion of local development through diversification and low-tech innovations (e.g., through "barefoot doctors") inspired many intellectuals in the West. At present, however, it appears that his leadership has created not a pure and immediate communism but at best an incipient welfare state, at worst an authoritarian capitalism.

Gandhi's approach was fundamentally different but equally successful in creating political change. Whereas Mao was philosophically a materialist, Gandhi was a spiritualist. He believed in non-violence and showed the power of civil disobedience and passive resistance. As did Mao, he believed that the organization of villagers should be a leading force in national development, but his approach involved more bottom-up cooperation and less industrialization. His view of development was alien to Western liberal and socialist thought. Gandhi succeeded in liberating India from the British, in 1947, but not from liberalism and remnants of feudalism. In this sense, his approach was less effective than Mao's in creating social change. The power of his ideas, however, may turn out to last longer. They are in harmony with those of the Buddhist ecologists, who, it will be argued below, appear to present the major alternative to the Keynesian welfare state.

Success of the Welfare State

While various fascist and Leninist (including Maoist) alternatives to the welfare state have had significant impacts on large numbers of people, none has had its equivalent staying power or has become as global in its application. The welfare state as prescribed by Mill and Keynes seems to be becoming universal.

Those countries that began their industrial development on a liberal path (Europe, North America) became more socialised in the middle of the 20th century: during the almost three decades from the end of World War II until the 1970's, growth was strong and relatively stable in these countries, and the scope and generosity of welfare programs grew correspondingly; while their economies have weakened in the last two decades, and welfare programs curtailed, the basic concept of the welfare state has continued to bound political discourse.

At the same time, countries that began their industrial development in this century on a revolutionary socialist path (e.g., USSR, China) are now becoming economically and/or politically liberalized. The pace and extent of this liberalization in many Marxist-Leninist countries provided dramatic television watching at the turn of decade into the 1990's.

The mainstream of political thought within both the fully developed welfare states and many of the still nominally socialist countries covers a modest range along the liberal-socialist continuum. In the West, "the right" wants a little less state control, "the left" a little more. In the Leninist socialist countries, "the right" wants to slow the conversion to a welfare state, the liberals want to speed it up. In both spheres, those who call for totally free markets and those who call for total state management are considered extremists on the fringe. Those whose politics are not even situated on the liberal-socialist continuum such as tradition-oriented conservatives or communal anarchists are considered to be on the lunatic fringe.

Challenges to the Welfare State

Although the welfare state appears to be widely accepted as providing the best possible resolution of thorny state-vs-individual questions, it has its challengers. The list of challengers still includes conservatives and revolutionary socialists, but increasingly these do not seem to pose major threats.

The two major challengers are "monetarism," and a complex of thought here termed "Buddhist ecology." Monetarists challenge the welfare state by essentially calling for a revival of a rather pure laissez-faire liberalism. Buddhist ecologists go beyond all 19th century political categories. They may trace their roots to the utopian socialists or anarchists, and incorporate elements of liberal, socialist and conservative thought, but in raising concerns about the social and environmental impacts of economic growth, and the fairness of distributing that growth through market or state trickle-down mechanisms, they break new ground.

The monetarists and Buddhist ecologists began to emerge as major threats in the 1970's as the mature welfare states began to manifest signs of ill health: stagflation (simultaneously high levels of unemployment and inflation), and pollution.

Monetarism: Among economists, there are many debates about the fine points of Keynesian theory, its proper application, and, to some degree, its fundamental validity. The most direct attack on Keynesian theory from within the economics profession has come from the monetarists who, always lurking in the background, came to prominence in the 1970's through the work of their own guru Milton Friedman. Friedman's prescription for economic stability, growth, and fairness, is simple and attractive to those with nostalgia for the days of laissez-faire. It was fully presented in his 1962 *Capitalism and Freedom* then popularized in the 1979 *Free to Choose*.

The monetarist prescription for good government is to replace ineffective and often counter-productive Keynesian fiscal tinkering with a clear consistent policy of maintaining slow constant growth in money supply, to eschew deficits, to privatize and minimize government operations and to insist people adjust to this reality no matter how much they complain about unemployment or demand new government programs. Friedman himself also recommended simplifying income assistance programs for the poor by instituting a guaranteed annual income to be administered though a negative income tax.

The general monetarist prescription became particularly attractive to a new breed of right-wing politicians, most notably the United Kingdom's Margaret Thatcher and the United States' Ronald Reagan, as the 1970's turned into a period of growing stagflation. Stagflation is theoretically impossible if governments follow either classical or Keynesian economic theory. It became a reality in the 1970's with shortages of some crucial commodities, particularly petroleum and some foods. These resulted in varying degrees from natural disasters (droughts, changing ocean currents), man-made disasters (e.g., desertification), production cartels (most notably the Organization of Petroleum Exporting Countries), resource exhaustion (e.g., United States oil), and surges in demand due to worldwide population and consumption growth.

Since such shortages were not provided for in Keynes' General Theory, welfare state governments could not rely on this theory to develop an effective response. They were no longer totally in control of the pace of overall production and thus could not create employment-filling growth with minimal inflation. In each country, the growth rate was being determined more by God, cartels, feedback from past decisions, and other states, than by that country's own government. The problem was not the same as it had been in the 1930's. Then, Keynes showed, the problem was lack of effective demand in an economy with high productive potential. In the 1970's, the problem was shortages of raw materials and too much effective demand, a combination which produces inflation. The Keynesian finetuning options for welfare state governments were limited: either take money out of the economy and increase unemployment, or meet demands of citizens for more money to cope with inflation and thus contribute further to that inflation. An extreme move in either direction would produce either very high unemployment or very high inflation; the moderate course, which was adopted by most welfare state governments during the 1970's, was to allow moderate increases of both unemployment and inflation.

A non-Keynesian alternative which was tried briefly in Canada then abandoned, but which was successfully applied in the more socialistic Sweden, was the application of wage and price controls. Both unemployment (which mostly affects the young) and inflation (which particularly affects retirees) could be reduced through such a fair measure, but of course standards of living for all would fall proportionately with the supply shortages. Swedish society could establish a social contract to distribute cutbacks fairly because it had the necessary combination of mutual trust, social control, self-discipline, a sense that distribution patterns were fair to begin with, and a willingness to accept the prospect of a lower standard of living. In Canada, the wage and price controls were imposed rather than developed through a consensual process. Correctly perceiving the unfairness of the existing distribution of income (let alone of wealth), lower paid workers and recipients of transfer payments refused to accept lower real dollar wages and support payments such as pensions. Loosely controlled businesses had ways of getting around the constraint. Middle class professionals used their power to maintain their financial status.

Keynesian theory having no solution for stagflation caused by material shortages, and most welfare states being more competitively liberal than consensually or coercively socialistic, it was necessary to find a school of political economy that could replace Keynes in guiding the economic management of welfare states. For those who saw stagflation as resulting from lazy and grasping workers, inefficient and bloated government, and/or the chicanery and degeneracy of businesses corrupted and straightjacketed by government handouts and rules, monetarism seemed to offer the perfect prescription.

By the early 1980's, the monetarist medicine was being administered in much of the Western world. What the monetarists labelled as "Keynesianism," continuous economic stimulation to avoid unemployment, was out. As a result, interest rates, bankruptcies and unemployment soared in 1981-82, as money became scarcer. There began the worst "recession" (there being no official definition for depression because it is considered a scourge of the past) since the 1930's.

Policies within the mature welfare states during the remainder of the 1980's were confused. Many aspects of monetarism were maintained: the rate of growth in money supply was much more carefully limited than it had been in the 1970's, many public services and government-controlled corporations were privatized, others were cut back, and there were even some moves toward a simplified negative income tax (e.g., as reflected in Canada's child tax credit). At the same time, government deficits quickly rose to meet ongoing welfare state commitments as unemployment rose and society aged, and in some countries, particularly the United States, to support growing military budgets.

The combination of high deficits and stable money supply has created high interest rates, high unemployment levels in most countries (particularly among the youth) with an historically high level of corresponding inflation, and virtually no real increases in wages despite lower commodity prices resulting from lags in production cut backs after the booming 1970's. Growth in real family incomes revived somewhat in the mid to late 1980's, but at a slower pace than in previous decades even though the percentage of women participating in the non-domestic labour force continued to grow. Statistics for Canada illustrate the situation. (See Appendix.)

There has been virtually no expansion of social programs in the welfare states of the 1980's. While fairly steady if slow growth, as measured by gross domestic product (GDP), resumed after 1982, this growth did not translate into a higher standard of living for the average person.

It has been a fundamental tenet of the welfare state that the distribution of incomes should reflect disparities that are the natural result of competition but that incomes for the poor should not fall below some defined minimum. Perhaps as an intentional or unintentional consequence, the shares of total national income accruing to the various classes within the welfare states have shown remarkable consistency. The distribution of incomes among quintiles is the one economic indicator that has not changed significantly over the life of the welfare state. (See Appendix, Table 6.) In short, income in the welfare state has never been, and is not now being, *re*distributed. The lot of the poor improved in the 1950's and 1960's because incomes shares were at least constant as total national income (as reflected in GDP) grew. However, as national growth tapered off from the 1970's into the 1980's, it tapered off proportionately for all classes. For people on the margin in high rent urban areas, or in chronically depressed areas, the slowing of growth has meant hardship neither expected nor seen since the 1940's. Food banks, unthinkable as necessary two decades ago, are now standard features of city life across Canada, for example.

Internationally, the influence of monetarism rose throughout the 1980's as welfare state governments and their international agencies (IMF, World Bank, etc.) pushed for "economic restructuring" in the poorer countries. Economic restructuring means privatization, ending subsidies to both producers and consumers, releasing market forces, adopting "realistic" official currency exchange rates (usually meaning devaluation of the poor country's currency in order to reduce consumption of imports), increasing exports, and paying off the international debts that were originally incurred in the 1970's when commodity prices were high and appeared to be going higher and that were exacerbated by the monetarist high interest rate policies of the 1980's. It is a solution to the economic malaise of debt, inefficiency, corruption, and resource exhaustion that increases inequity within and between countries and that promotes further environmental destruction. International debt levels remain high and standards of living deteriorate in most of Latin America, Africa and parts of Asia.

Economically, the promises of the welfare state have been broken nationally and internationally. It is seen increasingly as inherently unable to deliver growth, stability, or security. The major alternative to Keynesianism that is being entertained by those with power within the welfare states is monetarism. To the degree monetarism succeeds in influencing welfare state and international policies, its impacts add to the pain of decline. The poorer the person, the greater the pain.

Politically, the welfare state continues without any major challenge. For most people who love freedom and fairness, Mill's system still seems the best. Nevertheless, there are growing rumblings of discontent with representative democracy. On the one hand, governments seem too remote and beyond the influence of the average citizen; on the other, they appear inefficient and unable to solve growing economic, social and environmental problems.

Ironically, both the welfare state and the monetarist alternative seem to be gaining favour in the de-Leninizing countries at the same time as both are losing favour among large numbers of people in the industrialized and would-be industrializing world. Apart from the former Leninists, only in a few Newly Industrialized Countries (NICs) of Asia does either the welfare or monetarist state seem to enjoy widespread popular support and credibility as a realisable vision.

Possible Futures for the Welfare State

If the welfare state is in decline, and if the alternative offered by the establishment, monetarism, can only deliver more by promising less to most people, what are the choices for the future? The choices seem to fit into five categories.

One choice is to give up on liberalism in both its classical and welfare state variants and agree with Marx that the contradictions of capitalism will lead to its demise in industrially advanced nations, (as compared to the more agricultural nations where Marxism-Leninism has in fact been successful until now). This idea would appear to be an atavism that will not attract much support.

A second choice is to take the authoritarian right wing approach-- a frightening but plausible scenario if the welfare state continues to decay, and one which is potentially compatible with environmentalism.

A third choice is to attempt to carry on with the welfare state, enhancing its growth and preserving public services by finetuning the application of Keynesian principles, by: raising taxes to meet growing social service and income security demands as the population grows and ages, our capital plant runs down, and resources are exhausted; and/or, increasing government deficits still further in an attempt to stimulate growth regardless of the ecological costs. This could be called the social democratic choice.

Fourth, there is the possibility of cutting taxes and reducing social welfare programs to the minimum, i.e., returning to the pre-Keynesian economy and the hope that lower taxes and interest rates will stimulate growth which will trickle down to the masses. Such a revival of classical liberalism is what is proposed by the monetarists and close allies such as the "supply-siders" who contrast themselves with the Keynesians who focus on demand management.

The final possibility is to take an ecologically sound compassionate development approach which involves radical redistributions of wealth, income, and power, on global as well as national and local levels. This "Buddhist ecology" approach seems to offer the best hope: it recognizes the limitations of the welfare state without reverting to authoritarianism or laissez-faire irresponsibility. From a Buddhist ecology perspective, competition and inequalities are not essential to efficiency or freedom, nor is the state the sole level at which governance should occur.

The Buddhist Ecological Alternative to the Welfare State: The essence of what might be called the Buddhist ecological development approach was expressed and widely disseminated in the 1970's by E.F. Schumacher's popular 1973 book *Small is Beautiful*. The book called for human scale and environmental appropriateness in the design of technology and social organization. It challenged the welfare state assumption that the fulfilment of the individual and the economic management responsibility of the state lies in increasing consumption.

Schumacher (1911-1977) was only one of many social theorists expressing such thoughts in the early 1970's. Some, like Meadows et al.in their equally famous 1972 book *Limits to Growth*, and the assortment of writers in Herman Daly's more academic 1973 compendium *Toward a Steady-State Economy*, focused on the incompatibility of our addiction to growth with the finitude of our globe. Others like Catholic philosopher Ivan Illich (1973) showed that top-down technocratic welfare state institutions, such as our medical and educational systems, can create more problems than they solve, and that Western-biased development approaches and technologies, i.e, those funded by welfare states and their agencies such as the World Bank, tend to exacerbate conditions for most people in poor countries. What set Schumacher apart is that he went beyond critique of the growth-oriented welfare state to outline a theory for an alternative form of society.

Schumacher's "Buddhist" assumptions about the nature of human beings and their conception of the good life were at odds with the utilitarianism of Mill and Keynes which underlies "modern economics:"

> ...let us take some fundamentals and see what they look like when viewed by a modern economist and a Buddhist economist... Now, the modern economist has been brought up to consider 'labour' or work as little more than a necessary

evil. From the point of view of the employer, it is in any case simply an item of cost, to be reduced to a minimum if it cannot be eliminated altogether, say, by automation. From the point of view of the workman, it is a 'disutility'; to work is to make a sacrifice of one's leisure and comfort, and wages are a kind of compensation for the sacrifice. Hence the ideal from the point of view of the employer is to have output without employees, and the ideal from the point of view of the employee is to have income without employment.... If the ideal with regard to work is to get rid of it, every method that 'reduces the work load' is a good thing. The most potent method, short of automation, is the so-called 'division of labour' and the classical example is the pin factory eulogised in Adam Smith's *Wealth of Nations*...

The Buddhist point of view takes the function of work to be at least threefold: to give a man a chance to utilize and develop his faculties; to enable him to overcome his egocentredness by joining with other people in a common task; and to bring forth the goods and services needed for a becoming existence. ...

From the Buddhist point of view, there are therefore two types of mechanisation which must be clearly distinguished: one that enhances a man's skill and power and one that turns the work of man over to a mechanical slave, leaving man in a position of having to serve the slave. ...

If a man has no chance of obtaining work he is in a desperate position, not simply because he lacks an income but because he lacks this nourishing and enlivening factor of disciplined work which nothing can replace. A modern economist may engage in highly sophisticated calculations on whether full employment 'pays' or whether it might be more 'economic' to run an economy at less than full employment so as to ensure a greater mobility of labour, a better stability of wages, and so forth. His fundamental criterion of success is simply the total quantity of goods produced during a given period of time. ...

From a Buddhist point of view, this is standing the truth on its head by considering goods as more important than people and consumption as more important than creative activity. ...

> While the materialist is mainly interested in goods, the Buddhist is mainly interested in liberation. But Buddhism is 'The Middle Way' and therefore in no way antagonistic to physical well-being. It is not wealth that stands in the way of liberation but the attachment to wealth; not the enjoyment of pleasurable things but the craving for them. The keynote of Buddhist economics, therefore, is simplicity and non-violence... [T]he modern economist...is used to measuring the 'standard of living' by the amount of annual consumption, assuming all the time that a man who consumes more is 'better off' than a man who consumes less. A Buddhist economist would consider this approach excessively irrational: since consumption is merely a means to human well-being, the aim should be to obtain the maximum of well-being with the minimum of consumption. ... (Schumacher 1973 44-48)

As well as offering an alternative to modern economists' assumptions about human nature and the meaning of life, Schumacher's Buddhist economics began from a different starting point in its assumptions about natural resources. Schumacher rejected the (usually implicit) view of modern economists that the finitude of natural resources as a barrier to growth can be overcome by human inventiveness. Just as his conception of human nature led him to question division of labour as a basis for modern industry, so his recognition of ecological context for production led him to question the value of international free trade and inter-community specialization based on comparative advantage.

> As physical resources are everywhere limited, people satisfying their needs by means of a modest use of resources are obviously less likely to be at each other's throats than people depending on a high rate of use. Equally, people who live in highly self-sufficient local communities are less likely to get involved in large-scale violence than people whose existence depends on world-wide systems of trade. From the point of view of Buddhist economics, therefore, production from local resources for local needs is the most rational way of economic life, while dependence on imports from afar and the consequent need to produce for export to unknown and distant peoples is highly uneconomic and justifiable only in exceptional cases and on a small scale. (Schumacher 1973 48-49)

Schumacher's break with modern economics in all its forms, liberal and socialist, is all the more startling when one learns that he was not only an economist himself, but was in fact the Economic Adviser to Britain's National Coal Board from 1950 to 1970. Certainly, his break with his profession was more radical than Keynes', but it is interesting that Keynes, like Schumacher, was somewhat repulsed by the greed and self-centredness of modern people, and also like Schumacher dared to consider the impacts of free trade on the ability of nations to manage their own affairs and choose their economic goals. However, Keynes did not see modern consumption as being insidious, nor did he pay attention to the quality of working life. His questioning of free trade was circumspect.

Small is Beautiful, *Limits to Growth*, Illich's books, the essays in *Toward a Steady-State Economy*, and other works in the early to mid 1970's, presented a fundamental challenge to the growth-oriented Keynesian welfare state. The stagflation precipitated by the oil crisis of 1973 added to the popularity of these works. New kinds of social movements emerged. In the 1960's, movements had aimed to perfect the welfare state by extending the benefits of citizenship (e.g., the civil rights, student, and women's liberation movements), or by protecting citizens from direct threats to their enjoyment of the good life whether these were posed by nuclear war, urban freeways, or dirty water. Social movements in the 1970's were more low key in their tactics but more fundamental in their goals. They sought to improve gender relations, decentralize urban government, replace freeways with public transit, involve the public in decision-making on megaprojects, replace fossil fuels with solar energy, and protect farmlands. In general, the movements of the 1970's aimed at increasing participation in resource conservation and social development. These goals reflected dissatisfaction with the technocracy and gluttony of the Keynesian welfare state and a general sympathy with Buddhist ecology.

The monetarist shock in 1982 and the consequent crash of commodity prices took the wind from the Buddhist ecology sails. Steady-state academics and environmental activists had trouble explaining how gluts had replaced shortages as our major problem. Fossil fuels, now cheap again, made a comeback and solar energy was put on the back burner. At the same time, many people had to cope with the shift to a leaner and meaner economy: the welfare state, though still fundamentally intact, was being chopped at the edges through cutbacks and privatizations of public services, wage restraints, and continuously high unemployment levels. Foodbanks, set up in the early 1980's in response to the 1982 crisis, were institutionalized. Communities that had spurned industrial development because of its environmental impacts in the 1970's now sought industry for its economic benefits. Women increasingly stayed in the labour force because of the exigencies of the mortgage and rental market as much as to meet their career aspirations.

Despite the setbacks, there were two important developments in the 1980's from a Buddhist ecology perspective. First was the grassroots organization of community institutions to create local economies. Communities replaced reactive protests with proactive institution-building and comprehensive strategic planing. Community economic development (CED) and bottom-up development became household words. Secondly was an awareness of our planet's ecological fragility which in its intensity and extent exceeded the awareness of most people in the 1970's. Evidence of global warming from the green house effect of fossil fuels and deforestation, plus threats to the protective atmospheric ozone layer, showed that environmental problems were now not only local matters of aesthetics and health but also matters of global ecology.

In 1987, the World Commission on Economy and Development, headed by former Norwegian Prime Minister Brundtland released *Our Common Future*, the report of its findings on the environmental impact of economic development. To study such an issue would never have occurred to Keynes. The report's call for *sustainable development*, and the phrase itself, quickly became famous.

Many countries, not the least Canada, have responded to the call by investigating ways to make economic practices less environmentally malignant.

As the phrase "sustainable development" has gained currency, it has become less and less clear what it actually means. The definition in the Brundtland report was seemingly unambiguous: development is sustainable if it "meets the needs of the present without compromising the ability of future generations to meet their own needs." But the implications of this definition are subject to debate.

At one extreme, many ecologists tend to interpret sustainable development as meaning developing our society in a way that permits life-supporting ecological sustainability, and necessarily, therefore, ending *growth* in material consumption; at the other extreme many economists think of sustainable development as finding the means to permit economic growth to continue. The ecologists, looking at finite ecosystems, see a need to cut back now in order to leave something for future generations; the economists, looking at human ingenuity, see no intrinsic barrier to growth. The Brundtland report itself was a classic compromise. It listed the problems identified by the ecologists and came up with a solution that would comfort the economists: more growth.

The sustainable development debate-- to grow or not to grow-- is now heating up. In many countries, welfare state growth vs Buddhist ecology has replaced socialism vs. liberalism as the basic intellectual cleavage.

The "ecologists" are no longer just specialist biologists but comprise a mixed but largely compatible bag of conservative anti-materialists, decentralists in the anarchist tradition, communitarians, community developers, aboriginal peoples, feminists, and environmental activists-- people who are concerned with the connections among culture, gender, politics at all levels, natural resources, and technology. In Europe, and to a lesser extent in the welfare states of other regions, they have often coalesced their political energies through the Green Party.

The "economists" are not limited to utilitarian number-crunchers. They include many business people, trade unionists, consumer advocates, and the politicians of mainstream political parties. But the division between ecologists and economists is not just between those on one side of the fence and those on the other, those with black hats and those with white. The division appears in fact within each individual. In real life, most of us in our thinking and behaviour are part Buddhist ecologist, part economist.

The either-or cast of the 19th century debate between liberals and socialists, was compromised through the thinking of Mill, Keynes, and others contributing to the welfare state. Political debate shifted from individualism *or* collectivism to debates over the proper balance of each. The sustainable development debate between ecologists and economists, and between the greedy and altruistic side of individuals, does not seem to be compromising in this way. If anything, positions may be polarizing further. The radical Buddhist ecologists are increasingly daring to argue that not only must growth cease, but that overall consumption must be reduced and therefore radically equalized intra- and inter-nationally, i.e., that many people, certainly most Canadians, must consume much less if more of the very poor are not to starve. The economists' reply, as exemplified by the Brundtland report, is increasingly to call for more growth to give us the means to deal with environmental problems and more trickle-down of the fruits of this growth to the poor.

The Buddhist ecologists see the economists' solution as digging ourselves deeper into the mess we have created, the economists see the Buddhist ecologists as irresponsible fatalists. At this point, it does not appear that there will be a compromise similar to the welfare state compromise. More likely, we will continue to see individual compromises between the growing values of simplicity and equality and involvement, and our personal desires for luxury, getting ahead and privacy. The analogy with the welfare state lies in the process of change, i.e., a series of small scale compromises taking place over decades, but with the crucial compromises this time being made at the individual and community level as well as by the state. The debate this time will be resolved from the bottom rather than through state-level policy changes resulting from the parliamentary outcomes of electoral politics.

Perhaps the best known recent work on the Buddhist ecology side is the 1989 compendium of Buddhist ecology ideas presented in *For the Common Good: Redirecting the Economy Toward Community, the Environment, and a Sustainable Future* by economist Herman Daly and theologian John Cobb.

Daly and Cobb are more discursive and less incisive than Schumacher in their critique of utilitarian economics, but they address a wider range of specific issues: population, urban form, free trade, theology, taxes, income security, and so on. Like Schumacher they start from assumptions about human nature and ecology which are fundamentally different than those presented by most professional economists. Their assumptions reflect, they say, Christian theism, particularly theism in the Catholic tradition. As did Schumacher, who in fact was also a Christian, they believe that humans should live more in harmony with each other and with nature and less as consumption-maximizing individuals. They therefore share Schumacher's belief in strengthening the autonomy and self-sufficiency of the small community. Perhaps it is as much due to Daly's longstanding credentials as an academic economist and recent acceptance by the international development establishment-- he is an employee of the World Bank-- as to its radically appealing content that *For the Common Good* has quickly become a best seller. Their religious self-identification notwithstanding, Daly and Cobb can thus be seen as among the most contemporary popularizers of what is being called here, in deference to Schumacher's impact on our own society, Buddhist ecology.

Contemporary Buddhist ecology is not just a Christian pipedream. In Thailand, where Buddhism is not only the official religion but still has many truly spiritual adherents, Buddhist philosophy is seen by many community developers as offering exactly the development prescription outlined by Schumacher. Most concretely at the rural level, Buddhist development philosophy translates into farming/forestry that is more integrated (crop diversification with minimal industrial chemicals), self-sufficient, low-tech, local-knowledge-based and sometimes communal than the industrialized export-oriented monoculture that dispossess the "inefficient" poor from their land, than has been the mainstream agricultural development approach prescribed for poor countries since Bretton Woods, and that culminated in Asian countries' overly promoted "Green Revolutions." (See Pongphit 1986 1989.) Buddhist ecology in Thailand is not restricted to the villages. The Governor of metropolitan Bangkok (8 million population), Srimuang Chamlong, runs on a platform promising to provide leadership in helping people to make sacrifices, reduce their desires and share their wealth. He wins his elections because he practices what he preaches.

In cases such as Thailand, the Buddhist ecology grows in reaction to social upheaval created by a rapid evolution from feudalism through liberalism with growing features of a welfare state. Countries such as Vietnam and China are providing an alternative to revive Buddhist ecological principles of voluntary co-operation and integrated farming. In the many countries of Latin America, Africa and parts of Asia where development on the Western industrial Keynesian welfare state model has resulted in land commodification and consolidation by the rich, an indebted and proletarianized poor, unmanageable rural-to-urban migration, violence, corruption, capital flight, pollution, and the destruction of natural capital, Buddhist ecology provides hope in its practicality, fairness and satisfaction of needs.

In the industrialized welfare states still essentially operating on Millian and Keynesian utilitarian principles, the growing interest in Buddhist ecology suggests we are finding a way to end our rapaciousness and growing anxieties about our individual economic and physical futures. Where Mill and Keynes, those who ushered in the welfare state, and those who benefited from it as it flowered in the 1960's were fully optimistic, pessimism is the dominant mood of today. While the modern economist may blame people such as Schumacher, Daly and Cobb, and other "neo-Malthusians" for spreading a message of doom in predicting we cannot carry on our growing rates of consumption, the Buddhist ecological message in fact gives hope that we can organize ourselves in a way which is kinder, gentler and ultimately more satisfying.

Conclusion

Drawing on liberalism and socialism as synthesized in the utilitarian, democratic, and economic management theories of John Stuart Mill and John Maynard Keynes, the welfare state has given us much: prosperity, stability, security, freedom, optimism, and some measure of democracy. It is no wonder that it has been seen as the ideal form of political economy by increasing numbers of people worldwide. Its success, however, has rested on some assumptions that no longer seem self-evident: that growth can continue until all needs are met; that thanks to this growth the poor can advance without the need for fundamental redistribution; that the state and the market are society's only significant political economic institutions; that once the right balance between these two institutions is created, no fundamental ideological tensions remain to be resolved.

The Buddhist ecological approach to development may pose the greatest longrun threat to the welfare state. Two decades ago, E.F. Schumacher popularized the social theory on which this approach is based. Today it is being expanded and applied through the work of community developers such as Seri Pongphit and economists such as Herman Daly. Buddhist ecological development starts from assumptions radically different than those underlying the welfare state: there are indeed limits to growth; money-making and ever-increasing consumption must therefore give way to other sources of meaning; wealth and power must be redistributed; cooperative community must increasingly replace the competitive market and coercive state as the basis for governance, production, and socialization.

In the end, the most lasting thought of Keynes may that expressed in the famous final passage of *The General Theory*.

> The ideas of economists and political philosophers, both when they are right and when they are wrong, are more powerful than is commonly understood. Indeed the world is ruled by little else. Practical men, who believe themselves to be quite exempt from any intellectual influences, are usually the slaves of some defunct economist. Madmen in authority, who hear voices in the air, are distilling their frenzy from some academic scribbler of a few years back. I am sure that the power of vested interests is vastly exaggerated compared with the gradual encroachment of ideas. Not indeed, immediately, but after a certain interval; for in the field of economic and political philosophy there are not many who are influenced by new theories after they are twenty-five or thirty years of age, so that the ideas which civil servants and politicians and even agitators apply to current events are not likely to be the newest. But, soon or late, it is ideas, not vested interests, which are dangerous for good or evil. (Keynes 1936 382-3)

Keynes, of course, thought his own ideas would become the new orthodoxy for practical men, and he turned out to be right. But if we judge his ideas and those of his welfare state colleagues in terms of their relevance to present ecological, economic and social realities, in the same spirit that Keynes applied the reality test to his classical predecessors, we increasingly find these ideas too narrow and too mean. Our current problems require richer, more comprehensive, and more spiritual solutions than Keynes was able to provide with his utilitarian calculus.

At this point, the Buddhist ecologists seem to be pointing us in a more fruitful direction, but one that is difficult for many of us to accept today because of its implications for lifestyle change. We should hope Keynes was right in his conviction that the power of vested interests is vastly exaggerated compared with the gradual encroachment of ideas.

Bibliography

Daly, Herman E. 1971. "The Stationary-State Economy: Toward a Political Economy of Biophysical Equilibirum and Moral Growth." In Daly, Herman E. (ed.) 1973. *Toward a Steady-State Economy*. San Francisco: W.H. Freeman and Co.

Daly, Herman E. and John B. Cobb Jr. 1989. *For the Common Good: Redirecting the Economy Toward Community, the Environment, and a Sustainable Future*. Boston: Beacon Press.

Friedman, Milton. 1962. *Capitalism and Freedom*. Chicago: University of Chicago Press.

Friedman, Milton, and Rose Friedman. 1979. *Free to Choose*. New York: Harcourt Brace Jovanovich.

Illich, Ivan. 1973. *Tools for Conviviality*. New York: Harper & Row.

Keynes, John Maynard. 1936. *The General Theory of Employment, Interest, and Money*. Reprint. San Diego: Harcourt Brace Jovanovich. 1964

Meadows, Donella H. et al. 1972. *The Limits to Growth: A report for the Club of Rome's Project on the Predicament of Mankind*. New York: Universe Books.

Moggridge, D. E. 1976. *Keynes*. Glasgow: Fontana/Collins.

Pongphit, Seri. (ed.) 1986. *Back to the Roots: Village and self-reliance in a Thai context*. Bangkok: Rural Development Documentation Centre.

Pongphit, Seri. 1989. *Development Paradigm: Strategy, Activities and Reflection*. Bangkok: Thai Institute for Rural Development.

Samuelson, Paul A. and Anthony Scott. 1968. *Economics: An Introductory Analysis*. (2nd Canadian ed.). Toronto: McGraw-Hill.

Schumacher, E.F. 1973. *Small is Beautiful: A Study of Economics as if People Mattered*. London: Abacus (Sphere Books Ltd.).

World Commission on Environment and Development (WCED). 1987. *Our Common Future*. New York: Oxford University Press.

Appendix
THE CANADIAN WELFARE STATE IN DECLINE-- ECONOMIC STATISTICS

Table 1. *Mean Annual Growth in Real Family Income and Real Gross Domestic Product* (Mean annual percentage increase)

	Gross Family Income	Per Capita Income	GDP
1951-61	3.28	2.74	2.77
1961-71	4.60	5.30	5.45
1971-81	2.61	4.19	4.39
1981-89	0.89	1.25	3.20

Data Sources: Statistics Canada. 1990. *Income Distributions by Size in Canada 1989* (Catalogue 13-207 Annual).
Statistic Canada GDP data presented in *Canadian World Almanac and Book of Facts 1990*. Agincourt, Ont.: Global Press. (GDP data source)

Table 2. *Mean Federal Government Deficit as Percentage of GDP*

1960-69	1.27
1970-79	2.38
1980-88	6.12

Data Source: Canada, Department of Finance. 1990. *Quarterly Economic Review: Annual Reference Tables*.

Table 3. *Canadian Discomfort Index (Unemployment + Inflation)*
(mean annual rate)

	Unemployment Rate %	Inflation Rate (Change in CPI)	Discomfort Index (Sum of two columns)
1961-70	4.9	2.7	7.6
1971-80	6.9	8.1	15.0
1981-90	9.5	6.0	15.5

Data Sources: Canada, Department of Finance. 1981. *Economic Review*.
Canada, Department of Finance. 1985. *Economic Review*.
Canada, Department of Finance. 1990. *Quarterly Economic Review: Annual Reference Tables*. Statistics Canada

Table 4. *Labour Force Participation Rates, Selected Years*
(percentage of eligible population in labour force)

	Female	Male
1966	35.4	79.8
1971	39.4	77.3
1981	51.7	78.4
1989	57.9	76.7

Data Source: Canada, Department of Finance. 1990. *Quarterly Economic Review: Annual Reference Tables*.

Table 5. *Low-income Rates by Family Categories*
(percentage of families in category who are defined as "low-income")

	Young (head under age 25)	Two-parent, One-earner	Two-earner	Three-earner
1980	19.5	15.8	5.3	3.1
1989	25.1	18.2	5.2	2.3

Data Sources: Statistics Canada. 1980. *Perspectives Canada III*.
Statistics Canada. 1990. *Income Distributions by Size in Canada 1989* (Catalogue 13-207 Annual).

Table 6. *Income Shares of Families and Unattached Individuals in Canada*
(per cent of total income)

	Poorest Quintile	Richest Quintile
1951	4.4	42.8
1961	4.2	41.3
1971	3.6	43.3
1981	4.6	41.7
1989	4.8	43.2

Sources: Statistics Canada. 1980. *Perspectives Canada III*.
Statistics Canada. 1990. *Income Distributions by Size in Canada 1989* (Catalogue 13-207 Annual).

BIBLIOGRAPHY

Addams, Jane. *Peace and Bread in Time of War.* New York: 1922.

Aurelius, Marcus. *Meditations.*

Bentham, Jeremy. *An Introduction to the Principles of Morals and Legislation.* 1789.

Bernstein, Edward. *Evolunatary Socialism.* 1899.

Bismarck, Otto von. "State Socialism". Speech of 15 March 1884.

Bosanquet, Charles B.P. *London: Some Account of its Growth, Charitable Agencies and Wants.* London: 1868, pp. 197-207.

Bourne, Randolph. "Twilight of Idols". In *The New Republic*, Vol. IV, September 4, 1915, pp. 117-119.

Burke, Edmund. *Thoughts on the Cause of the Present Discontent: Letters on a Regicide Peace.* pp. 208-9.

Burkenhardt, Jakob. "On War". *Reflections on History.*

Defoe, Daniel. *A Journal of the Plague Year.* 1722.

Disraeli, Benjamin. *Sybil, or The Two Nations.* London: 1840, pp. 60-66.

Eighth Annual Report of the Poor Law Commission. *Parliamentary Papers*, 1842, Vol. XIX, Appendix pp. 48-51.

George, Henry. *Social Problems.* London: 1884, pp. 100-111.

Hegel, G.W.F. *Reason in History.*

Hobbes, Thomas. *Leviathan.* London: 1651.

Kropotkin, Prince Peter. Revolutionary Pamphlets. ed. by Roger Baldwin. New York: 1927.

Lassalle, Ferdinand. *What is Capital?* New York, 1900.

Lenin, V.I. "Left Wing Communism, An Infantile Disorder". Moscow: 1920, pp. 158-164.

Luxemburg, Rosa. *Reform or Revolution.* 1899.

Machavelli, Nicolo. *The Prince.*

Malthus, "A Summary View of the Principle of Population". London: 1830.

Marx, Karl & Engels, Frederick. "The Communist Manifesto". 1848.

Mill, John Stuart. *On Liberty.*

More, Sir Thomas. *Utopia.* 1516.

Mussolini, Benito. *The Doctrine of Fascism.* Firenze: 1937.

Nietzsche, Friedrich. *The Will to Power.* Seyszig: 1901.

Owen, Robert. *New View of Society.* 1813.

Plato. *The Republic.*

Proudhoun. *What is Property?* 1840, pp. 133-5.

Ricardo, David. *On the Principles of Political Economy and Taxation.* London: 1817, pp. 104-109.

Rousseau, Jean-Jacques. *The Social Contract and Discourse on the Origin of Inequality.* 1767, pp. 7-19.

Saint Simon. *The Organizer.* 1819.

Say, J.B. *A Treatise on Political Economy or the Production, Distribution and Consumption of Wealth.* Philadelphia: 1880, pp. 181-2.

Schopenhauer, Arthur. "Studies in Pessimism: On the Sufferings of the World". T. Bailey Saunders translation, New York: approx. 1900 (no date), pp. 381-393.

Smith, Adam. *An Inquiry into the Nature and Causes of the Wealth of Nations.* London: 1776, Numbers 13-26.

Sorel, Georges. *Reflections on Violence.* 1906.

Spencer, Herbert. *The Study of Sociology.* 1890.

Veblen, Thorstein. *The Theory of the Leisure Class.* 1899.

Voltaire. (Francois-Marie Arouet, Philosophical Dictionary). Paris: 1776.

Weber, Max. *The Protestant Ethic and the Spirit of Capitalism.* Archiv fur Sozialwissenschaft und Sozialpolitik, Vol. XX, 1904, p. 71.

Wilde, Oscar. *The Soul of Man.* London: 1909, pp. 2-13.

Winstanley, Gerrard. *The Laws of Freedom in a Platform; or, True Magistry Restored.* 1652.

Wollstonecraft, Mary. *A Vindication of the Rights of Men.* London: 1790.